SUSE OpenStack Cloud 6 - Deployment Guide

A catalogue record for this book is available from the Hong Kong Public Libraries.

Published in Hong Kong by Samurai Media Limited.

Email: info@samuraimedia.org

ISBN 978-988-8406-45-6

Contents

About This Guide

SUSE® OpenStack Cloud is an open source software solution that provides the fundamental capabilities to deploy and manage a cloud infrastructure based on SUSE Linux Enterprise. SUSE OpenStack Cloud is powered by OpenStack, the leading community-driven, open source cloud infrastructure project. It seamlessly manages and provisions workloads across a heterogeneous cloud environment in a secure, compliant, and fully-supported manner. The product tightly integrates with other SUSE technologies and with the SUSE maintenance and support infrastructure.

In SUSE OpenStack Cloud, there are several high-level user roles (or viewpoints) that we need to discriminate:

SUSE OpenStack Cloud Operator

Installs and deploys SUSE OpenStack Cloud, starting with bare-metal, then installing the operating system and the OpenStack components. For detailed information about the operator's tasks and how to solve them, refer to SUSE OpenStack Cloud *Deployment Guide*.

SUSE OpenStack Cloud Administrator

Manages projects, users, images, flavors, and quotas within SUSE OpenStack Cloud. For detailed information about the administrator's tasks and how to solve them, refer to the OpenStack *Admin User Guide* and the SUSE OpenStack Cloud *Supplement to Admin User Guide and End User Guide*.

SUSE OpenStack Cloud User

End user who launches and manages instances, can create snapshots, and use volumes for persistent storage within SUSE OpenStack Cloud. For detailed information about the user's tasks and how to solve them, refer to OpenStack *End User Guide* and the SUSE OpenStack Cloud *Supplement to Admin User Guide and End User Guide*.

This guide provides cloud operators with the information needed to deploy and maintain SUSE OpenStack Cloud administrative units, the Administration Server, the Control Nodes, and the Compute and Storage Nodes. The Administration Server provides all services needed to manage and deploy all other nodes in the cloud. The Control Node hosts all OpenStack services needed to operate virtual machines deployed on the Compute Nodes in the SUSE OpenStack Cloud. Each virtual machine (instance) started in the cloud will be hosted on one of the Compute Nodes. Object storage is managed by the Storage Nodes.

Many chapters in this manual contain links to additional documentation resources. These include additional documentation that is available on the system and documentation available on the Internet.

For an overview of the documentation available for your product and the latest documentation updates, refer to http://www.suse.com/documentation.

1 Available Documentation

The following manuals are available for this product:

Deployment Guide

Gives an introduction to the SUSE® OpenStack Cloud architecture, lists the requirements, and describes how to set up, deploy, and maintain the individual components. Also contains information about troubleshooting, support, and a glossary listing the most important terms and concepts for SUSE OpenStack Cloud.

Admin User Guide

Guides you through management of projects and users, images, flavors, quotas, and networks. Also describes how to migrate instances.
To complete these tasks, either use the graphical Web interface (based on OpenStack Dashboard, code name `Horizon`) or the OpenStack command line clients.

End User Guide

Describes how to manage images, instances, networks, volumes, and track usage.
To complete these tasks, either use the graphical Web interface (based on OpenStack Dashboard, code name `Horizon`) or the OpenStack command line clients.

Supplement to Admin User Guide and End User Guide

A supplement to the SUSE OpenStack Cloud *Admin User Guide* and SUSE OpenStack Cloud *End User Guide*. It contains additional information for admin users and end users guides that is specific to SUSE OpenStack Cloud.

HTML versions of the product manuals can be found in the installed system under `/usr/share/doc/manual`. Additionally, you can access the product-specific manuals and the upstream documentation from the *Help* links in the graphical Web interfaces. Find the latest documentation updates at http://www.suse.com/documentation where you can download the manuals for your product in multiple formats.

2 Feedback

Several feedback channels are available:

Services and Support Options

For services and support options available for your product, refer to http://www.suse.com/support/.

User Comments/Bug Reports

We want to hear your comments about and suggestions for this manual and the other documentation included with this product. If you are reading the HTML version of this guide, use the Comments feature at the bottom of each page in the online documentation at http://www.suse.com/documentation/.

If you are reading the single-page HTML version of this guide, you can use the *Report Bug* link next to each section to open a bug report at https://bugzilla.suse.com/. A user account is needed for this.

Mail

For feedback on the documentation of this product, you can also send a mail to doc-team@suse.de. Make sure to include the document title, the product version, and the publication date of the documentation. To report errors or suggest enhancements, provide a concise description of the problem and refer to the respective section number and page (or URL).

3 Documentation Conventions

The following notices and typographical conventions are used in this documentation:

Warning

Vital information you must be aware of before proceeding. Warns you about security issues, potential loss of data, damage to hardware, or physical hazards.

Important

Important information you should be aware of before proceeding.

Note

Additional information, for example about differences in software versions.

 Tip

Helpful information, like a guideline or a piece of practical advice.

- ```
  tux > command
  ```

  Commands than can be run by any user, including the root user.

- ```
  root # command
  ```

  Commands that must be run with root privileges. Often you can also prefix these commands with the **sudo** command to run them.

- /etc/passwd: directory names and file names

- *PLACEHOLDER*: replace *PLACEHOLDER* with the actual value

- PATH: the environment variable PATH

- **ls**, --help: commands, options, and parameters

- user: users or groups

- Alt, Alt–F1: a key to press or a key combination; keys are shown in uppercase as on a keyboard

- *File, File > Save As*: menu items, buttons

- *Dancing Penguins* (Chapter *Penguins*, ↑Another Manual): This is a reference to a chapter in another manual.

4 About the Making of This Manual

This documentation is written in SUSEDoc, a subset of DocBook 5 [http://www.docbook.org]. The XML source files were validated by **jing [https://code.google.com/p/jing-trang/]**, processed by **xsltproc**, and converted into XSL-FO using a customized version of Norman

Walsh's stylesheets. The final PDF is formatted through FOP [https://xmlgraphics.apache.org/fop] from Apache Software Foundation. The open source tools and the environment used to build this documentation are provided by the DocBook Authoring and Publishing Suite (DAPS). The project's home page can be found at https://github.com/openSUSE/daps.

The XML source code of this documentation can be found at https://github.com/SUSE/doc-cloud.

I Architecture and Requirements

1 The SUSE OpenStack Cloud Architecture

SUSE OpenStack Cloud is a cloud infrastructure solution that can easily be deployed and managed. It offers a cloud management solution that helps organizations to centralize virtual machine deployment.

SUSE OpenStack Cloud 6 provides the following features:

- Open source software that is based on the OpenStack Liberty release.

- Centralized resource tracking providing insight into activities and capacity of the cloud infrastructure for optimized automated deployment of services.

- A self-service portal enabling end users to configure and deploy services as necessary, also offering the ability to track resource consumption (Horizon).

- An image repository from which standardized, preconfigured virtual machines can be published (Glance).

- Automated installation processes via Crowbar using pre-defined scripts for configuring and deploying the Control Node(s) and Compute and Storage Nodes.

- Multi-tenant, role-based provisioning and access control for multiple departments and users within your organization.

- APIs enabling the integration of third-party software, such as identity management and billing solutions.

- Heterogeneous hypervisor support (Xen and KVM).

SUSE OpenStack Cloud is based on SUSE Linux Enterprise Server, OpenStack, Crowbar, and Chef. SUSE Linux Enterprise Server is used as the underlying operating system for all cloud infrastructure machines (also called nodes). The cloud management layer, OpenStack, works as the "Cloud Operating System". Crowbar and Chef are used to automatically deploy and manage the OpenStack nodes from a central Administration Server.

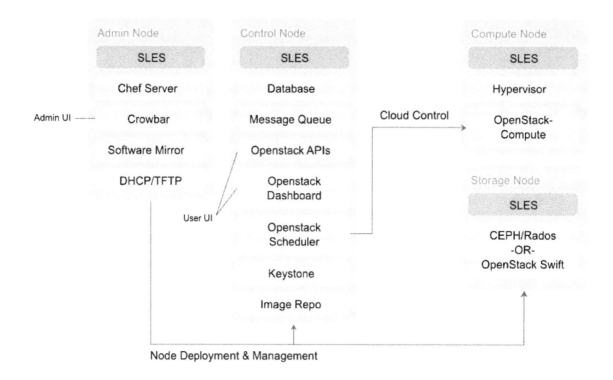

FIGURE 1.1: SUSE OPENSTACK CLOUD INFRASTRUCTURE

SUSE OpenStack Cloud is deployed to four different types of machines:

- one Administration Server for node deployment and management

- one or more Control Nodes hosting the cloud management services

- several Compute Nodes on which the instances are started

- several Storage Nodes for block and object storage

1.1   The Administration Server

The Administration Server provides all services needed to manage and deploy all other nodes in the cloud. Most of these services are provided by the Crowbar tool that—together with Chef —automates all the required installation and configuration tasks. Among the services provided by the server are DHCP, DNS, NTP, PXE, TFTP.

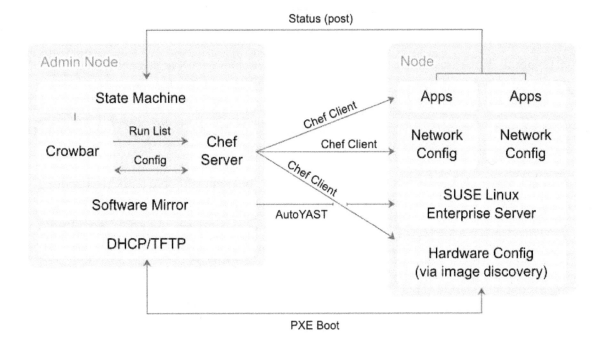

The Administration Server also hosts the software repositories for SUSE Linux Enterprise Server and SUSE OpenStack Cloud. They are needed for node deployment. If no other sources for the software repositories are available it can optionally also host the Subscription Management Tool (SMT), providing up-to-date repositories with updates and patches for all nodes.

1.2 The Control Node(s)

The Control Node(s) hosts all OpenStack services needed to orchestrate virtual machines deployed on the Compute Nodes in the SUSE OpenStack Cloud. OpenStack on SUSE OpenStack Cloud uses a PostgreSQL database, which is also hosted on the Control Node(s). The following OpenStack components—if deployed—run on the Control Node(s):

- PostgreSQL database

- Image (Glance) for managing virtual images

- Identity (Keystone), providing authentication and authorization for all OpenStack services

- Networking (Neutron), providing "networking as a service" between interface devices managed by other OpenStack services

- Block Storage (Cinder), providing block storage

- OpenStack Dashboard (Horizon), providing the Dashboard, a user Web interface for the OpenStack services

- Compute (Nova) management (Nova controller) including API and scheduler

- Message broker (RabbitMQ)

- Swift proxy server plus dispersion tools (health monitor) and Swift ring (index of objects, replicas, and devices). Swift provides object storage.

- Ceph master cluster monitor (Calamari), needs to be deployed on a dedicated node

- Hawk, a monitor for a pacemaker cluster (HA setup)

- Heat, an orchestration engine

- Ceilometer server and agents. Ceilometer collects CPU and networking data for billing purposes.

- Trove, a Database-as-a-Service, needs to be deployed on a dedicated node

Being a central point in the SUSE OpenStack Cloud architecture that runs a lot of services, a single Control Node can quickly become a performance bottleneck, especially in large SUSE OpenStack Cloud deployments. It is possible to distribute the services listed above on more than one Control Node, up to a setup where each service runs on its own node.

Deploying certain parts of Networking (Neutron) on a distinct node is a general recommendation for production clouds. See *Section 10.11, "Deploying Neutron"* for details.

Hosting Identity (Keystone) on a distinct node enables you to separate authentication and authorization services from other cloud services for security reasons. Another "good candidate" to be hosted on a separate node is Block Storage (Cinder, particularly the cinder-volume role) when using local disks for storage. Deploying it on one or more separate node enables you to equip the node with storage and network hardware best suiting the service. Trove, the Database-as-a-Service for SUSE OpenStack Cloud and Calamari, the server for Ceph management and monitoring, always need to be deployed on dedicated Control Nodes.

 Note: Moving Services in an Existing Setup

In case you plan to move a service in an already deployed SUSE OpenStack Cloud from one Control Node to another, it is strongly recommended to shut down or save *all* instances before doing so. Restart them after having successfully re-deployed the services. Moving services also requires to stop them manually on the original Control Node.

1.3   The Compute Nodes

The Compute Nodes are the pool of machines on which the instances are running. These machines need to be equipped with a sufficient number of CPUs and enough RAM to start several instances. They also need to provide sufficient hard disk space, see *Section 2.2.2.3, "Compute Nodes"* for details. The Control Node effectively distributes instances within the pool of Compute Nodes and provides the necessary network resources. The OpenStack service Compute (Nova) runs on the Compute Nodes and provides means for setting up, starting, and stopping virtual machines.

SUSE OpenStack Cloud supports several hypervisors such as Hyper-V, KVM, VMware vSphere, Xen and—as a technology preview—Docker. Each image that can be started with an instance is bound to one hypervisor. Each Compute Node can only run one hypervisor at a time. You can choose which hypervisor to run on which Compute Node when deploying the Nova barclamp.

1.4   The Storage Nodes

The Storage Nodes are the pool of machines providing object or block storage. Object storage is provided by the OpenStack Swift component, while block storage is provided by Cinder which supports several different back-ends, among them Ceph, which can be deployed during the installation. Deploying Swift and Ceph is optional.

1.5   HA Setup

A failure of components in SUSE OpenStack Cloud can lead to system downtime and/or data loss. To prevent this, SUSE OpenStack Cloud 6 allows you to make all functions provided by the Control Node(s) highly available. During cloud deployment, you can set up a High Availability (HA) cluster consisting of several nodes. You can assign certain roles to this cluster instead of assigning them to individual nodes. As of SUSE OpenStack Cloud 6, Control Nodes and Compute Nodes can be made highly available.

For all HA-enabled roles, the respective functions are automatically handled by the clustering software SUSE Linux Enterprise High Availability Extension. The High Availability Extension uses the Pacemaker cluster stack with Pacemaker as cluster resource manager and Corosync as messaging/infrastructure layer.

You can view the cluster status and configuration with the cluster management tools HA Web Console (Hawk) or the `crm` shell.

 Important: Do Not Change the Configuration

Use the cluster management tools only for *viewing*. All of the clustering configuration is done automatically via Crowbar and Chef. If you change anything via the cluster management tools you risk breaking the cluster. Changes done there may be reverted by the next run of Chef anyway.

A failure of the OpenStack infrastructure services (running on the Control Nodes) is the most crucial point of failure that can cause downtimes within the cloud. For more information on how to make those services highly-available and on how to avoid other potential points of failure in your cloud setup, refer to *Section 2.6, "High Availability"*.

2 Considerations and Requirements

Before deploying SUSE OpenStack Cloud, there are a few requirements to be met and considerations to be made. Make sure to thoroughly read this chapter—some decisions need to be made *before* deploying SUSE OpenStack Cloud, since you cannot change them afterwards.

2.1 Network

SUSE OpenStack Cloud requires a complex network setup consisting of several networks that are configured during installation. These networks are for exclusive cloud usage. To access them from an existing network, a router is needed.

The network configuration on the nodes in the SUSE OpenStack Cloud network is entirely controlled by Crowbar. Any network configuration not done with Crowbar (for example, with YaST) will automatically be overwritten. After the cloud is deployed, network settings cannot be changed anymore!

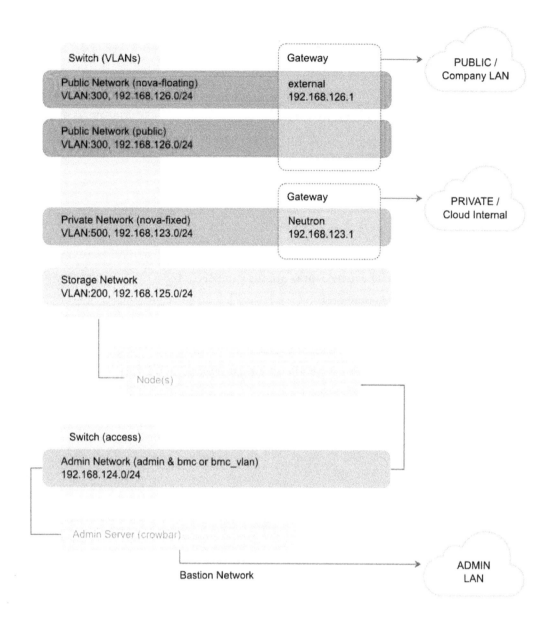

FIGURE 2.1: SUSE OPENSTACK CLOUD NETWORK: OVERVIEW

The following networks are pre-defined when setting up SUSE OpenStack Cloud. The IP addresses listed are the default addresses and can be changed using the YaST Crowbar module (see *Chapter 7, Crowbar Setup*). It is also possible to completely customize the network setup. This requires to manually edit the network barclamp template. See *Appendix D, The Network Barclamp Template File* for detailed instructions.

Admin Network (192.168.124/24)

A private network to access the Administration Server and all nodes for administration purposes. The default setup lets you also access the BMC (Baseboard Management Controller) data via IPMI (Intelligent Platform Management Interface) from this network. If required, BMC access can be swapped to a separate network.

You have the following options for controlling access to this network:

- do not allow access from the outside and keep the admin network completely separated

- allow access to the Administration Server from a single network (for example, your company's administration network) via the "bastion network" option configured on an additional network card with a fixed IP address

- allow access from one or more networks via a gateway

Storage Network (192.168.125/24)

Private, SUSE OpenStack Cloud internal virtual network. This network is used by Ceph and Swift only. It should not be accessed by users.

Private Network (nova-fixed, 192.168.123/24)

Private, SUSE OpenStack Cloud internal virtual network. This network is used for inter-instance communication and provides access to the outside world for the instances. The gateway required is also automatically provided by SUSE OpenStack Cloud.

Public Network (nova-floating, public, 192.168.126/24)

The only public network provided by SUSE OpenStack Cloud. You can access the Nova Dashboard and all instances (provided they have been equipped with a floating IP) on this network. This network can only be accessed via a gateway, which needs to be provided externally. All SUSE OpenStack Cloud users and administrators need to be able to access the public network.

Software Defined Network (os_sdn, 192.168.130/24)

Private, SUSE OpenStack Cloud internal virtual network. This network is used when Neutron is configured to use openvswitch with GRE tunneling for the virtual networks. It should not be accessed by users.

Warning: Protect Networks from External Access

For security reasons, protect the following networks from external access:

- *Admin Network (192.168.124/24)*

- *Storage Network (192.168.125/24)*

- *Software Defined Network (os_sdn, 192.168.130/24)*

Especially traffic from the cloud instances must not be able to pass through these networks.

 Important: VLAN Settings

As of SUSE OpenStack Cloud 6, using a VLAN for the admin network is only supported on a native/untagged VLAN. If you need VLAN support for the admin network, it must be handled at switch level.

When deploying Compute Nodes with Microsoft Hyper-V or Windows Server, you must *not* use openvswitch with gre. Use openvswitch with VLAN (recommended) or linuxbridge as a plugin for Neutron instead.

When changing the network configuration with YaST or by editing `/etc/crowbar/network.json` you can define VLAN settings for each network. For the networks `nova-fixed` and `nova-floating`, however, special rules apply:

nova-fixed: The *USE VLAN* setting will be ignored. However, VLANs will automatically be used if deploying Neutron with VLAN support (using the plugins linuxbridge, openvswitch plus VLAN or cisco plus VLAN). In this case, you need to specify a correct *VLAN ID* for this network.

nova-floating: When using a VLAN for `nova-floating` (which is the default), the *USE VLAN* and *VLAN ID* settings for *nova-floating* and *public* need to be the same. When not using a VLAN for `nova-floating`, it needs to use a different physical network interface than the `nova_fixed` network.

 Note: No IPv6 Support

As of SUSE OpenStack Cloud 6, IPv6 is not supported. This applies to the cloud internal networks and to the instances.

The following diagram shows the pre-defined SUSE OpenStack Cloud network in more detail. It demonstrates how the OpenStack nodes and services use the different networks.

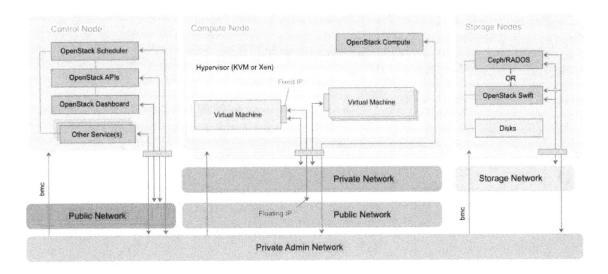

FIGURE 2.2: SUSE OPENSTACK CLOUD NETWORK: DETAILS

2.1.1 Network Address Allocation

The default networks set up in SUSE OpenStack Cloud are class C networks with 256 IP addresses each. This limits the maximum number of instances that can be started simultaneously. Addresses within the networks are allocated as outlined in the following table. Use the YaST Crowbar module to customize (see *Chapter 7, Crowbar Setup*). The last address in the IP range of each network is always reserved as the broadcast address. This assignment cannot be changed.

 Note: Limitations of the Default Network Proposal

The default network proposal as described below limits the maximum number of Compute Nodes to 80, the maximum number of floating IP addresses to 61 and the maximum number of addresses in the nova_fixed network to 204.

To overcome these limitations you need to reconfigure the network setup by using appropriate address ranges. Do this by either using the YaST Crowbar module as described in *Chapter 7, Crowbar Setup* or by manually editing the network template file as described in *Appendix D, The Network Barclamp Template File*.

TABLE 2.1: 192.168.124.0/24 (ADMIN/BMC) NETWORK ADDRESS ALLOCATION

Function	Address	Remark
router	192.168.124.1	Provided externally.
admin	192.168.124.10 - 192.168.124.11	Fixed addresses reserved for the Administration Server.
DHCP	192.168.124.21 - 192.168.124.80	Address range reserved for node allocation/installation. Determines the maximum number of parallel allocations/installations.
host	192.168.124.81 - 192.168.124.160	Fixed addresses for the OpenStack nodes. Determines the maximum number of OpenStack nodes that can be deployed.
bmc vlan host	192.168.124.161	Fixed address for the BMC VLAN. Used to generate a VLAN tagged interface on the Administration Server that can access the BMC network. The BMC VLAN needs to be in the same ranges as BMC, and BMC needs to have VLAN enabled.
bmc host	192.168.124.162 - 192.168.124.240	Fixed addresses for the OpenStack nodes. Determines the maximum number of OpenStack nodes that can be deployed.
switch	192.168.124.241 - 192.168.124.250	This range is not used in current releases and might be removed in the future.

TABLE 2.2: 192.168.125/24 (STORAGE) NETWORK ADDRESS ALLOCATION

Function	Address	Remark
host	192.168.125.10 - 192.168.125.239	Each Storage Node will get an address from this range.

TABLE 2.3: 192.168.123/24 **(PRIVATE NETWORK/NOVA-FIXED) NETWORK ADDRESS ALLOCATION**

Function	Address	Remark
DHCP	192.168.123.1 - 192.168.123.254	Address range for instances, routers and DHCP/DNS agents.

TABLE 2.4: 192.168.126/24 **(PUBLIC NETWORK NOVA-FLOATING, PUBLIC) NETWORK ADDRESS ALLOCATION**

Function	Address	Remark
router	192.168.126.1	Provided externally.
public host	192.168.126.2 - 192.168.126.127	Public address range for external SUSE OpenStack Cloud services such as the OpenStack Dashboard or the API.
floating host	192.168.126.129 - 192.168.126.254	Floating IP address range. Floating IPs can be manually assigned to a running instance to allow to access the guest from the outside. Determines the maximum number of instances that can concurrently be accessed from the outside. The nova_floating network is set up with a netmask of 255.255.255.192, allowing a maximum number of 61 IP addresses. This range is pre-allocated by default and managed by Neutron.

TABLE 2.5: 192.168.130/24 **(SOFTWARE DEFINED NETWORK) NETWORK ADDRESS ALLOCATION**

Function	Address	Remark
host	192.168.130.10 - 192.168.130.254	If Neutron is configured with open-vswitch and gre, each network node and all Compute Nodes will get an IP from this range.

Note: Addresses for Additional Servers

Addresses not used in the ranges mentioned above, can be used to add additional servers with static addresses to SUSE OpenStack Cloud. Such servers can be used to provide additional services. A SUSE Manager server inside SUSE OpenStack Cloud, for example, needs to be configured using one of these addresses.

2.1.2 Network Modes

SUSE OpenStack Cloud supports different network modes: single, dual, and teaming. As of SUSE OpenStack Cloud 6, the networking mode is applied to all nodes and the Administration Server. That means that all machines need to meet the hardware requirements for the chosen mode. The network mode can be configured using the YaST Crowbar module (*Chapter 7, Crowbar Setup*). The network mode cannot be changed after the cloud is deployed.

Other, more flexible network mode setups can be configured by manually editing the Crowbar network configuration files. See *Appendix D, The Network Barclamp Template File* for more information. SUSE or a partner can assist you in creating a custom setup within the scope of a consulting services agreement (see http://www.suse.com/consulting/ for more information on SUSE consulting).

 Important: Teaming Network Mode is Required for HA

Teaming network mode is required for an HA setup of SUSE OpenStack Cloud. If you are planning to move your cloud to an HA setup at a later point in time, make sure to deploy SUSE OpenStack Cloud with teaming network mode from the beginning. Otherwise a migration to an HA setup is not supported.

2.1.2.1 Single Network Mode

In single mode you just use one Ethernet card for all the traffic:

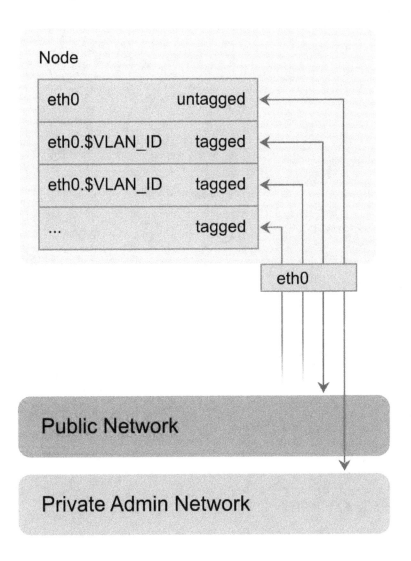

2.1.2.2 Dual Network Mode

Dual mode needs two Ethernet cards (on all nodes but Administration Server). It allows you to completely separate traffic to/from the Admin Network and to/from the public network:

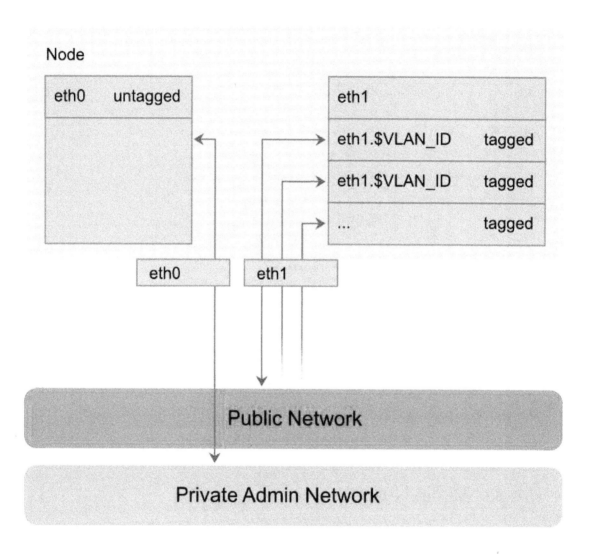

2.1.2.3 Teaming Network Mode

Teaming mode is almost identical to single mode, except that you combine several Ethernet cards to a "bond" (network device bonding). Teaming mode needs two or more Ethernet cards.

Team Mode

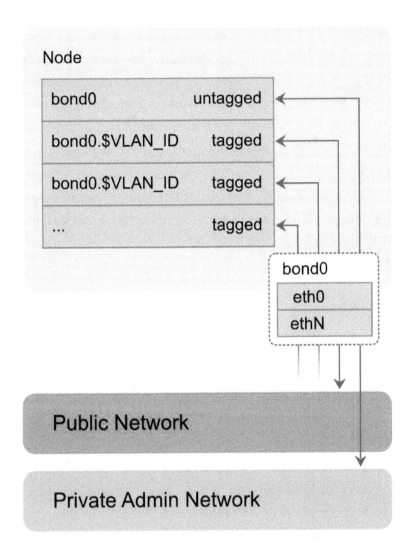

When using teaming mode, you also need to choose a "bonding policy" that defines how to use the combined Ethernet cards. You can either set them up for fault tolerance, performance (load balancing) or for a combination of both.

2.1.3 Accessing the Administration Server via a Bastion Network

If you want to enable access to the Administration Server from another network, you can do so by providing an external gateway. This option offers maximum flexibility, but requires additional machines and may be less secure than you require. Therefore SUSE OpenStack Cloud offers a second option for accessing the Administration Server: the bastion network. You only need a dedicated Ethernet card and a static IP address from the external network to set it up.

The bastion network setup enables you to log in to the Administration Server via SSH (see *Section 2.1.3, "Accessing the Administration Server via a Bastion Network"* for setup instructions). A direct login to other nodes in the cloud is not possible. However, the Administration Server can act as a "jump host": To log in to a node, first log in to the Administration Server via SSH. From there, you can log in via SSH to other nodes.

2.1.4 DNS and Host Names

The Administration Server acts as a name server for all nodes in the cloud. If the Administration Server has access to the outside, then you can add additional name servers that will automatically be used to forward requests. If additional name servers are found on cloud deployment, the name server on the Administration Server will automatically be configured to forward requests for non-local records to those servers.

The Administration Server needs to be configured to have a fully qualified host name. The domain name you specify will be used for the DNS zone. It is required to use a sub-domain such as `cloud.example.com`. The Administration Server needs to have authority on the domain it is working on (to be able to create records for discovered nodes). As a result it will not forward requests for names it cannot resolve in this domain and thus cannot resolve names for `example.com` other than the ones in the cloud.

This host name must not be changed after SUSE OpenStack Cloud has been deployed. The OpenStack nodes will be named after their MAC address by default, but you can provide aliases, which are easier to remember when allocating the nodes. The aliases for the OpenStack nodes can be changed at any time. It is useful to have a list of MAC addresses and the intended use of the corresponding host at hand when deploying the OpenStack nodes.

2.2   Persistent Storage

When talking about "persistent storage" on SUSE OpenStack Cloud, there are two completely different aspects to discuss: the block and object storage services SUSE OpenStack Cloud offers on the one hand and the hardware related storage aspects on the different node types.

 Note: Persistent vs. Ephemeral Storage

Block and object storage are persistent storage models where files or images are stored until they are explicitly deleted. SUSE OpenStack Cloud also offers ephemeral storage for images attached to instances. These ephemeral images only exist during the life of an instance and are deleted when the guest is terminated. See *Section 2.2.2.3, "Compute Nodes"* for more information.

2.2.1   Cloud Storage Services

As mentioned above, SUSE OpenStack Cloud offers two different types of services for persistent storage: object and block storage. Object storage lets you upload and download files (similar to an FTP server), whereas a block storage provides mountable devices (similar to a hard-disk partition). Furthermore SUSE OpenStack Cloud provides a repository to store the virtual disk images used to start instances.

Object Storage with Swift

The OpenStack object storage service is called Swift. The storage component of Swift (swift-storage) needs to be deployed on dedicated nodes where no other cloud services run. To be able to store the objects redundantly, it is required to deploy at least two Swift nodes. SUSE OpenStack Cloud is configured to always use all unused disks on a node for storage. Swift can optionally be used by Glance, the service that manages the images used to boot the instances. Offering object storage with Swift is optional.

Block Storage

Block storage on SUSE OpenStack Cloud is provided by Cinder. Cinder can use a variety of storage back-ends, among them network storage solutions like NetApp or EMC. It is also possible to use local disks for block storage. A list of drivers available for Cinder and the features supported for each driver is available from the *CinderSupportMatrix* at https://wiki.openstack.org/wiki/CinderSupportMatrix. SUSE OpenStack Cloud 6 is shipping with OpenStack Liberty.

Alternatively, Cinder can use Ceph RBD as a back-end. Ceph offers data security and speed by storing the devices redundantly on different servers. Ceph needs to be deployed on dedicated nodes where no other cloud services run. Ceph requires at least four dedicated nodes. If deploying the optional Calamari server for Ceph management and monitoring, an additional dedicated node is required.

The Glance Image Repository

Glance provides a catalog and repository for virtual disk images used to start the instances. Glance is installed on a Control Node. It either uses Swift, Ceph or a directory on the Control Node to store the images. The image directory can either be a local directory or an NFS share.

2.2.2   Storage Hardware Requirements

Apart from sufficient disk space to install the SUSE Linux Enterprise Server operating system, each node in SUSE OpenStack Cloud needs to store additional data. Requirements and recommendations for the various node types are listed below.

❗ Important: Choose a Hard Disk for the Operating System Installation

The operating system will always be installed on the *first* hard disk, the one that is recognized as /dev/sda. This is the disk that is listed *first* in the BIOS, the one from which the machine will boot. If you have nodes with a certain hard disk you want the operating system to be installed on, make sure it will be recognized as the first disk.

2.2.2.1   Administration Server

If you store the update repositories directly on the Administration Server (see *Section 2.5.2, "Product and Update Repositories"* for details), it is recommended to mount /srv to a separate partition or volume with a minimum of 30 GB space.

Log files from all nodes in SUSE OpenStack Cloud are stored on the Administration Server under /var/log (see *Section A.1, "On the Administration Server"* for a complete list). Furthermore, the message service RabbitMQ requires 1 GB of free space in /var. Make sure sufficient space is available under /var.

2.2.2.2 Control Nodes

Depending on how the services are set up, Glance and Cinder may require additional disk space on the Control Node on which they are running. Glance may be configured to use a local directory, whereas Cinder may use a local image file for storage. For performance and scalability reasons this is only recommended for test setups. Make sure there is sufficient free disk space available if you use a local file for storage.

Cinder may be configured to use local disks for storage (configuration option `raw`). If you choose this setup, it is recommended to deploy the *cinder-volume* role to one or more dedicated Control Nodes. Those should be equipped with several disks providing sufficient storage space. It may also be necessary to equip this node with two or more bonded network cards, since it will generate heavy network traffic. Bonded network cards require a special setup for this node. For details, refer to *Appendix D, The Network Barclamp Template File*.

Live migration for Xen instances requires to export `/var/lib/nova/instances` on the Control Node hosting `nova-controller`. This directory will host a copy of the root disk of *all* Xen instances in the cloud and needs to have sufficient disk space. It is strongly recommended to use a separate block device for this directory, preferably a RAID device to ensure data security.

2.2.2.3 Compute Nodes

Unless an instance is started via "Boot from Volume", it is started with at least one disk—a copy of the image from which it has been started. Depending on the flavor you start, the instance may also have a second, so-called "ephemeral" disk. The size of the root disk depends on the image itself. Ephemeral disks are always created as sparse image files that grow (up to a defined size) when being "filled". By default ephemeral disks have a size of 10 GB.

Both disks, root images and ephemeral disk, are directly bound to the instance and are deleted when the instance is terminated. Therefore these disks are bound to the Compute Node on which the instance has been started. The disks are created under `/var/lib/nova` on the Compute Node. Your Compute Nodes should be equipped with enough disk space to store the root images and ephemeral disks.

Note: Ephemeral Disks vs. Block Storage

Do not confuse ephemeral disks with persistent block storage. In addition to an ephemeral disk, which is automatically provided with most instance flavors, you can optionally add a persistent storage device provided by Cinder. Ephemeral disks are deleted when the instance terminates, while persistent storage devices can be reused in another instance.

The maximum disk space required on a compute node depends on the available flavors. A flavor specifies the number of CPUs, RAM and disk size of an instance. Several flavors ranging from *tiny* (1 CPU, 512 MB RAM, no ephemeral disk) to *xlarge* (8 CPUs, 8 GB RAM, 10 GB ephemeral disk) are available by default. Adding custom flavors, editing and deleting existing flavors is also supported.

To calculate the minimum disk space needed on a compute node, you need to determine the highest "disk space to RAM" ratio from your flavors. Example:

Flavor small: 2 GB RAM, 100 GB ephemeral disk = > 50 GB disk /1 GB RAM
Flavor large: 8 GB RAM, 200 GB ephemeral disk = > 25 GB disk /1 GB RAM

So, 50 GB disk /1 GB RAM is the ratio that matters. If you multiply that value by the amount of RAM in GB available on your compute node, you have the minimum disk space required by ephemeral disks. Pad that value with sufficient space for the root disks plus a buffer that enables you to create flavors with a higher disk space to RAM ratio in the future.

 ## Warning: Overcommitting Disk Space

The scheduler that decides in which node an instance is started does not check for available disk space. If there is no disk space left on a compute node, this will not only cause data loss on the instances, but the compute node itself will also stop operating. Therefore you must make sure all compute nodes are equipped with enough hard disk space!

2.2.2.4 Storage Nodes (optional)

The block-storage service Ceph RBD and the object storage service Swift need to be deployed onto dedicated nodes—it is not possible to mix these services. Swift service requires at least two machines (more are recommended) to be able to store data redundantly. For Ceph at least four machines are required (more are recommended). If deploying the optional Calamari server for Ceph management and monitoring, an additional machine (with moderate CPU and RAM requirements) needs to be supplied.

Each Ceph/Swift Storage Node needs at least two hard disks. The first one will be used for the operating system installation, while the others can be used for storage purposes. It is recommended to equip the storage nodes with as many disks as possible.

Using RAID on Swift storage nodes is not supported. Swift takes care of redundancy and replication on its own. Using RAID with Swift would also result in a huge performance penalty.

2.3 SSL Encryption

Whenever non-public data travels over a network it needs to be encrypted. Encryption protects the integrity and confidentiality of data. Therefore you should enable SSL support when deploying SUSE OpenStack Cloud to production. (SSL is not enabled by default since it requires certificates to be provided). The following services (and their APIs if available) can use SSL:

- Cinder

- Dashboard

- Glance

- Heat

- Keystone

- Manila

- Neutron

- Nova

- Trove

- VNC

Using SSL requires an SSL certificate either for each node on which the services that uses encryption run (services sharing a certificate). Alternatively, you need a dedicated certificate for each service. A single certificate for the Control Node is the minimum requirement, where all services listed above are installed on the Control Node and are sharing the certificate.

Certificates must be signed by a trusted authority. Refer to http://www.suse.com/documentation/sles-12/book_sle_admin/data/sec_apache2_ssl.html for instructions on how to create and sign them.

 Important: Host Names

Each SSL certificate is issued for a certain host name and, optionally, for alternative host names (via the `AlternativeName` option). Each publicly available node in SUSE OpenStack Cloud has two host names—an internal and a public one. The SSL certificate needs to be issued for both names.

The internal name has the following scheme:

```
dMAC ADDRESS.FQDN
```

`MAC ADDRESS` is the MAC address of the interface used to boot the machine via PXE. All letters are turned lowercase and all colons are replaced with dashes. For example, `52-54-00-8e-ce-e3`. `FQDN` is the fully qualified domain name. An example name looks like this:

```
d52-54-00-8e-ce-e3.example.com
```

Unless you have entered a custom *Public Name* for a client (see *Section 9.2, "Node Installation"* for details), the public name is the same as the internal name prefixed by `public`:

```
public.d52-54-00-8e-ce-e3.example.com
```

To look up the node names open the Crowbar Web interface and click the name of a node in the *Node Dashboard*. The names are listed as *Full Name* and *Public Name*.

2.4 Hardware Requirements

Precise hardware requirements can only be listed for the Administration Server and the OpenStack Control Node. The requirements of the OpenStack Compute and Storage Nodes depends on the number of concurrent instances and their virtual hardware equipment.

The minimum number of machines required for a SUSE OpenStack Cloud setup is three: one Administration Server, one Control Node, and one Compute Node. In addition to that, a gateway providing access to the public network is required. Deploying storage requires additional nodes: at least two nodes for Swift and a minimum of four nodes for Ceph.

> ⓘ **Important: Physical Machines and Architecture**
>
> All SUSE OpenStack Cloud nodes need to be physical machines. Although the Administration Server and the Control Node can be virtualized in test environments, this is not supported for production systems.
>
> SUSE OpenStack Cloud currently only runs on x86_64 hardware.

2.4.1 Administration Server

- Architecture: x86_64

- RAM: at least 2 GB, 4 GB recommended

- Hard disk: at least 50 GB. It is recommended to put /srv on a separate partition with at least additional 30 GB of space. Alternatively, you can mount the update repositories from another server (see *Section 2.5.2, "Product and Update Repositories"* for details).

- Number of network cards: 1 for single and dual mode, 2 or more for team mode. Additional networks such as the bastion network and/or a separate BMC network each need an additional network card. See *Section 2.1, "Network"* for details.

2.4.2 Control Node

- Architecture: x86_64

- RAM: at least 2 GB, 12 GB recommended (when deploying a single Control Node)

- Number of network cards: 1 for single mode, 2 for dual mode, 2 or more for team mode. See *Section 2.1, "Network"* for details.

- Hard disk: See *Section 2.2.2.2, "Control Nodes"*.

2.4.3 Compute Node

The Compute Nodes need to be equipped with a sufficient amount of RAM and CPUs, matching the numbers required by the maximum number of instances running concurrently. An instance started in SUSE OpenStack Cloud cannot share resources from several physical nodes. It uses the resources of the node on which it was started. So if you offer a flavor (see *Flavor* for a definition) with 8 CPUs and 12 GB RAM, at least one of your nodes should be able to provide these resources.

See *Section 2.2.2.3, "Compute Nodes"* for storage requirements.

2.4.4 Storage Node

The Storage Nodes are sufficiently equipped with a single CPU and 1 or 2 GB of RAM. See *Section 2.2.2.4, "Storage Nodes (optional)"* for storage requirements.

2.5 Software Requirements

All nodes and the Administration Server in SUSE OpenStack Cloud run on SUSE Linux Enterprise Server 12 SP1. A SUSE OpenStack Cloud subscription will include the following:

- SUSE OpenStack Cloud 6 for an unlimited number of nodes

- an entitlement for SUSE Linux Enterprise Server 12 SP1 for a single Administration Server

- an entitlement for SUSE Linux Enterprise Server 12 SP1 for a single Control Node

- an entitlement for the SUSE Linux Enterprise Server 12 SP1 High Availability Extension for an unlimited number of Control Nodes

SUSE Linux Enterprise Server 12 SP1 entitlements for additional nodes (such as Compute Nodes, storage nodes and additional Control Nodes) need to be purchased in addition to the SUSE OpenStack Cloud subscription. Refer to http://www.suse.com/products/suse-openstack-cloud/how-to-buy/ for more information.

Running Ceph within SUSE OpenStack Cloud (optional) requires an additional SUSE Enterprise Storage subscription. Refer to https://www.suse.com/products/suse-enterprise-storage/ for more information.

> **Important: SUSE Account**
>
> A SUSE account is needed for product registration and access to update repositories. If you do not already have one, go to http://www.suse.com/login to create it.

2.5.1 Optional Component: SUSE Enterprise Storage

SUSE OpenStack Cloud can be extended by SUSE Enterprise Storage for setting up a Ceph cluster providing block storage services. To store virtual disks for instances SUSE OpenStack Cloud uses block storage provided by the Cinder module. Cinder itself needs a back-end providing storage. In production environments this usually is a network storage solution. Cinder can use a variety of network storage back-ends, among them solutions from EMC, Fujitsu or NetApp. In case your organization does not provide a network storage solution that can be used with SUSE OpenStack Cloud, you can set up a Ceph cluster with SUSE Enterprise Storage. SUSE Enterprise Storage provides a reliable and fast distributed storage architecture using commodity hardware platforms.

Deploying SUSE Enterprise Storage (Ceph) within SUSE OpenStack Cloud is fully supported. Ceph nodes can be deployed using the same interface as for all other SUSE OpenStack Cloud services. It requires a SUSE Enterprise Storage subscription. See https://www.suse.com/products/suse-enterprise-storage/ for more information on SUSE Enterprise Storage.

2.5.2 Product and Update Repositories

To deploy SUSE OpenStack Cloud and to be able to keep a running SUSE OpenStack Cloud up-to-date, a total of seven software repositories is needed. This includes the static product repositories, which do not change over the product life cycle and the update repositories, which constantly change. The following repositories are needed:

MANDATORY REPOSITORIES

SUSE Linux Enterprise Server 12 SP1 Product
> The SUSE Linux Enterprise Server 12 SP1 product repository is a copy of the installation media (DVD #1) for SUSE Linux Enterprise Server. As of SUSE OpenStack Cloud 6 it is required to have it available locally on the Administration Server. This repository requires approximately 3.5 GB of hard disk space.

SUSE OpenStack Cloud 6 Product

The SUSE OpenStack Cloud 6 product repository is a copy of the installation media (DVD #1) for SUSE OpenStack Cloud. It can either be made available remote via HTTP or locally on the Administration Server. The latter is recommended, since it makes the setup of the Administration Server easier. This repository requires approximately 500 MB of hard disk space.

PTF

A repository created automatically on the Administration Server upon the SUSE OpenStack Cloud add-on product installation. It serves as a repository for "Program Temporary Fixes" (PTF) which are part of the SUSE support program.

SLES12-SP1-Pool and SUSE-OpenStack-Cloud-6-Pool

The SUSE Linux Enterprise Server and SUSE OpenStack Cloud repositories contain all binary RPMs from the installation media, plus pattern information and support status metadata. These repositories are served from SUSE Customer Center and need to be kept in synchronization with their sources. They can be made available remotely via an existing SMT or SUSE Manager server. Alternatively, make them available locally on the Administration Server by installing a local SMT server, by mounting or synchronizing a remote directory or by copying them.

SLES12-SP1-Updates and SUSE-OpenStack-Cloud-6-Updates

These repositories contain maintenance updates to packages in the corresponding Pool repositories. These repositories are served from SUSE Customer Center and need to be kept synchronized with their sources. They can be made available remotely via an existing SMT or SUSE Manager server or locally on the Administration Server by installing a local SMT server, by mounting or synchronizing a remote directory or by regularly copying them.

As explained in *Section 2.6, "High Availability"*, Control Nodes in SUSE OpenStack Cloud can optionally be made highly available with the help of the SUSE Linux Enterprise High Availability Extension. SUSE OpenStack Cloud also comes with full support for installing a storage cluster running Ceph provided by the SUSE Enterprise Storage extension. Deploying Ceph is optional. The following repositories are required to deploy SLES High Availability Extension and SUSE Enterprise Storage nodes:

OPTIONAL REPOSITORIES

SLE-HA12-SP1-Pool and SUSE-Enterprise-Storage-2.1-Pool

The pool repositories contain all binary RPMs from the installation media, plus pattern information and support status metadata. These repositories are served from SUSE Customer Center and need to be kept in synchronization with their sources. They can be made available remotely via an existing SMT or SUSE Manager server. Alternatively, make them available locally on the Administration Server by installing a local SMT server, by mounting or synchronizing a remote directory or by copying them.

SLE-HA12-SP1-Updates and SUSE-Enterprise-Storage-2.1-Updates

These repositories contain maintenance updates to packages in the corresponding pool repositories. These repositories are served from SUSE Customer Center and need to be kept synchronized with their sources. They can be made available remotely via an existing SMT or SUSE Manager server or locally on the Administration Server by installing a local SMT server, by mounting or synchronizing a remote directory or by regularly copying them.

The product repositories (for SUSE Linux Enterprise Server 12 SP1 and SUSE OpenStack Cloud 6) do not change during the life cycle of a product. Thus, they can be copied to the destination directory from the installation media. However, the pool and update repositories need to be kept synchronized with their sources on the SUSE Customer Center. SUSE offers two products taking care of synchronizing repositories and making them available within your organization: SUSE Manager (http://www.suse.com/products/suse-manager/ and Subscription Management Tool (shipping with SUSE Linux Enterprise Server 12 SP1).

All repositories need to be served via `http` to be available for SUSE OpenStack Cloud deployment. Repositories that are directly available on the Administration Server are made available by the Apache Web server running on the Administration Server. If your organization already uses SUSE Manager or SMT, you can use the repositories provided by these servers.

Making the repositories locally available on the Administration Server has the advantage of a simple network setup within SUSE OpenStack Cloud. It also allows you to seal off the SUSE OpenStack Cloud network from other networks in your organization. Using a remote server as a source for the repositories has the advantage of using existing resources and services. It also makes setting up the Administration Server much easier. However, this requires a custom network setup for SUSE OpenStack Cloud, since the Administration Server needs to be able to access the remote server.

Installing a Subscription Management Tool (SMT) Server on the Administration Server

The SMT server, shipping with SUSE Linux Enterprise Server 12 SP1, regularly synchronizes repository data from SUSE Customer Center with your local host. Installing the SMT server on the Administration Server is recommended if you do not have access to update repositories from elsewhere within your organization. This option requires the Administration Server to be able to access the Internet.

Using a Remote SMT Server

If you already run an SMT server within your organization, you can use it within SUSE OpenStack Cloud. When using a remote SMT server, update repositories are served directly from the SMT server. Each node is configured with these repositories upon its initial setup. The SMT server needs to be accessible from the Administration Server and all nodes in SUSE OpenStack Cloud (via one or more gateways). Resolving the server's host name also needs to work.

Using a SUSE Manager Server

Each client that is managed by SUSE Manager needs to register with the SUSE Manager server. Therefore the SUSE Manager support can only be installed after the nodes have been deployed. To also be able to use repositories provided by SUSE Manager during node deployment, SUSE Linux Enterprise Server 12 SP1 must be set up for autoinstallation on the SUSE Manager server.

The server needs to be accessible from the Administration Server and all nodes in SUSE OpenStack Cloud (via one or more gateways). Resolving the server's host name also needs to work.

Utilizing Existing Repositories

If you can access existing repositories from within your company network from the Administration Server, you have the following options: either mount or synchronize or manually transfer these repositories to the required locations on the Administration Server.

2.6 High Availability

Several components and services in SUSE OpenStack Cloud can become single points of failure that may cause system downtime and/or data loss if they fail.

SUSE OpenStack Cloud provides various mechanisms which can ensure that the crucial components and services are highly available. The following sections provide an overview of which components on each node you should consider to make highly available. For making the Control Node functions and the Compute Nodes highly available, SUSE OpenStack Cloud uses the cluster software SUSE Linux Enterprise High Availability Extension. Make sure to thoroughly read *Section 2.6.5, "Cluster Requirements and Recommendations"* that lists additional requirements with regard to that.

2.6.1 High Availability of the Administration Server

The Administration Server provides all services needed to manage and deploy all other nodes in the cloud. If the Administration Server is not available, new cloud nodes cannot be allocated, and you cannot add new roles to cloud nodes.

However, only two services on the Administration Server are single point of failures, without which the cloud cannot continue to run properly: DNS and NTP.

2.6.1.1 Administration Server—Avoiding Points of Failure

To avoid DNS and NTP as potential points of failure, deploy the roles `dns-server` and `ntp-server` to multiple nodes.

 Note: Access to External Network

If any configured DNS forwarder or NTP external server is not reachable through the admin network from these nodes, allocate an address in the public network for each node that has the `dns-server` and `ntp-server` roles:

```
crowbar network allocate_ip default `hostname -f` public host
```

That way, the nodes can use the public gateway to reach the external servers. The change will only become effective after the next run of **chef-client** on the affected nodes.

2.6.1.2 Administration Server—Recovery

To minimize recovery time for the Administration Server, follow the backup and restore recommendations described in *Section 11.5, "Backing Up and Restoring the Administration Server"*.

2.6.2 High Availability of the Control Node(s)

The Control Node(s) usually run a variety of services without which the cloud would not be able to run properly.

2.6.2.1 Control Node(s)—Avoiding Points of Failure

To prevent the cloud from avoidable downtime in case one or more Control Nodes fail, you can make the following roles highly available:

- database-server (database barclamp)

- keystone-server (keystone barclamp)

- rabbitmq-server (rabbitmq barclamp)

- swift-proxy (swift barclamp)

- glance-server (glance barclamp)

- cinder-controller (cinder barclamp)

- neutron-server (neutron barclamp)

- neutron-network (neutron barclamp)

- nova-controller (nova barclamp)

- nova_dashboard-server (nova_dashboard barclamp)

- ceilometer-server (ceilometer barclamp)

- ceilometer-polling (ceilometer barclamp)

- heat-server (heat barclamp)

Instead of assigning these roles to individual cloud nodes, you can assign them to one or several High Availability clusters. SUSE OpenStack Cloud will then use the Pacemaker cluster stack (shipped with the SUSE Linux Enterprise High Availability Extension) to manage the services. In case one Control Node fails, the services will fail over to another Control Node. For details on the Pacemaker cluster stack and the SUSE Linux Enterprise High Availability Extension, refer to the Administration Guide, available at http://www.suse.com/documentation/sle-ha-12/. However, whereas SUSE Linux Enterprise High Availability Extension includes Linux Virtual Server as load-balancer, SUSE OpenStack Cloud uses HAProxy for this purpose (http://haproxy.1wt.eu/).

 Note: Recommended Setup

Though it is possible to use the same cluster for all of the roles above, the recommended setup is to use three clusters and to deploy the roles as follows:

- `data` cluster: `database-server` and `rabbitmq-server`

- `network` cluster: `neutron-network` (as the `neutron-network` role may result in heavy network load and CPU impact)

- Trove (always needs to be deployed on a dedicated node)

- `services` cluster: all other roles listed above (as they are related to API/schedulers)

SUSE OpenStack Cloud does not support High Availability for the LBaaS service plug-in. Thus, failover of a neutron load-balancer to another node can only be done manually by editing the database.

 Important: Cluster Requirements and Recommendations

For setting up the clusters, some special requirements and recommendations apply. For details, refer to *Section 2.6.5, "Cluster Requirements and Recommendations"*.

2.6.2.2 Control Node(s)—Recovery

Recovery of the Control Node(s) is done automatically by the cluster software: if one Control Node fails, Pacemaker will fail over the services to another Control Node. If a failed Control Node is repaired and rebuilt via Crowbar, it will be automatically configured to join the cluster, at which point Pacemaker will have the option to fail services back if required.

2.6.3 High Availability of the Compute Node(s)

If a Compute Node fails, all VMs running on that node will go down, too. While it cannot protect against failures of individual VMs, a High Availability setup for Compute Nodes helps you to minimize VM downtime caused by Compute Node failures. If the `nova-compute` service or `libvirtd` fail on a Compute Node, Pacemaker will try to automatically recover them. If recovery fails, or the node itself should become unreachable, the node will be fenced and the VMs will be moved to a different Compute Node.

If you decide to use High Availability for Compute Nodes, your Compute Node will be run as Pacemaker remote nodes. With the `pacemaker-remote` service, High Availability clusters can be extended to control remote nodes without any impact on scalability, and without having to install the full cluster stack (including `corosync`) on the remote nodes. Instead, each Compute Node only runs the `pacemaker-remote` servic. The service acts as a proxy, allowing the cluster stack on the "normal" cluster nodes to connect to it and to control services remotely. Thus, the node is effectively integrated into the cluster as a remote node. In this way, the services running on the OpenStack compute nodes can be controlled from the core Pacemaker cluster in a lightweight, scalable fashion.

Find more information about the `remote_pacemaker` service in *Pacemaker Remote—Extending High Availability into Virtual Nodes*, available at http://www.clusterlabs.org/doc/.

To configure High Availability for Compute Nodes, you need to adjust the following barclamp proposals:

* Pacemaker—for details, see *Section 10.2, "Deploying Pacemaker (Optional, HA Setup Only)"*.

* Nova—for details, see *Section 10.12.1, "HA Setup for Nova"*.

2.6.4 High Availability of the Storage Node(s)

SUSE OpenStack Cloud offers two different types of storage that can be used for the Storage Nodes: object storage (provided by the OpenStack Swift component) and block storage (provided by Ceph).

Both already consider High Availability aspects by design, therefore it does not require much effort to make the storage highly available.

2.6.4.1 Swift—Avoiding Points of Failure

The OpenStack Object Storage replicates the data by design, provided the following requirements are met:

- The option *Replicas* in the Swift barclamp is set to 3, the tested and recommended value.

- The number of Storage Nodes needs to be greater than the value set in the *Replicas* option.

1. To avoid single points of failure, assign the `swift-storage` role to multiple nodes.

2. To make the API highly available, too, assign the `swift-proxy` role to a cluster instead of assigning it to a single Control Node. See *Section 2.6.2.1, "Control Node(s)—Avoiding Points of Failure"*. Other swift roles must not be deployed on a cluster.

2.6.4.2 Ceph—Avoiding Points of Failure

Ceph is a distributed storage solution that can provide High Availability. For High Availability redundant storage and monitors need to be configured in the Ceph cluster. For more information refer to the SUSE Enterprise Storage documentation at http://www.suse.com/documentation/ses-2/.

2.6.5 Cluster Requirements and Recommendations

When considering to set up one ore more High Availability clusters, refer to the chapter *System Requirements* in the Administration Guide for SUSE Linux Enterprise High Availability Extension. The guide is available at http://www.suse.com/documentation/sle-ha-12/.

If you want to make the Control Node functions highly available, the requirements listed there also apply to SUSE OpenStack Cloud. Note that by buying SUSE OpenStack Cloud, you automatically get an entitlement for SUSE Linux Enterprise High Availability Extension.

Especially note the following requirements:

Number of Cluster Nodes
    Each cluster needs to consist of at least two cluster nodes.

 **Important: Odd Number of Cluster Nodes**

It is strongly recommended to use an *odd* number of cluster nodes with a *minimum* of three nodes.

A cluster needs *Quorum* to keep services running. Therefore a three-node cluster can tolerate only failure of one node at a time, whereas a five-node cluster can tolerate failures of two nodes etc.

STONITH

The cluster software will shut down "misbehaving" nodes in a cluster to prevent them from causing trouble. This mechanism is called `fencing` or *STONITH*.

 **Important: No Support Without STONITH**

A cluster without STONITH is not supported.

For a supported HA setup, ensure the following:

* Each node in the High Availability cluster needs to have at least one STONITH device (usually a piece of hardware). We strongly recommend multiple STONITH devices per node, unless SBD is used.

* The global cluster options `stonith-enabled` and `startup-fencing` needs to be set to `true`. These options are set automatically when deploying the `Pacemaker` barclamp. As soon as you change them, you will lose support.

* When deploying the `Pacemaker` service, select a *STONITH: Configuration mode for STONITH* that matches your setup. If your STONITH devices support the IPMI protocol, choosing the IPMI option is the easiest way to configure STONITH. Another alternative is SBD (STONITH Block Device). It provides a way to enable STONITH and fencing in clusters without external power switches, but it requires shared storage. For SBD requirements, see http://linux-ha.org/wiki/SBD_Fencing, section *Requirements*.

For more information, refer to the Administration Guide, available at http://www.suse.com/documentation/sle-ha-12/. Especially read the following chapters: *Configuration and Administration Basics*, and *Fencing and STONITH, Storage Protection*.

Important: Redundant Communication Paths

For a supported HA setup, it is required to set up cluster communication via two or more redundant paths. For this purpose, use teaming network mode in your network setup. For details, see *Section 2.1.2.3, "Teaming Network Mode"*. At least two Ethernet cards per cluster node are required for network redundancy. It is advisable to use teaming network mode everywhere (not just between the cluster nodes) to ensure redundancy.

For more information, refer to the Administration Guide, available at http://www.suse.com/documentation/sle-ha-12/. Especially read the following chapters: *Network Device Bonding*, and *Installation and Basic Setup* (section *Defining the Communication Channels*).

Storage Requirements

The following services require shared storage: `database-server` and `rabbitmq-server`. For this purpose, use either an external NFS share or DRBD.

If using an external NFS share, the following additional requirements are important:

- The share needs to be reliably accessible from all cluster nodes via redundant communication paths. See *Network Configuration*.

- The share needs to have certain settings in `/etc/exports` to be usable by the `database` barclamp. For details, see *Section 10.3.1, "HA Setup for the Database"* **and** *Section 10.4.1, "HA Setup for RabbitMQ"*.

If using DRDB, the following additional requirements are important:

- Because of a DRBD limitation, the cluster used for `database-server` and `rabbitmq-server` is restricted to two nodes.

- All nodes of the cluster that is used for `database-server` and `rabbitmq-server` needs to have an additional hard disk that will be used for DRBD. For more information on DRBD, see the *DRBD* chapter in the Administration Guide, which is available at http://www.suse.com/documentation/sle-ha-12/.

When using SBD as STONITH device, additional requirements apply for the shared storage. For details, see http://linux-ha.org/wiki/SBD_Fencing, section *Requirements*.

2.6.6 For More Information

For a basic understanding and detailed information on the SUSE Linux Enterprise High Availability Extension (including the Pacemaker cluster stack), read the Administration Guide. It is available at http://www.suse.com/documentation/sle-ha-12/.

In addition to the chapters mentioned in *Section 2.6.5, "Cluster Requirements and Recommendations"*, especially the following chapters are recommended:

* *Product Overview*

* *Configuration and Administration Basics*

The Administration Guide also provides comprehensive information about the cluster management tools with which you can view and check the cluster status in SUSE OpenStack Cloud. They can also be used to look up details like configuration of cluster resources or global cluster options. Read the following chapters for more information:

* HA Web Console: *Configuring and Managing Cluster Resources (Web Interface)*

* `crm.sh`: *Configuring and Managing Cluster Resources (Command Line)*

2.7 Summary: Considerations and Requirements

As outlined above, there are some important considerations to be made before deploying SUSE OpenStack Cloud. The following briefly summarizes what was discussed in detail in this chapter. Keep in mind that as of SUSE OpenStack Cloud 6 it is not possible to change some aspects such as the network setup when SUSE OpenStack Cloud is deployed!

NETWORK

* If you do not want to stick with the default networks and addresses, define custom networks and addresses. You need five different networks. If you need to separate the admin and the BMC network, a sixth network is required. See *Section 2.1, "Network"* for details. Networks that share interfaces need to be configured as VLANs.

* The SUSE OpenStack Cloud networks are completely isolated, therefore it is not required to use public IP addresses for them. A class C network as used in this documentation may not provide enough addresses for a cloud that is supposed to grow. You may alternatively choose addresses from a class B or A network.

- Determine how to allocate addresses from your network. Make sure not to allocate IP addresses twice. See *Section 2.1.1, "Network Address Allocation"* for the default allocation scheme.

- Define which network mode to use. Keep in mind that all machines within the cloud (including the Administration Server) will be set up with the chosen mode and therefore need to meet the hardware requirements. See *Section 2.1.2, "Network Modes"* for details.

- Define how to access the admin and BMC network(s): no access from the outside (no action is required), via an external gateway (gateway needs to be provided), or via bastion network. See *Section 2.1.3, "Accessing the Administration Server via a Bastion Network"* for details.

- Provide a gateway to access the public network (public, nova-floating).

- Make sure the Administration Server's host name is correctly configured (`hostname -f` needs to return a fully qualified host name). If this is not the case, run *YaST › Network Services › Hostnames* and add a fully qualified host name.

- Prepare a list of MAC addresses and the intended use of the corresponding host for all OpenStack nodes.

UPDATE REPOSITORIES

- Depending on your network setup you have different options on how to provide up-to-date update repositories for SUSE Linux Enterprise Server and SUSE OpenStack Cloud for SUSE OpenStack Cloud deployment: using an existing SMT or SUSE Manager server, installing SMT on the Administration Server, synchronizing data with an existing repository, mounting remote repositories or using a "Sneakernet". Choose the option that best matches your needs.

STORAGE

- Decide whether you want to deploy the object storage service Swift. If so, you need to deploy at least two nodes with sufficient disk space exclusively dedicated to Swift.

- Decide which back-end to use with Cinder. If using the *raw* back-end (local disks) it is strongly recommended to use a separate node equipped with several hard disks for deploying `cinder-volume`. If using Ceph, you need to deploy at least four nodes with sufficient disk space exclusively dedicated to it.

- Make sure all Compute Nodes are equipped with sufficient hard disk space.

- Decide whether to use different SSL certificates for the services and the API or whether to use a single certificate.

- Get one or more SSL certificates certified by a trusted third party source.

HARDWARE AND SOFTWARE REQUIREMENTS

- Make sure the hardware requirements for the different node types are met.

- Make sure to have all required software at hand.

2.8 Overview of the SUSE OpenStack Cloud Installation

Deploying and installing SUSE OpenStack Cloud is a multi-step process, starting by deploying a basic SUSE Linux Enterprise Server installation and the SUSE OpenStack Cloud add-on product to the Administration Server. Now the product and update repositories need to be set up and the SUSE OpenStack Cloud network needs to be configured. Next the Administration Server setup will be finished. After the Administration Server is ready, you can start deploying and configuring the OpenStack nodes. The complete node deployment is done automatically via Crowbar and Chef from the Administration Server. All you need to do is to boot the nodes using PXE and to deploy the OpenStack services to them.

1. Install SUSE Linux Enterprise Server 12 SP1 on the Administration Server with the add-on product SUSE OpenStack Cloud. Optionally select the Subscription Management Tool pattern for installation. See *Chapter 3, Installing the Administration Server*.

2. Optionally set up and configure the SMT server on the Administration Server. See *Chapter 4, Installing and Setting Up an SMT Server on the Administration Server (Optional)*.

3. Make all required software repositories available on the Administration Server. See *Chapter 5, Software Repository Setup*.

4. Set up the network on the Administration Server See *Chapter 6, Service Configuration: Administration Server Network Configuration*.

5. Perform the Crowbar setup to configure the SUSE OpenStack Cloud network and to make the repository locations known. When the configuration is done, start the SUSE OpenStack Cloud Crowbar installation. See *Chapter 7, Crowbar Setup*.

6. Boot all nodes onto which the OpenStack components should be deployed using PXE and allocate them in the Crowbar Web interface to start the automatic SUSE Linux Enterprise Server installation. See *Chapter 9, Installing the OpenStack Nodes*.

7. Configure and deploy the OpenStack services via the Crowbar Web interface or command line tools. See *Chapter 10, Deploying the OpenStack Services*.

8. When all OpenStack services are up and running, SUSE OpenStack Cloud is ready. The cloud administrator can now upload images to enable users to start deploying instances. See the *Admin User Guide* and the *Supplement to Admin User Guide and End User Guide*.

II Setting Up the Administration Server

3 Installing the Administration Server

In this chapter you will learn how to install the Administration Server from bare-metal. It will run on SUSE Linux Enterprise Server 12 SP1 and include the SUSE OpenStack Cloud extension and, optionally, the Subscription Management Tool (SMT) server. Prior to starting the installation, refer to *Section 2.4, "Hardware Requirements"* and *Section 2.5, "Software Requirements"* for the requirements.

3.1 Starting the Operating System Installation

Start the installation by booting into the SUSE Linux Enterprise Server 12 SP1 installation system. For an overview of a default SUSE Linux Enterprise Server installation, refer to the SUSE Linux Enterprise Server *Installation Quick Start* [http://www.suse.com/documentation/sles-12/book_quickstarts/data/art_sle_installquick.html]. Detailed installation instructions [http://www.suse.com/documentation/sles-12/book_sle_deployment/data/cha_inst.html] are available in the SUSE Linux Enterprise Server *Deployment Guide*. Both documents are available at http://www.suse.com/documentation/sles-12/.

The following sections will only cover the differences from the default installation process.

3.2 Registration and Online Updates

Registering SUSE Linux Enterprise Server 12 SP1 during the installation process is required for getting product updates and for installing the SUSE OpenStack Cloud extension. Refer to the SUSE Customer Center Registration [http://www.suse.com/documentation/sles-12/book_sle_deployment/data/sec_i_yast2_conf_manual_cc.html] section of the SUSE Linux Enterprise Server 12 SP1 *Deployment Guide* for further instructions.

After having successfully registered you will be asked whether to add the update repositories. If you agree, the latest updates will automatically be installed, ensuring that your system is on the latest patch level after the initial installation. It is strongly recommended to add the update repositories now. If you choose to skip, you need to perform an online update later, before starting the SUSE OpenStack Cloud Crowbar installation.

 Note: SUSE Login Required

To register a product, you need to have a SUSE login. If you do not have such a login, create it at http://www.suse.com/login.

3.3 Installing the SUSE OpenStack Cloud Extension

SUSE OpenStack Cloud is an extension to SUSE Linux Enterprise Server. Installing it during the SUSE Linux Enterprise Server installation is the easiest and recommended way to set up the Administration Server. In order to get access to the extension selection dialog, you need to register SUSE Linux Enterprise Server 12 SP1 during the installation. After a successful registration, the SUSE Linux Enterprise Server 12 SP1 installation continues with the *Extension & Module Selection*. Choose *SUSE OpenStack Cloud 6* and provide the registration key you have obtained by purchasing SUSE OpenStack Cloud. The registration and the extension installation require an Internet connection.

Alternatively, install the SUSE OpenStack Cloud after the SUSE Linux Enterprise Server 12 SP1 installation via *YaST* › *Software* › *Add-On Products*. For details, refer to the section Installing Modules and Extensions from Online Channels [https://www.suse.com/documentation/sles-12/book_sle_deployment/data/sec_add-ons_extensions.html] of the SUSE Linux Enterprise Server 12 SP1 *Deployment Guide*.

3.4 Partitioning

Currently, Crowbar requires /opt to be writable. It is also recommended to create a separate partition or volume formatted with XFS for /srv with a size of at least 30 GB.

The default file system on SUSE Linux Enterprise Server 12 SP1 is Btrfs with snapshots enabled. SUSE OpenStack Cloud installs into /opt, a directory that is excluded from snapshots. Reverting to a snapshot may therefore break the SUSE OpenStack Cloud installation. It is recommended to disable Btrfs snapshots on the Administration Server.

Help on using the partitioning tool is available at the section Using the YaST Partitioner [http://www.suse.com/documentation/sles11/book_sle_deployment/data/sec_yast2_i_y2_part_expert.html] of the SUSE Linux Enterprise Server 12 SP1 *Deployment Guide*.

3.5 Installation Settings

The final installation step, *Installation Settings*, lets you configure various settings. For the Administration Server setup, you need to adjust the software selection and the firewall settings. For more information refer to the Installation Settings [http://www.suse.com/documentation/sles-12/book_sle_deployment/data/sec_i_yast2_proposal.html] section of the SUSE Linux Enterprise Server 12 SP1 *Deployment Guide*.

3.5.1 Software Selection

Installing a minimal base system is sufficient to set up the Administration Server. The following patterns are the minimum requirement:

- *Base System*

- *Minimal System (Appliances)*

- *Meta Package for Pattern cloud_admin*

Tip: Installing a Local SMT Server (Optional)

In case you do not have a SUSE Manager or SMT server in your organization or are planning to manually update the repositories needed to deploy the SUSE OpenStack Cloud nodes, you need to set up an SMT server on the Administration Server. Choose the pattern *Subscription Management Tool* in addition to the patterns listed above to install the SMT server software.

3.5.2 Firewall Settings

SUSE OpenStack Cloud requires to disable the firewall on the Administration Server. You can disable the firewall now in the *Firewall and SSH* section. In case your environment requires a firewall to be active at this stage of the installation, you can postpone disabling the firewall until doing the final network configuration (see *Chapter 6, Service Configuration: Administration Server Network Configuration*).

4 Installing and Setting Up an SMT Server on the Administration Server (Optional)

One way of providing the repositories needed to set up the nodes in SUSE OpenStack Cloud is to install an SMT server on the Administration Server. Then mirror all repositories from SUSE Customer Center via this server. Installing an SMT server on the Administration Server is optional. If your organization already provides an SMT server or a SUSE Manager server that can be accessed from the Administration Server, skip this step.

4.1 SMT Installation

If you have not installed the SMT server during the initial Administration Server installation as suggested in *Section 3.5.1, "Software Selection"*, run the following command to install it:

```
sudo zypper in -t pattern smt
```

4.2 SMT Configuration

No matter whether the SMT server was installed during the initial installation or in the running system, it needs to be configured with the following steps.

 Note: Prerequisites

To configure the SMT server, a SUSE account is required. If you do not have such an account, register at http://www.suse.com/login. Furthermore, all products and extensions for which you want to mirror updates with the SMT server, should be registered at the SUSE Customer Center (http://scc.suse.com/).

1. Configuring the SMT server requires you to have your mirroring credentials (user name and password) and your registration e-mail address at hand. To access them, proceed as follows:

    a. Open a Web browser and log in to the SUSE Customer Center at http://scc.suse.com/.

b. Click your name to see the e-mail address which you have registered.

c. Click *Organization* › *Organization Credentials* to obtain your mirroring credentials (user name and password).

2. Start *YaST* › *Network Services* › *SMT Configuration Wizard*.

3. Activate *Enable Subscription Management Tool Service (SMT)*.

4. Enter the *Customer Center Configuration* data as follows:

   Use Custom Server: Do *not* activate this option
   User: The user name you retrieved from the SUSE Customer Center
   Password:The password you retrieved from the SUSE Customer Center
   Check your input with *Test*. If the test does not return `success`, check the credentials you entered.

5. Enter the e-mail address you retrieved from the SUSE Customer Center at *SCC E-Mail Used for Registration*.

6. *Your SMT Server URL* shows the HTTP address of your server. Usually it should not be necessary to change it.

7. Proceed to step two of the *SMT Configuration Wizard* with *Next*.

8. Enter a *Database Password for SMT User* and confirm it by entering it once again.

9. Enter one or more e-mail addresses to which SMT status reports are sent by selecting *Add*.

10. Write the SMT configuration with *Next*. When setting up the database, you will be prompted for the MariaDB root password. If you have already configured it earlier on, provide the existing password. Otherwise enter a new password. Note, that this is the global MariaDB root password, not the database password for the SMT user you specified before.
    The SMT server requires a server certificate at `/etc/pki/trust/anchors/YaST-CA.pem`. Choose *Run CA Management*, provide a password and choose *Next* to create such a certificate. If your organization already provides a CA certificate, *Skip* this step and import the certificate via *YaST* › *Security and Users* › *CA Management* after the SMT configuration is done. See http://www.suse.com/documentation/sles-12/book_security/data/cha_security_yast_ca.html for more information.
    The last step that is performed when writing the configuration, is a synchronization check with the SUSE Customer Center. It may take several minutes until it is finished.

4.3 Setting up Repository Mirroring on the SMT Server

The final step in setting up the SMT server is to configure it to mirror the repositories needed for SUSE OpenStack Cloud. The SMT server mirrors the repositories from the SUSE Customer Center. To access them, make sure to have appropriate subscriptions registered in SUSE Customer Center with the same e-mail address you have specified when configuring SMT. For details on the required subscriptions refer to *Section 2.5, "Software Requirements"*.

4.3.1 Adding Mandatory Repositories

Mirroring the SUSE Linux Enterprise Server 12 SP1 and SUSE OpenStack Cloud 6 repositories is mandatory. Run the following commands as user `root` to add them to the list of mirrored repositories:

```
for REPO in SLES12-SP1-{Pool,Updates} SUSE-OpenStack-Cloud-6-{Pool,Updates}; do
  smt-repos $REPO sle-12-x86_64 -e
done
```

4.3.2 Adding Optional Repositories

The following repositories are only required if wanting to install the respective optional functionality:

High Availability

For the optional HA setup you need to mirror the SLE-HA12-SP1 repositories. Run the following commands as user `root` to add them to the list of mirrored repositories:

```
for REPO in SLE-HA12-SP1-{Pool,Updates}; do
  smt-repos $REPO sle-12-x86_64 -e
done
```

SUSE Enterprise Storage

The SUSE Enterprise Storage repositories are needed if you plan to deploy Ceph with SUSE OpenStack Cloud. Run the following commands as user `root` to add them to the list of mirrored repositories:

```
for REPO in SUSE-Enterprise-Storage-2.1-{Pool,Updates}; do
  smt-repos $REPO sle-12-x86_64 -e
done
```

4.3.3 Mirroring the Repositories

Repositories added to SMT are updated automatically via cron job. However, to make repositories that have been added available, a manual mirroring run needs to be triggered initially. Do so by running the following command as user `root`:

```
smt-mirror -L /var/log/smt/smt-mirror.log
```

This command will download several GB of patches. This process may last up to several hours. A log file is written to `/var/log/smt/smt-mirror.log`. A list of all repositories and their location in the file system on the Administration Server can be found at *Table B.1, "SMT Repositories Hosted on the Administration Server"*.

4.4 For More Information

For detailed information about SMT refer to the Subscription Management Tool manual at http://www.suse.com/documentation/sles-12/book_smt/data/book_smt.html.

5 Software Repository Setup

Nodes in SUSE OpenStack Cloud are automatically installed from the Administration Server. To do so, software repositories containing products, extensions and the respective updates for all software need to be available on or accessible from the Administration Server. In this configuration step, these repositories are made available. Two types of repositories can be distinguished:

Product Media Repositories: Product media repositories are copies of the installation media. They need to be directly copied to the Administration Server, "loop-mounted" from an iso image or mounted from a remote server via NFS. Affected are SUSE Linux Enterprise Server 12 SP1 and SUSE OpenStack Cloud 6. The content of these repositories is static. See *Section 5.1, "Copying the Product Media Repositories"* for setup instructions.

Update and Pool Repositories: Update and Pool repositories are provided by the SUSE Customer Center. They contain all updates and patches for the products and extensions. To make them available for SUSE OpenStack Cloud they need to be mirrored from the SUSE Customer Center. Since their content is regularly updated, they need to be kept in synchronization with SUSE Customer Center. For these purposes, SUSE provides either the Subscription Management Tool (SMT) or the SUSE Manager.

5.1 Copying the Product Media Repositories

The files in the product repositories for SUSE Linux Enterprise Server and SUSE OpenStack Cloud do not change, therefore they do not need to be synchronized with a remote source. It is sufficient to either copy the data (from a remote host or the installation media), to mount the product repository from a remote server via NFS, or to loop mount a copy of the installation images.

 Important: No Symbolic Links for the SUSE Linux Enterprise Server Repository

Note that the SUSE Linux Enterprise Server product repository *must* be directly available from the local directory listed below. It is not possible to use a symbolic link to a directory located elsewhere, since this will cause booting using PXE to fail.

Tip: Providing the SUSE OpenStack Cloud Repository via HTTP

The SUSE Linux Enterprise Server product repositories needs to be made available locally to enable booting using PXE for node deployment. The SUSE OpenStack Cloud repository may also be served via `http` from a remote host. In this case, enter the URL to the `Cloud` repository as described in *Section 7.4, "Repositories"*.

However, copying the data to the Administration Server as described here, is recommended. It does not require much hard disk space (approximately 350 MB). Nor does it require the Administration Server to be able to access a remote host from a different network.

The following product media needs to be copied to the specified directories:

TABLE 5.1: LOCAL PRODUCT REPOSITORIES FOR SUSE OPENSTACK CLOUD

Repository	Directory
SUSE Linux Enterprise Server 12 SP1 DVD #1	`/srv/tftpboot/suse-12.1/x86_64/install`
SUSE OpenStack Cloud 6 DVD #1	`/srv/tftpboot/suse-12.1/x86_64/repos/Cloud`

The data can be copied by a variety of methods:

Copying from the Installation Media

It is recommended to use **rsync** for copying. If the installation data is located on a removable device, make sure to mount it first (for example, after inserting the DVD1 in the Administration Server and waiting for the device to become ready):

SUSE Linux Enterprise Server 12 SP1 DVD#1

```
mkdir -p /srv/tftpboot/suse-12.1/x86_64/install
mount /dev/dvd /mnt
rsync -avP /mnt/ /srv/tftpboot/suse-12.1/x86_64/install/
umount /mnt
```

SUSE OpenStack Cloud 6 DVD#1

```
mkdir -p /srv/tftpboot/suse-12.1/x86_64/repos/Cloud
```

```
mount /dev/dvd /mnt
rsync -avP /mnt/ /srv/tftpboot/suse-12.1/x86_64/repos/Cloud/
umount /mnt
```

Copying from a Remote Host

If the data is provided by a remote machine, log in to that machine and push the data to the Administration Server (which has the IP address 192.168.124.10 in the following example):

SUSE Linux Enterprise Server 12 SP1 DVD#1

```
mkdir -p /srv/tftpboot/suse-12.1/x86_64/install
rsync -avPz /data/SLES-12-SP1/DVD1/ 192.168.124.10:/srv/tftpboot/suse-12.1/
x86_64/install/
```

SUSE OpenStack Cloud 6 DVD#1

```
mkdir -p /srv/tftpboot/suse-12.1/x86_64/repos/Cloud
rsync -avPz /data/SUSE-OPENSTACK-CLOUD//DVD1/ 192.168.124.10:/srv/tftpboot/
suse-12.1/x86_64/repos/Cloud/
```

Mounting from an NFS Server

If the installation data is provided via NFS by a remote machine, mount the respective shares as follows. To automatically mount these directories either create entries in /etc/fstab or set up the automounter.

SUSE Linux Enterprise Server 12 SP1 DVD#1

```
mkdir -p /srv/tftpboot/suse-12.1/x86_64/install
mount -t nfs nfs.example.com:/exports/SLES-12-SP1/x86_64/DVD1/ /srv/tftpboot/
suse-12.1/x86_64/install
```

SUSE OpenStack Cloud 6 DVD#1

```
mkdir -p /srv/tftpboot/suse-12.1/x86_64/repos/Cloud/
mount -t nfs nfs.example.com:/exports/SUSE-OPENSTACK-CLOUD/DVD1/ /srv/tftpboot/
suse-12.1/x86_64/repos/Cloud
```

Mounting the ISO Images

The product repositories can also be made available by copying the respective iso images to the Administration Server and mounting them. To automatically mount these directories either create entries in /etc/fstab or set up the automounter.

SUSE Linux Enterprise Server 12 SP1 DVD#1

```
mkdir -p /srv/tftpboot/suse-12.1/x86_64/install/
mount -o loop /local/SLES-12-SP1-x86_64-DVD1.iso /srv/tftpboot/suse-12.1/
x86_64/install
```

SUSE OpenStack Cloud 6 DVD#1

```
mkdir -p /srv/tftpboot/suse-12.1/x86_64/repos/Cloud/
mount -o loop /local/SUSE-OPENSTACK-CLOUD-6-x86_64-DVD1.iso /srv/tftpboot/
suse-12.1/x86_64/repos/Cloud
```

5.2 Update and Pool Repositories

Update and Pool Repositories are required on the Administration Server to set up and maintain the SUSE OpenStack Cloud nodes. They are provided by SUSE Customer Center and contain all software packages needed to install SUSE Linux Enterprise Server 12 SP1 and the extensions (pool repositories). In addition, they contain all updates and patches (update repositories). Update repositories are already used when deploying the nodes that will build SUSE OpenStack Cloud to ensure they are initially equipped with the latest software versions available.

The repositories can be made available on the Administration Server using one of the following methods (or a mix of them):

- *Section 5.2.1, " Repositories Hosted on an SMT Server Installed on the Administration Server "*

- *Section 5.2.2, "Repositories Hosted on a Remote SMT Server"*

- *Section 5.2.3, "Repositories Hosted on a SUSE Manager Server"*

- *Section 5.2.4, "Alternative Ways to Make the Repositories Available"*

5.2.1 Repositories Hosted on an SMT Server Installed on the Administration Server

When all update and pool repositories are managed by an SMT server installed on the Administration Server (see *Chapter 4, Installing and Setting Up an SMT Server on the Administration Server (Optional)*), make sure the repository location in YaST Crowbar is set to *Local SMT Server* (this is the default). For details, see *Section 7.4, "Repositories"* . No further action is required. The SUSE OpenStack Cloud Crowbar installation automatically detects all available repositories.

5.2.2 Repositories Hosted on a Remote SMT Server

To use repositories from a remote SMT server you first need to make sure all required repositories are mirrored on the server. Refer to *Section 4.3, "Setting up Repository Mirroring on the SMT Server"* for more information. When all update and pool repositories are managed by a remote SMT server, make sure the repository location in YaST Crowbar is set to *Remote SMT Server*. For details, see *Section 7.4, "Repositories"*. No further action is required. The SUSE OpenStack Cloud Crowbar installation automatically detects all available repositories.

 Note: Accessing an External SMT Server

In SUSE OpenStack Cloud, only the Administration Server needs to be able to access the external SMT server. A network connection can either be established via a bastion network (see *Section 7.3.1, "Setting Up a Bastion Network"* or an external gateway.

5.2.3 Repositories Hosted on a SUSE Manager Server

To use repositories from SUSE Manager you first need to make sure all required products and extensions are registered and the corresponding channels are mirrored in SUSE Manager (refer to *Table B.3, "SUSE Manager Repositories (Channels)"* for a list of channels).

 Important: Accessing a SUSE Manager Server

An external SUSE Manager server needs to be accessed from *all* nodes in SUSE OpenStack Cloud. To be able to access it, the network hosting the SUSE Manager server needs to be added to the network definitions as described in *Section 7.5.1, "Providing Access to External Networks"*.

By default SUSE Manager does not expose repositories for direct access. To access them via `https`, you need to create a *Distribution* for auto-installation for the SUSE Linux Enterprise Server 12 SP1 (x86_64) product. Creating this distribution makes the update repositories for this product available, including the repositories for all registered add-on products (like SUSE OpenStack Cloud, SLES High Availability Extension and SUSE Enterprise Storage). Instructions on how to create a distribution can be found in the SUSE Manager documentation in http://www.suse.com/documentation/suse_manager/.

During the distribution setups you need to provide a *Label* for each the distribution. This label will be part of the URL under which the repositories are available. It is recommended to choose a name consisting of characters that do not need to be URL-encoded. In *Table B.3, "SUSE Manager Repositories (Channels)"* we assume the following label has been provided: `sles12-sp1-x86_64`.

When all update and pool repositories are managed by a SUSE Manager server, make sure the repository location in YaST Crowbar is set to *SUSE Manager Server*. For details, see *Section 7.4, "Repositories"*. No further action is required. The SUSE OpenStack Cloud Crowbar installation automatically detects all available repositories.

The autoinstallation tree provided by SUSE Manager does not provide the SLES Pool repository. Although this repositories is not used for node installation, it needs to be present. To work around this issue, it is sufficient to create an empty Pool repository for SUSE Linux Enterprise Server 12 SP1:

```
mkdir /srv/tftpboot/suse-12.1/x86_64/repos/SLES12-SP1-Pool/
createrepo /srv/tftpboot/suse-12.1/x86_64/repos/SLES12-SP1-Pool/
```

5.2.4 Alternative Ways to Make the Repositories Available

If you want to keep your SUSE OpenStack Cloud network as isolated from the company network as possible, or your infrastructure does not allow accessing a SUSE Manager or an SMT server, you can alternatively provide access to the required repositories by one of the following ways:

- mounting the repositories from a remote server

- synchronizing the repositories from a remote server (for example via `rsync` and cron)

- manually synchronize the update repositories from removable media ("sneakernet").

It is strongly recommended to make the repositories available at the default locations on the Administration Server as listed in *Table B.4, "Default Repository Locations on the Administration Server"*. When choosing these locations, it is sufficient to set the repository location in YaST Crowbar to *Custom*. You do not need to specify a detailed location for each repository. Refer to *Section 7.4, "Repositories"* for details. If you prefer to use different locations, you need to announce each location with YaST Crowbar.

5.3 Software Repository Sources for the Administration Server Operating System

During the installation of the Administration Server repository locations for SUSE Linux Enterprise Server 12 SP1 have been automatically added to the Administration Server. They point to the source used to install the Administration Server and to the SUSE Customer Center. These repository locations have no influence on the repositories used to set up nodes in the cloud. They are solely used to maintain and update the Administration Server itself.

However, as the Administration Server and all nodes in the cloud use the same operating system—SUSE Linux Enterprise Server 12 SP1—it makes sense to use the same repositories for the cloud and the Administration Server. To avoid downloading the same patches twice: Change this setup in a way that the repositories set up for SUSE OpenStack Cloud deployment are also used on the Administration Server.

To do so, you need to disable or delete all services. In a second step all SUSE Linux Enterprise Server and SUSE OpenStack Cloud repositories need to be edited to point to the alternative sources. Editing the repository setup can either be done with Zypper or YaST. Note that changing the repository setup on the Administration Server is optional.

6 Service Configuration: Administration Server Network Configuration

Prior to starting the SUSE OpenStack Cloud Crowbar installation, make sure the first network interface (`eth0`) gets a fixed IP address from the admin network. A host and domain name also needs to be provided. Other interfaces will automatically be configured during the SUSE OpenStack Cloud Crowbar installation.

To configure the network interface proceed as follows:

1. Start *YaST > System > Network Settings*.

2. Switch to the *Overview* tab and select the interface with the *Device* identifier `eth0` and choose *Edit*.

3. Switch to the *Address* tab and activate *Statically Assigned IP Address* and provide an IPv4 *IP Address*, a *Subnet Mask* and a fully qualified *Hostname*. Examples in this book assume the default IP address of `192.168.124.10` and a network mask of `255.255.255.0`. Using a different IP address requires to adjust the Crowbar configuration in a later step as described in *Chapter 7, Crowbar Setup*.

4. Check the settings on the *General* tab. The device needs to be activated *At Boot Time*. Confirm your settings with *Next*.

5. Back on the *Network Settings* dialog, switch to the *Routing* tab and enter a *Default IPv4 Gateway*. The address depends on whether you have provided an external gateway for the admin network. In that case, use the address of that gateway. If not, use *xxx.xxx.xxx*.1, for example, `192.168.124.1`. Confirm your settings with *OK*.

6. Choose *Hostname/DNS* from the *Network Settings* dialog and set the *Hostname* and *Domain Name*. Examples in this book assume and `admin.cloud.example.com` for the host/domain name.

   If the Administration Server has access to the outside, you can add additional name servers here that will automatically be used to forward requests. The Administration Server's name server will automatically be configured during the SUSE OpenStack Cloud Crowbar installation to forward requests for non-local records to those server(s).

7. Last, check if the firewall is disabled. Return to YaST's main menu (*YaST Control Center*) and start *Security and Users* › *Firewall*. On *Start-Up* › *Service Start*, the firewall needs to be disabled. Confirm your settings with *Next*.

> **❗ Important: Administration Server Domain Name and Host name**
>
> Setting up the SUSE OpenStack Cloud will also install a DNS server for all nodes in the cloud. The domain name you specify for the Administration Server will be used for the DNS zone. It is required to use a sub-domain such as `cloud.example.com`. See *Section 2.1.4, "DNS and Host Names"* for more information.
>
> The host name and the FQDN need to be resolvable with `hostname` `-f`. Double-check whether `/etc/hosts` contains an appropriate entry for the Administration Server. It should look like the following:
>
> ```
> 192.168.124.10 admin.cloud.example.com admin
> ```
>
> It is *not* possible to change the Administration Server host name or the FQDN after the SUSE OpenStack Cloud Crowbar installation has been completed.

7 Crowbar Setup

The YaST Crowbar module enables you to configure all networks within the cloud, to set up additional repositories and to manage the Crowbar users. This module should be launched before starting the SUSE OpenStack Cloud Crowbar installation. To start this module, either run `yast crowbar` or *YaST › Miscellaneous › Crowbar*.

7.1 User Settings

On this tab you can manage users for the Crowbar Web interface. The user `crowbar` (password `crowbar`) is preconfigured. Use the *Add*, *Edit* and *Delete* buttons to manage user accounts. Users configured here have no relations to existing system users on the Administration Server.

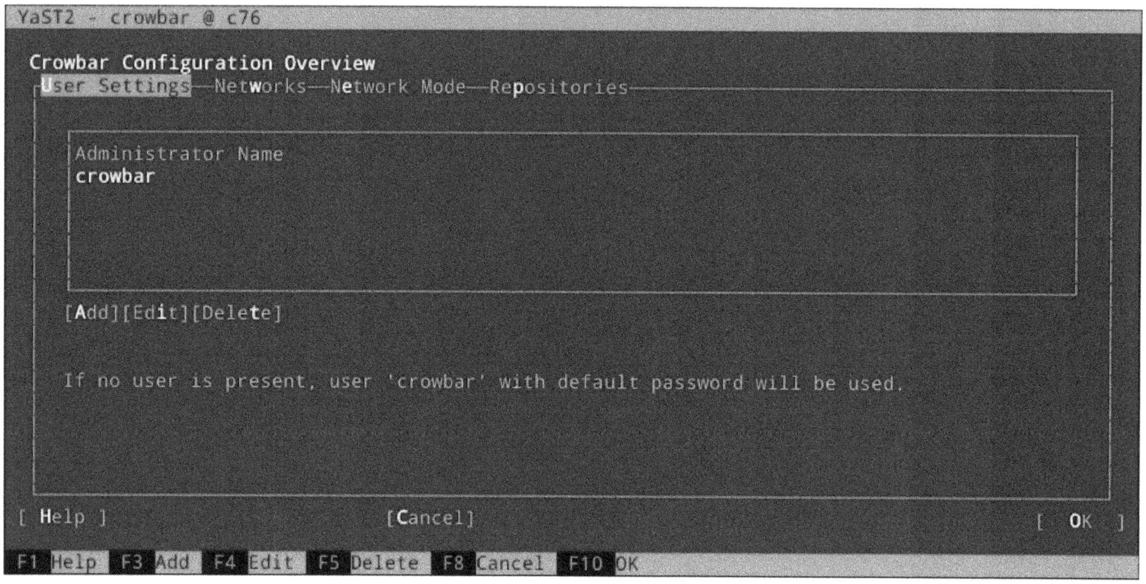

```
YaST2 - crowbar @ c76

Crowbar Configuration Overview
  User Settings──Networks──Network Mode──Repositories─────────────

   ┌─────────────────────────────────────────────────────────────┐
   │ Administrator Name                                           │
   │ crowbar                                                      │
   │                                                             │
   │                                                             │
   │                                                             │
   └─────────────────────────────────────────────────────────────┘

   [Add][Edit][Delete]


   If no user is present, user 'crowbar' with default password will be used.




[ Help ]                      [Cancel]                            [  OK  ]
F1 Help  F3 Add  F4 Edit  F5 Delete  F8 Cancel  F10 OK
```

FIGURE 7.1: YAST CROWBAR SETUP: USER SETTINGS

7.2 Networks

Use the *Networks* tab to change the default network setup (described in *Section 2.1, "Network"*). Change the IP address assignment for each network under *Edit Ranges*. You may also add a bridge (*Add Bridge*) or a VLAN (*Use VLAN, VLAN ID*) to a network. Only change the latter two settings if you really know what you require; sticking with the defaults is recommended.

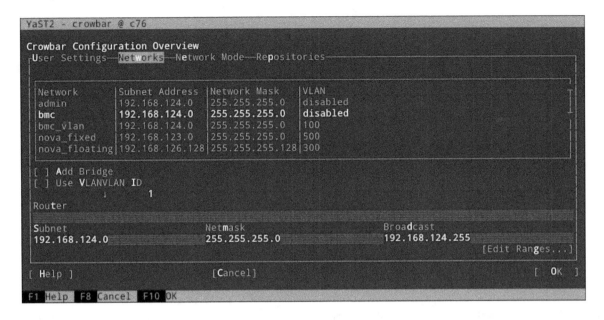

FIGURE 7.2: YAST CROWBAR SETUP: NETWORK SETTINGS

> ## Warning: No Network Changes After Having Completed the SUSE OpenStack Cloud Crowbar installation
>
> After you have completed the SUSE OpenStack Cloud Crowbar installation, you cannot change the network setup anymore. If you did, you would need to completely set up the Administration Server again.

> ## Important: VLAN Settings
>
> As of SUSE OpenStack Cloud 6, using a VLAN for the admin network is only supported on a native/untagged VLAN. If you need VLAN support for the admin network, it must be handled at switch level.
>
> When deploying Compute Nodes with Microsoft Hyper-V or Windows Server, you must *not* use openvswitch with gre. Instead, use openvswitch with VLAN (recommended) or linuxbridge as a plugin for Neutron.

When changing the network configuration with YaST or by editing `/etc/crow-bar/network.json` you can define VLAN settings for each network. For the networks `nova-fixed` and `nova-floating`, however, special rules apply:

nova-fixed: The *USE VLAN* setting will be ignored. However, VLANs will automatically be used if deploying Neutron with VLAN support (using the plugins linuxbridge, openvswitch plus VLAN or cisco plus VLAN). In this case, you need to specify a correct *VLAN ID* for this network.

nova-floating: When using a VLAN for `nova-floating` (which is the default), the *USE VLAN* and *VLAN ID* settings for *nova-floating* and *public* need to be the same. When not using a VLAN for `nova-floating`, it needs to use a different physical network interface than the `nova_fixed` network.

Other, more flexible network mode setups, can be configured by manually editing the Crowbar network configuration files. See *Appendix D, The Network Barclamp Template File* for more information. SUSE or a partner can assist you in creating a custom setup within the scope of a consulting services agreement. See http://www.suse.com/consulting/ for more information on SUSE consulting.

7.2.1   Separating the Admin and the BMC Network

If you want to separate the admin and the BMC network, you must change the settings for the networks *bmc* and *bmc_vlan*. The *bmc_vlan* is used to generate a VLAN tagged interface on the Administration Server that can access the *bmc* network. The *bmc_vlan* needs to be in the same ranges as *bmc*, and *bmc* needs to have *VLAN* enabled.

TABLE 7.1: SEPARATE BMC NETWORK EXAMPLE CONFIGURATION

	bmc	bmc_vlan
Subnet	192.168.128.0	
Netmask	255.255.255.0	
Router	192.168.128.1	
Broadcast	192.168.128.255	

	bmc	bmc_vlan
Host Range	`192.168.128.10` - `192.168.128.100`	`192.168.128.101` - `192.168.128.101`
VLAN	yes	
VLAN ID	100	
Bridge	no	

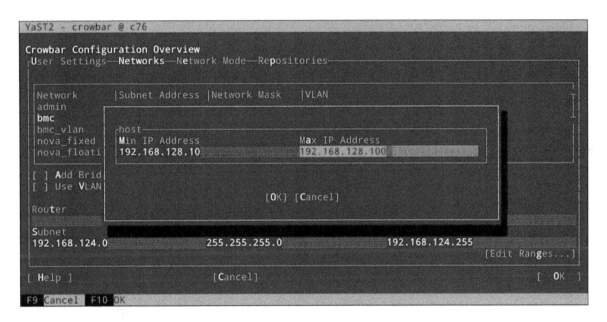

FIGURE 7.3: YAST CROWBAR SETUP: NETWORK SETTINGS FOR THE BMC NETWORK

7.3 Network Mode

On the *Network Mode* tab you can choose between *single*, *dual*, and *team*. In single mode, all traffic is handled by a single Ethernet card. Dual mode requires two thernet cards and seperates traffic for private and public networks. See *Section 2.1.2, "Network Modes"* for details.

Teaming mode is almost identical to single mode, except that you combine several Ethernet cards to a "bond". It is required for a HA setup of SUSE OpenStack Cloud. When choosing this mode, you also have to specify a *Bonding Policy*. This option lets you define whether to focus on reliability (fault tolerance), performance (load balancing), or a combination of both. The following modes can be chosen (see https://www.kernel.org/doc/Documentation/networking/bonding.txt for a more detailed description):

0 (balance-rr)

Packets are transmitted in round-robin fashion from the first to the last available interface. Provides fault tolerance and load balancing.

1 (active-backup)

Only one network interface is active. If it fails, a different interface becomes active. This setting is the default for SUSE OpenStack Cloud. Provides fault tolerance.

2 (balance-xor)

Traffic is split between all available interfaces absed on the following policy: `[(source MAC address XOR'd with destination MAC address XOR packet type ID) modulo slave count]`. Provides fault tolerance and load balancing.

3 (broadcast)

The complete traffic is broadcasted on all interfaces. Provides fault tolerance.

4 (802.3ad)

Aggregates interfaces into groups that share the same speed and duplex settings. Requires `ethtool` support in the interface drivers and a switch that supports and is configured for IEEE 802.3ad Dynamic link aggregation. Provides fault tolerance and load balancing.

5 (balance-tlb)

Adaptive transmit load balancing. Requires `ethtool` support in the interface drivers but no switch support. Provides fault tolerance and load balancing.

6 (balance-alb)

Adaptive load balancing. Requires `ethtool` support in the interface drivers but no switch support. Provides fault tolerance and load balancing.

7.3.1   Setting Up a Bastion Network

The *Network Mode* tab of the YaST Crowbar module also lets you set up a Bastion network. As outlined in *Section 2.1, "Network"*, one way to access the Administration Server from a defined external network is via a Bastion network and a second network card (as opposed to providing an external gateway).

To set up the Bastion network, you need to have a static IP address for the Administration Server from the external network. The example configuration used below assumes that the external network from which to access the admin network has the following addresses. Adjust them according to your needs.

TABLE 7.2: EXAMPLE ADDRESSES FOR A BASTION NETWORK

Subnet	10.10.1.0
Netmask	255.255.255.0
Broadcast	10.10.1.255
Gateway	10.10.1.1
Static Administration Server address	10.10.1.125

In addition to the values above, you need to enter the *Physical Interface Mapping*. With this value you specify the Ethernet card that is used for the bastion network. See *Section D.4, "Network Conduits"* for details on the syntax. The default value ?1g2 matches the second interface ("eth1") of the system.

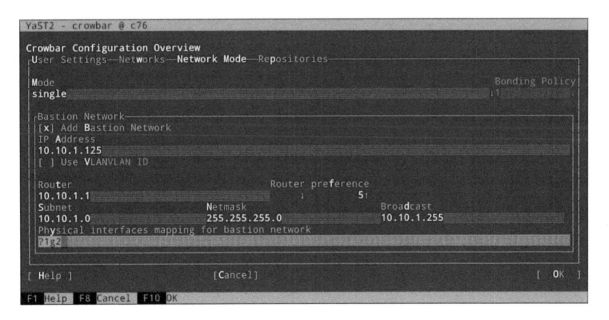

FIGURE 7.4: YAST CROWBAR SETUP: NETWORK SETTINGS FOR THE BASTION NETWORK

Warning: No Network Changes After Having Completed the SUSE OpenStack Cloud Crowbar installation

After you have completed the SUSE OpenStack Cloud Crowbar installation, you cannot change the network setup anymore. If you did, you would need to completely set up the Administration Server again.

Important: Accessing Nodes From Outside the Bastion Network

The example configuration from above allows to access SUSE OpenStack Cloud nodes from *within* the bastion network. If you want to access nodes from outside the bastion network, make the router for the bastion network the default router for the Administration Server. This is achieved by setting the value for the bastion network's *Router preference* entry to a lower value than the corresponding entry for the admin network. By default no router preference is set for the Administration Server—in this case, set the preference for the bastion network to 5.

If you use a Linux gateway between the outside and the bastion network, you also need to disable route verification (rp_filter) on the Administration Server. Do so by running the following command on the Administration Server:

```
echo 0 > /proc/sys/net/ipv4/conf/all/rp_filter
```

That command disables route verification for the current session, so the setting will not "survive" a reboot. Make it permanent by editing /etc/sysctl.conf and setting the value for *net.ipv4.conf.all.rp_filter* to 0.

7.4 Repositories

This dialog lets you announce the locations of the product, pool, and update repositories (see *Chapter 5, Software Repository Setup* for details). You can choose between four alternatives:

Local SMT Server

> If you have an SMT server installed on the Administration Server as explained in *Chapter 4, Installing and Setting Up an SMT Server on the Administration Server (Optional)*, choose this option. The repository details do not need to be provided, they will be configured automatically. This option will be applied by default in case the repository configuration has net been changed manually.

Remote SMT Server

> If you use a remote SMT for *all* repositories, choose this option and provide the *Sever URL* (in the form of `http://smt.example.com`). The repository details do not need to be provided, they will be configured automatically.

SUSE Manager Server

> If you use a remote SUSE Manager server for *all* repositories, choose this option and provide the *Sever URL* (in the form of `http://manager.example.com`).

Custom

> If you use different sources for your repositories or are using non-standard locations, choose this option and manually provide a location for each repository. This can either be a local directory (`/srv/tftpboot/suse-12.1/x86_64/repos/SLES12-SP1-Pool/`) or a remote location (`http://manager.example.com/ks/dist/child/sles12-sp1-updates-x86_64/sles12-sp1-x86_64/`). Activating *Ask On Error* ensures that you will be informed, if a repository is not available during node deployment (otherwise errors will be silently ignored).
>
> The *Add Repository* dialog allows to add additional repositories. See *Q:* for instructions.

> Tip: Default Locations
>
> In case you have made the repositories available in the default locations on the Administration Server (see *Table B.4, "Default Repository Locations on the Administration Server"* for a list), choose *Custom* and leave the *Repository URL* empty (default). The repositories will automatically be detected.

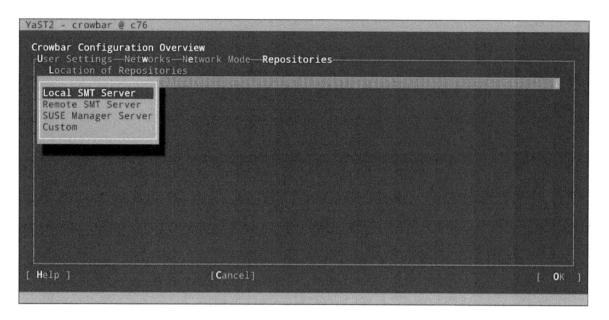

FIGURE 7.5: YAST CROWBAR SETUP: REPOSITORY SETTINGS

7.5 Custom Network Configuration

In case you need to adjust the pre-defined network setup of SUSE OpenStack Cloud beyond the scope of changing IP address assignments (as described in *Chapter 7, Crowbar Setup*), you need to manually modify the network barclamp template. Refer to *Appendix D, The Network Barclamp Template File* for details.

7.5.1 Providing Access to External Networks

By default, external networks cannot be reached from nodes in the SUSE OpenStack Cloud. To access external services such as a SUSE Manager server, an SMT server, or a SAN, you need to make the external network(s) known to SUSE OpenStack Cloud. Do so by adding a network definition for each external network to `/etc/crowbar/network.json`. Refer to *Appendix D, The Network Barclamp Template File* for setup instructions.

EXAMPLE 7.1: EXAMPLE NETWORK DEFINITION FOR THE EXTERNAL NETWORK 192.168.150.0/16

```
"external" : {
    "add_bridge" : false,
```

```
            "vlan" : XXX,
            "ranges" : {
                "host" : {
                    "start" : "192.168.150.1",
                    "end" : "192.168.150.254"
                }
            },
            "broadcast" : "192.168.150.255",
            "netmask" : "255.255.255.0",
            "conduit" : "intf1",
            "subnet" : "192.168.150.0",
            "use_vlan" : true
        }
```

Replace the value *XXX* for the VLAN by a value not used within the SUSE OpenStack Cloud network and not used by Neutron. By default, the following VLANs are already used:

TABLE 7.3: VLANS USED BY THE SUSE OPENSTACK CLOUD DEFAULT NETWORK SETUP

VLAN ID	Used by
100	BMC VLAN (bmc_vlan)
200	Storage Network
300	Public Network (nova-floating, public)
400	Software-defined network (os_sdn)
500	Private Network (nova-fixed)
501 - 2500	Neutron (value of nova-fixed plus 2000)

7.5.2 Split Public and Floating Networks on Different VLANs

For custom setups, the public and floating networks can be separated. For this, configure your own separate floating network which will not be a subnet of public network. The floating network also needs to have its own router defined.

7.5.3 Adjusting the Maximum Transmission Unit for the Admin and Storage Network

If you need to adjust the Maximum Transmission Unit (MTU) for the Admin and/or Storage Network, adjust `/etc/crowbar/network.json` as shown below. You can also enable jumbo frames this way by setting the MTU to 9000. The following example enables jumbo frames for both, the storage and the admin network by setting `"mtu": 9000`.

```
"admin": {
  "add_bridge": false,
  "broadcast": "192.168.124.255",
  "conduit": "intf0",
  "mtu": 9000,
  "netmask": "255.255.255.0",
  "ranges": {
    "admin": {
      "end": "192.168.124.11",
      "start": "192.168.124.10"
    },
    "dhcp": {
      "end": "192.168.124.80",
      "start": "192.168.124.21"
    },
    "host": {
      "end": "192.168.124.160",
      "start": "192.168.124.81"
    },
    "switch": {
      "end": "192.168.124.250",
      "start": "192.168.124.241"
    }
  },
  "router": "192.168.124.1",
  "router_pref": 10,
  "subnet": "192.168.124.0",
  "use_vlan": false,
```

```
      "vlan": 100
    },
    "storage": {
      "add_bridge": false,
      "broadcast": "192.168.125.255",
      "conduit": "intf1",
      "mtu": 9000,
      "netmask": "255.255.255.0",
      "ranges": {
        "host": {
          "end": "192.168.125.239",
          "start": "192.168.125.10"
        }
      },
      "subnet": "192.168.125.0",
      "use_vlan": true,
      "vlan": 200
    },
```

 Warning: No Network Changes After Having Completed the SUSE
OpenStack Cloud Crowbar installation

After you have completed the SUSE OpenStack Cloud Crowbar installation, you cannot
change the network setup anymore. This also includes changing the MTU size.

7.6 Starting the SUSE OpenStack Cloud Crowbar installation

Before starting the SUSE OpenStack Cloud Crowbar installation to finish the configuration of
the Administration Server make sure to double-check the following items.

FINAL CHECK POINTS

- Make sure the network configuration is correct. Run *YaST* › *Crowbar* to review/change the
  configuration. See *Chapter 7, Crowbar Setup* for further instructions.

Important: An HA Setup Requires Teaming Network Mode

In case you are planning to make SUSE OpenStack Cloud highly available upon the initial setup or at a later point in time, make sure to set up the network in teaming mode. Such a setup requires at least two network cards for each node.

- Make sure `hostname -f` returns a fully qualified host name. See *Chapter 6, Service Configuration: Administration Server Network Configuration* for further instructions.

- Make sure all update and product repositories are available. See *Chapter 5, Software Repository Setup* for further instructions.

- Make sure the operating system and SUSE OpenStack Cloud are up-to-date and have the latest patches installed. Run `zypper patch` to install them.

Now everything is in place to finally configure the Administration Server. This is done by either running the script `install-suse-cloud` on the command line or starting the installation via Web interface. This routine will install and configure Chef, and use it to complete the installation of Crowbar and all required barclamps. It will take several minutes to complete.

 Warning: No Network Changes After Having Run the Cloud Installation Script

After you have run the cloud installation script, you cannot change the network setup anymore. If you did, you would need to completely set up the Administration Server again.

7.6.1 Starting the SUSE OpenStack Cloud Crowbar Installation from the Web Interface

To use the Web interface you need network access to the Administration Server via a second network interface. As the network will be reconfigured during the SUSE OpenStack Cloud Crowbar installation, make sure to either have a bastion network or an external gateway configured. (For details on bastion networks, see *Section 7.3.1, "Setting Up a Bastion Network".*) Before you can access the Web interface start the Crowbar service:

```
systemctl start crowbar
```

If you have installed SMT on the Administration Server you also need to restart the Apache Web server:

```
systemctl reload apache2
```

When Crowbar is running, you can access the Web interface from a Web browser by the address `http://ADDRESS`. Replace `ADDRESS` either with the IP address of the second network interface or its associated host name.

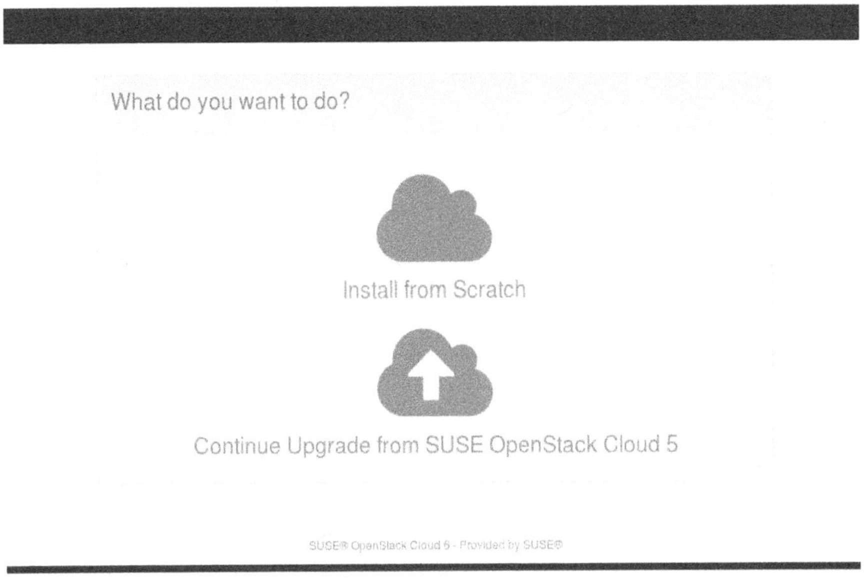

What do you want to do?

Install from Scratch

Continue Upgrade from SUSE OpenStack Cloud 5

SUSE® OpenStack Cloud 5 · Provided by SUSE®

FIGURE 7.6: THE SUSE OPENSTACK CLOUD INSTALLER

To start the installation procedure, click *Install from Scratch*. The installation progress is shown in the table detailing the installation steps.

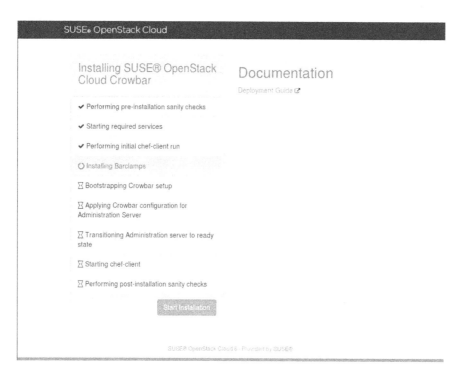

FIGURE 7.7: THE SUSE OPENSTACK CLOUD CROWBAR INSTALLATION WEB INTERFACE

7.6.2 Starting the SUSE OpenStack Cloud Crowbar Installation from the Command Line

To start the SUSE OpenStack Cloud Crowbar installation execute the following command:

```
screen install-suse-cloud
```

install-suse-cloud will produce a lot of output that gets written to a log file located at `/var/log/crowbar/install.log`. Check this log file in case something goes wrong. You can run **install-suse-cloud** multiple times as long as you have not started to deploy the OpenStack services. It is also possible to run **install-suse-cloud** in verbose mode with the `-v` switch. It will show the same output that goes to the log file on STDOUT, too.

> **❗ Important: Use a Terminal Multiplexer to Run the Cloud Installation Script**
>
> Run the installation script `install-suse-cloud` inside of a terminal multiplexer like GNU Screen (provided by the `screen` package).

During the run of this script the network will be reconfigured. This may result in interrupting the script when being run from a network connection (like SSH). Using **screen** will continue running the script in a session to which you can reconnect via **screen -r** if you lose the connection.

7.6.3 Log in to the Crowbar Web Interface

If the installation via Web interface has been successfully finished, you will be redirected to the Crowbar Web interface. If you have started the installation from the command line, start a browser. Point it to the Crowbar Web interface available on the Administration Server, for example `http://192.168.124.10/`.

Logging in to the Web interface requires the credentials you configured with YaST Crowbar (see *Section 7.1, "User Settings"*). If you have not changed the defaults, user name and password are both `crowbar`. Refer to *Chapter 8, The Crowbar Web Interface* for details.

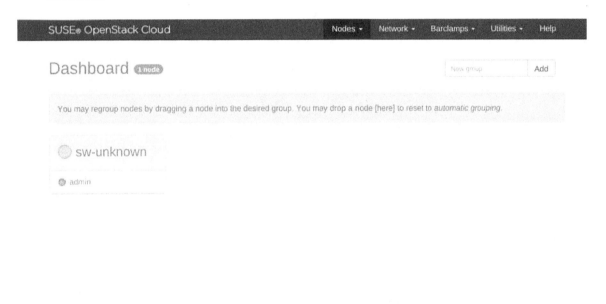

FIGURE 7.8: CROWBAR WEB INTERFACE: INITIAL STATE

III Setting Up OpenStack Nodes and Services

8 The Crowbar Web Interface

The Crowbar Web interface runs on the Administration Server. It provides an overview of the most important deployment details in your cloud, including a view on the nodes and which roles are deployed on which nodes, and on the barclamp proposals that can be edited and deployed. In addition, the Crowbar Web interface shows details about the networks and switches in your cloud. It also provides graphical access to some tools with which you can manage your repositories, back up or restore the Administration Server, export the Chef configuration, or generate a `supportconfig` TAR archive with the most important log files.

8.1 Logging In

The Crowbar Web interface uses the HTTP protocol and port `80`.

PROCEDURE 8.1: LOGGING IN TO THE CROWBAR WEB INTERFACE

1. On any machine, start a Web browser and make sure that JavaScript and cookies are enabled.

2. As URL, enter the IP address of the Administration Server, for example:

   ```
   http://192.168.124.10/
   ```

3. Log in as user `crowbar`. If you have not changed the password, it is `crowbar` by default.

PROCEDURE 8.2: CHANGING THE PASSWORD FOR THE CROWBAR WEB INTERFACE

1. After being logged in to the Crowbar Web interface, select *Barclamp* › *Crowbar*.

2. Select the `Crowbar` barclamp entry and *Edit* the proposal.

3. In the *Attributes* section, click *Raw* to edit the configuration file.

4. Search for the following entry:

   ```
   "crowbar": {
        "password": "crowbar"
   ```

5. Change the password.

6. Confirm your change by clicking *Save* and *Apply*.

8.2 Overview: Main Elements

After logging in to Crowbar, you will see a navigation bar at the top-level row. Its menus and the respective views are described in the following sections.

FIGURE 8.1: CROWBAR UI—DASHBOARD (MAIN SCREEN)

8.2.1 Nodes

Dashboard

> This is the default view after logging in to the Crowbar Web interface. The Dashboard shows the groups (which you can create to arrange nodes according to their purpose), which nodes belong to each group and which state the nodes and groups are in. In addition, the total number of nodes is displayed in the top-level row.
>
> The color of the dot in front of each node or group indicates the status. If the dot for a group shows more than one color, hover the mouse pointer over the dot to view the total number of nodes and the statuses they are in.

- Gray means the node is being discovered by the Administration Server or that there is no up-to-date information about a deployed node. If the status is shown for a node longer than expected, check if the chef-client is still running on the node.

- Yellow means the node has been `Discovered`. As long as the dot is still blinking, the respective node is being installed and booted.

- Green means the node is in status `Ready`.

- Red means the node is in status `Problematic`.

During the initial state of the setup, the Dashboard only shows one group called `sw_unknown` into which the Administration Server is automatically sorted. Initially, all nodes (except the Administration Server) are listed with their MAC address as a name. However, it is recommended to create an alias for each node. This makes it easier to identify the node in the admin network and on the Dashboard. For details on how to create groups, how to assign nodes to a group and how to create node aliases, see *Section 9.2, "Node Installation"*.

Bulk Edit

This screen allows you to edit multiple nodes at once instead of editing them individually. It lists all nodes, including their *Name* (in form of the MAC address), their *Hardware* configuration, their *Alias* (used within the admin network), their *Public Name* (name used outside of the SUSE OpenStack Cloud network), their *Group*, their *Intended Role*, their *Platform* (the operating system that is going to be installed on the node), their *License* (if available), and their allocation status. You can toggle the list view between *Show unallocated* or *Show all* nodes.

For details on how to fill in the data for all nodes and how to start the installation process, see *Section 9.2, "Node Installation"*.

HA Clusters

This menu entry only appears if your cloud contains a High Availability setup. The overview shows all clusters in your setup, including the *Nodes* that are members of the respective cluster and the *Roles* assigned to the cluster. It also shows if a cluster contains *Remote Nodes* and which roles are assigned to the remote nodes.

Actives Roles

This overview shows which roles have been deployed on which node(s). The roles are grouped according to the service to which they belong. You cannot edit anything here. To change role deployment, you need to edit and redeploy the respective barclamp as described in *Chapter 10, Deploying the OpenStack Services*.

8.2.2 Barclamps

All Barclamps

This screen shows a list of all available barclamp proposals, including their *Status*, *Name* and a short *Description*. From here, you can *Edit* individual barclamp proposals as described in *Section 10.1, "Barclamps"*.

Crowbar

This screen only shows the barclamps that are included with the core Crowbar framework. They contain general recipes for setting up and configuring all nodes. From here, you can *Edit* individual barclamp proposals.

OpenStack

This screen only shows the barclamps that are dedicated to OpenStack service deployment and configuration. From here, you can *Edit* individual barclamp proposals.

Deployment Queue

If barclamps are applied to one or more nodes that are nor yet available for deployment (for example, because they are rebooting or have not been fully installed yet), the proposals will be put in a queue. This screen shows the proposals that are *Currently deploying* or *Waiting in queue*.

8.2.3 Utilities

Exported Items

The *Exported Files* screen allows you to export the Chef configuration and the `support-config` TAR archive. The `supportconfig` archive contains system information such as the current kernel version being used, the hardware, RPM database, partitions, and the most important log files for analysis of any problems. To access the export options, click *New Export*. After the export has been successfully finished, the *Exported Files* screen will show any files that are available for download.

Repositories

This screen shows an overview of the mandatory, recommended and optional repositories for all architectures of SUSE OpenStack Cloud. On each reload of the screen the Crowbar Web interface checks the availability and status of the repositories. If a mandatory repository is not present, it is marked red in the screen. Any repositories marked green are usable and available to each node in the cloud. If you activate the check box for a repository in the *Active* column, the managed nodes will automatically be configured to use this repository. You cannot edit any repositories in this screen. If you need additional, third-party repositories (or want to modify the repository metadata), edit `/etc/crowbar/repos.yml`. Find an example of a repository definition below:

```
suse-12.1:
  x86_64:
    Custom-Repo-12.1:
      url: 'http://example.com/12-SP1:/x86_64/custom-repo/'
      ask_on_error: true # sets the ask_on_error flag in the autoyast profile
 for that repo
      priority: 99 # sets the repo priority for zypper
```

Alternatively, use YaST Crowbar module to add or edit repositories as described in *Section 7.4, "Repositories"*.

Swift Dashboard

This screen allows you to run **swift-dispersion-report** on the node or nodes to which it has been deployed. Use this tool to measure the overall health of the swift cluster. For details, see http://docs.openstack.org/liberty/config-reference/content/object-storage-dispersion.html.

Backup & Restore

This screen lets you create a backup of the Administration Server and download it. You can also restore from a backup or upload a backup image from your local file system. For details, see *Section 11.5, "Backing Up and Restoring the Administration Server"*.

Cisco UCS

SUSE OpenStack Cloud can communicate with a Cisco UCS Manager instance via its XML-based API server to perform the following functions:

* Instantiate UCS service profiles for Compute Nodes and Storage Nodes from predefined UCS service profile templates

* Reboot, start, and stop nodes.

The following prerequisites need to be fulfilled on the Cisco UCS side:

* Templates for Compute Nodes and Storage Nodes need to be created. These service profile templates will be be used for preparing systems as SUSE Cloud nodes. Minimum requirements are a processor supporting AMD-V or Intel-VT, 8 GB RAM, one network interface and at least 20 GB of storage (more for Storage Nodes). The templates need to be named `suse-cloud-compute` and `suse-cloud-storage`.

* A user account with administrative permissions needs to be created for communicating with SUSE OpenStack Cloud. The account needs to have access to the service profile templates listed above. It also need permission to create service profiles and associate them with physical hardware.

To initially connect to the Cisco UCS Manager provide the login credentials of the user account mentioned above. The *API URL* has the form `http://UCSMANAGERHOST/nuova`. Click *Login* to connect. Once connected, you will see a list of servers and associated actions. Applying an action with the *Update* button can take up to several minutes.

8.2.4 Help

From this screen, you can access HTML and PDF versions of the SUSE OpenStack Cloud manuals. .

9 Installing the OpenStack Nodes

The OpenStack nodes represent the actual cloud infrastructure. Node installation and service deployment is done automatically from the Administration Server. Before deploying the OpenStack services, SUSE Linux Enterprise Server 12 SP1 will be installed on all Control Nodes and Storage Nodes. Compute Nodes can either run SUSE Linux Enterprise Server 12 SP1, Windows (see *Appendix F, Setting up a Netboot Environment for Microsoft* Windows* for installation instructions) or VMware vSphere (see *Appendix G, VMware vSphere Installation Instructions* for installation instructions).

To prepare the installation, each node needs to be booted using PXE, which is provided by the `tftp` server from the Administration Server. Afterwards you can allocate the nodes and trigger the operating system installation.

9.1 Preparations

Meaningful Node Names

Make a note of the MAC address and the purpose of each node (for example, controller, block storage, object storage, compute). This will make deploying the OpenStack services a lot easier and less error-prone—it enables you to assign meaningful names (aliases) to the nodes, which are otherwise listed with the MAC address by default.

BIOS Boot Settings

Make sure booting using PXE (booting from the network) is enabled and configured as the *primary* boot-option for each node. The nodes will boot twice from the network during the allocation and installation phase. Booting from the first hard disk needs to be configured as the second boot option.

Custom Node Configuration

All nodes are installed using AutoYaST with the same configuration located at `/opt/dell/chef/cookbooks/provisioner/templates/default/autoyast.xml.erb`. If this configuration does not match your needs (for example if you need special third party drivers) you need to make adjustments to this file. See the AutoYaST manual [http://

www.suse.com/documentation/sles-12/book_autoyast/data/book_autoyast.html] for details. Having changed the AutoYaST configuration file, you need to re-upload it to Chef, using the following command:

```
knife cookbook upload -o /opt/dell/chef/cookbooks/ provisioner
```

Direct root Login

By default, the root account on the nodes has no password assigned, so a direct root login is not possible. Logging in on the nodes as root is only possible via SSH public keys (for example, from the Administration Server).

If you want to allow direct root login, you can set a password via the Crowbar Provisioner barclamp before deploying the nodes. That password will be used for the root account on all OpenStack nodes. Using this method after the nodes are deployed is not possible. In that case you would need to log in to each node via SSH from the Administration Server and change the password manually with **passwd**.

SETTING A root PASSWORD FOR THE OPENSTACK NODES

1. Create an md5-hashed root-password, for example by using **openssl passwd** **-1**.

2. Open a browser and point it to the Crowbar Web interface on the Administration Server, for example `http://192.168.124.10`. Log in as user `crowbar`. The password is `crowbar` by default, if you have not changed it during the installation.

3. Open the barclamp menu by clicking *Barclamps* › *Crowbar*. Click the *Provisioner* barclamp entry and *Edit* the *Default* proposal.

4. Click *Raw* in the *Attributes* section to edit the configuration file.

5. Add the following line to the end of the file before the last closing curly bracket:

```
, "root_password_hash": "HASHED_PASSWORD"
```

replacing "*HASHED_PASSWORD*" with the password you generated in the first step.

6. Click *Apply*.

Preparing a Windows Netboot Environment

In case you plan to deploy Compute Nodes running either Microsoft Hyper-V Server or Windows Server 2012, you need to prepare a Windows Netboot Environment. Refer to *Appendix F, Setting up a Netboot Environment for Microsoft* Windows* for details.

9.2 Node Installation

To install a node, you need to boot it first using PXE. It will be booted with an image that enables the Administration Server to discover the node and make it available for installation. When you have allocated the node, it will boot using PXE again and the automatic installation will start.

1. Boot all nodes that you want to deploy using PXE. The nodes will boot into the "SLEShammer" image, which performs the initial hardware discovery.

    Important: Limit the Number of Concurrent Boots using PXE

   Booting many nodes using PXE at the same time will cause heavy load on the TFTP server, because all nodes will request the boot image at the same time. It is recommended to boot the nodes time-delayed.

2. Open a browser and point it to the Crowbar Web interface on the Administration Server, for example `http://192.168.124.10/`. Log in as user `crowbar`. The password is `crowbar` by default, if you have not changed it.
   Click *Nodes › Dashboard* to open the *Node Dashboard*.

3. Each node that has successfully booted will be listed as being in state `Discovered`, indicated by a yellow bullet. The nodes will be listed with their MAC address as a name. Wait until all nodes are listed as being `Discovered` before proceeding. In case a node does not report as being `Discovered`, it may need to be rebooted manually.

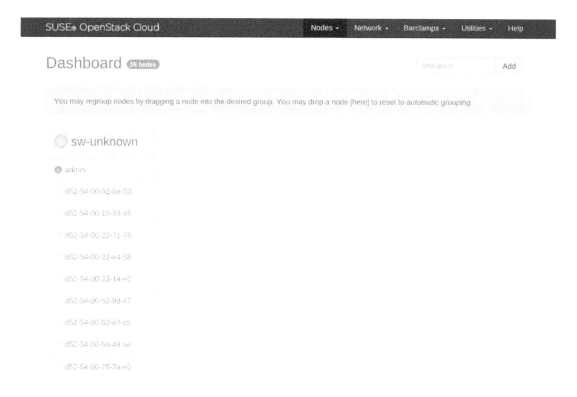

FIGURE 9.1: DISCOVERED NODES

4. Although this step is optional, it is recommended to properly group your nodes at this stage, since it lets you clearly arrange all nodes. Grouping the nodes by role would be one option, for example control, compute, object storage (Swift), and block storage (Ceph).

   a. Enter the name of a new group into the *New Group* text box and click *Add Group*.

   b. Drag and drop a node onto the title of the newly created group. Repeat this step for each node you want to put into the group.

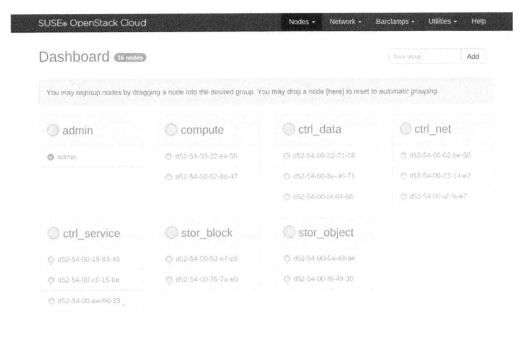

FIGURE 9.2: GROUPING NODES

5. To allocate all nodes, click *Nodes* › *Bulk Edit*. To allocate a single node, click the name of a node, then click *Edit*.

FIGURE 9.3: EDITING A SINGLE NODE

Important: Limit the Number of Concurrent Node Deployments

Deploying many nodes in bulk mode will cause heavy load on the Administration Server. The subsequent concurrent Chef client runs triggered by the nodes will require a lot of RAM on the Administration Server.

Therefore it is recommended to limit the number of concurrent "Allocations" in bulk mode. The maximum number depends on the amount of RAM on the Administration Server—limiting concurrent deployments to five up to ten is recommended.

6. In single node editing mode, you can also specify the *Filesystem Type* for the node. By default, it is set to `ext4` for all nodes. It is recommended to keep this default.

Note: Use Btrfs with `nova-compute-docker`

However, for Compute Nodes with the `nova-compute-docker` role assigned, set the *Filesystem Type* to Btrfs for those nodes. Docker has a better performance with Btrfs.

7. Provide a meaningful *Alias, Public Name* and a *Description* for each node and check the *Allocate* box. You can also specify the *Intended Role* for the node. This optional setting is used to make reasonable proposals for the barclamps.

By default *Target Platform* is set to *SLES 12 SP1*. Windows as a target platform for Compute Nodes only becomes available after having set up a Windows netboot environment as described in *Appendix F, Setting up a Netboot Environment for Microsoft* Windows*. After that is done, the platform options *Windows Server* or *HyperV Server* are available. When choosing *Windows Server* you also need to add a valid *License* key.

Tip: Alias Names

Providing an alias name will change the default node names (MAC address) to the name you provided, making it easier to identify the node. Furthermore, this alias will also be used as a DNS `CNAME` for the node in the admin network. As a result, you can access the node via this alias when, for example, logging in via SSH.

Tip: Public Names

A node's *Alias Name* is resolved by the DNS server installed on the Administration Server and therefore only available within the cloud network. The OpenStack Dashboard or some APIs (`keystone-server`, `glance-server`, `cinder-controller`, `neutron-server`, `nova-controller`, and `swift-proxy`) can be accessed from outside the SUSE OpenStack Cloud network. To be able to access them by name, these names need to be resolved by a name server placed outside of the SUSE OpenStack Cloud network. If you have created DNS entries for nodes, specify the name in the *Public Name* field.

The *Public Name* is never used within the SUSE OpenStack Cloud network. However, if you create an SSL certificate for a node that has a public name, this name must be added as an `AlternativeName` to the certificate. See *Section 2.3, "SSL Encryption"* for more information.

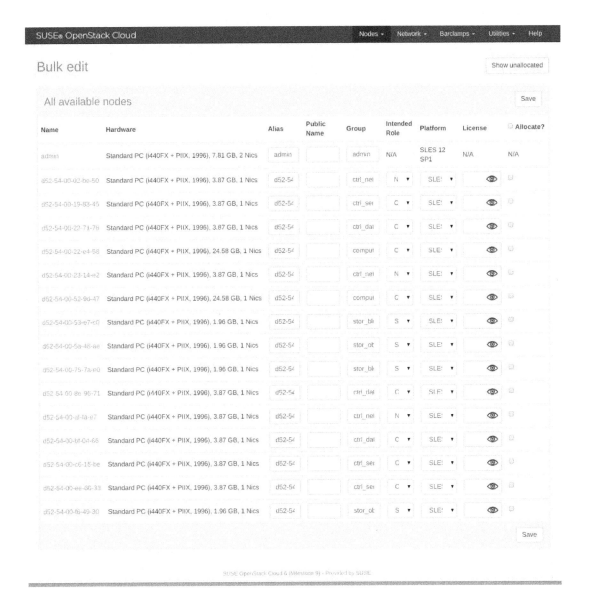

FIGURE 9.4: BULK EDITING NODES

8. When you have filled in the data for all nodes, click *Save*. The nodes will reboot and commence the AutoYaST-based SUSE Linux Enterprise Server installation (or installation of other target platforms, if selected) via a second boot using PXE. Click *Nodes › Dashboard* to return to the *Node Dashboard*.

9. Nodes that are being installed are listed with the status `Installing` (yellow/green bullet). When the installation of a node has finished, it is listed as being `Ready`, indicated by a green bullet. Wait until all nodes are listed as being `Ready` before proceeding.

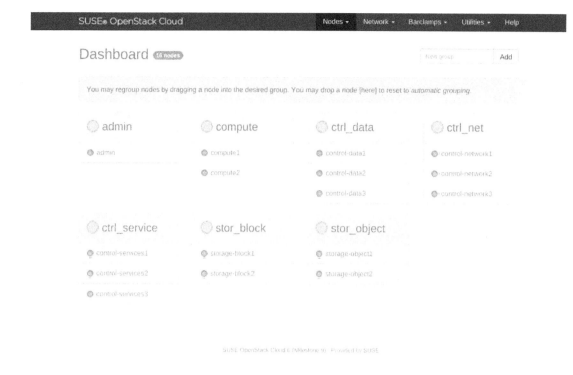

FIGURE 9.5: ALL NODES HAVE BEEN INSTALLED

9.3 Converting Existing SUSE Linux Enterprise Server 12 SP1 Machines Into SUSE OpenStack Cloud Nodes

SUSE OpenStack Cloud also allows to add existing machines installed with SUSE Linux Enterprise Server 12 SP1 to the pool of nodes. This enables you to use spare machines for SUSE OpenStack Cloud, and offers an alternative way of provisioning and installing nodes (via SUSE Manager for example). The machine must run SUSE Linux Enterprise Server 12 SP1.

The machine also needs to be on the same network as the Administration Server, because it needs to communicate with this server. Since the Administration Server provides a DHCP server, it is recommended to configure the respective network device with DHCP. If using a static IP address, make sure it is not already used in the admin network. Check the list of used IP addresses with the YaST Crowbar module as described in *Section 7.2, "Networks"*.

Proceed as follows to convert an existing SUSE Linux Enterprise Server 12 SP1 machine into a SUSE OpenStack Cloud node:

1. Download the `crowbar_register` script from the Administration Server at `http://192.168.124.10:8091/suse-12.1/x86_64/crowbar_register`. Replace the IP address with the IP address of your Administration Server using **curl** or **wget**. Note that the download only works from within the admin network.

2. Make the `crowbar_register` script executable (**chmod** `a+x` crowbar_register).

3. Run the `crowbar_register` script. If you have multiple network interfaces, the script tries to automatically detect the one that is connected to the admin network. You may also explicitly specify which network interface to use by using the `--interface` switch, for example **crowbar_register** `--interface eth1`.

4. After the script has successfully run, the machine has been added to the pool of nodes in the SUSE OpenStack Cloud and can be used as any other node from the pool.

9.4 Post-Installation Configuration

The following lists some *optional* configuration steps like configuring node updates, monitoring, access and SSL-enablement. You may entirely skip the following steps or perform any of them at a later stage.

9.4.1 Deploying Node Updates with the Updater Barclamp

To keep the operating system and the SUSE OpenStack Cloud software itself up-to-date on the nodes, you can deploy either the Updater barclamp or the SUSE Manager barclamp. The latter requires access to a SUSE Manager server. The Updater barclamp uses Zypper to install updates and patches from repositories made available on the Administration Server.

The easiest way to provide the required repositories on the Administration Server is to set up an SMT server as described in *Chapter 4, Installing and Setting Up an SMT Server on the Administration Server (Optional)*. Alternatives to setting up an SMT server are described in *Chapter 5, Software Repository Setup*.

The Updater barclamp lets you deploy updates that are available on the update repositories at the moment of deployment. Each time you deploy updates with this barclamp you can choose a different set of nodes to which the updates are deployed. This lets you exactly control where and when updates are deployed.

To deploy the Updater barclamp, proceed as follows. For general instructions on how to edit barclamp proposals refer to *Section 10.1, "Barclamps"*.

1. Open a browser and point it to the Crowbar Web interface on the Administration Server, for example `http://192.168.124.10/`. Log in as user `crowbar`. The password is `crowbar` by default, if you have not changed it during the installation.

2. Open the barclamp menu by clicking *Barclamps › Crowbar*. Click the *Updater* barclamp entry and *Create* to open the proposal.

3. Configure the barclamp by the following attributes. This configuration always applies to all nodes on which the barclamp is deployed. Individual configurations for certain nodes are only supported by creating a separate proposal.

   Use zypper

   Define which Zypper subcommand to use for updating. *patch* will install all patches applying to the system from the configured update repositories that are available. *update* will update packages from all configured repositories (not just the update repositories) that have a higher version number than the installed packages. *dist-upgrade* replaces each package installed with the version from the repository and deletes packages not available in the repositories.
   Using *patch* is recommended.

   Enable GPG Checks

   If set to true (recommended), checks if packages are correctly signed.

   Automatically Agree With Licenses

   If set to true (recommended), Zypper automatically accepts third party licenses.

   Include Patches that need Reboots (Kernel)

   Installs patches that require a reboot (for example Kernel or glibc updates). Only set this option to `true` when you can safely reboot the affected nodes. Refer to *Chapter 11, SUSE OpenStack Cloud Maintenance* for more information. Installing a new Kernel and not rebooting may result in an unstable system.

Reboot Nodes if Needed

Automatically reboots the system in case a patch requiring a reboot has been in-stalled. Only set this option to `true` when you can safely reboot the affected nodes. Refer to *Chapter 11, SUSE OpenStack Cloud Maintenance* for more information.

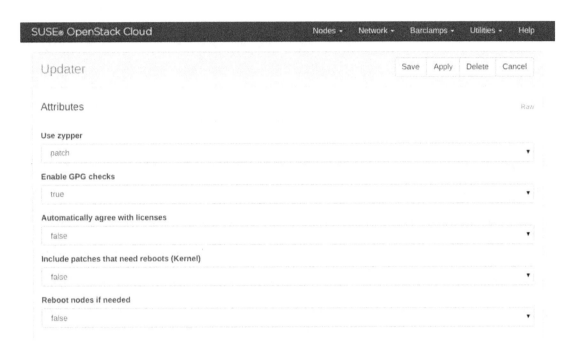

FIGURE 9.6: SUSE UPDATER BARCLAMP: CONFIGURATION

4. Choose the nodes on which the Updater barclamp should be deployed in the *Node Deployment* section by dragging them to the *Updater* column.

FIGURE 9.7: SUSE UPDATER BARCLAMP: NODE DEPLOYMENT

zypper keeps track of the packages and patches it installs in `/var/log/zypp/history`. Review that log file on a node to find out which updates have been installed. A second log file recording debug information on the **zypper** runs can be found at `/var/log/zypper.log` on each node.

 Warning: Updating Software Packages on Cluster Nodes

Before starting an update for a cluster node, either stop the cluster stack on that node or put the cluster into maintenance mode. If the cluster resource manager on a node is active during the software update, this can lead to unpredictable results like fencing of active nodes. For deatiled instructions refer to http://www.suse.com/documentation/sle-ha-12/book_sleha/data/sec_ha_migration_update.html.

9.4.2 Configuring Node Updates with the *SUSE Manager Client* Barclamp

To keep the operating system and the SUSE OpenStack Cloud software itself up-to-date on the nodes, you can deploy either *SUSE Manager Client* barclamp or the Updater barclamp. The latter uses Zypper to install updates and patches from repositories made available on the Administration Server.

To enable the SUSE Manager server to manage the SUSE OpenStack Cloud nodes, the respective SUSE OpenStack Cloud 6 channels, the SUSE Linux Enterprise Server 12 SP1 channels and the channels for extensions used with your deployment (High Availability Extension, SUSE Enterprise Storage) need to be made available via an activation key.

The *SUSE Manager Client* barclamp requires access to the SUSE Manager server from every node it is deployed to.

To deploy the *SUSE Manager Client* barclamp, proceed as follows. For general instructions on how to edit barclamp proposals refer to *Section 10.1, "Barclamps"*.

1. Generate an `Activation Key` for SUSE OpenStack Cloud on the SUSE Manager server. See the SUSE Manager documentation [http://www.suse.com/documentation/suse_manager/] for instructions.

2. Download the package `rhn-org-trusted-ssl-cert-VERSION-RELEASE.noarch.rpm` from https://*susemanager.example.com*/pub/. `VERSION` and `RELEASE` may vary, ask the administrator of the SUSE Manager for the correct values. `susemanager.example.com` needs to be replaced by the address of your SUSE Manager server. Copy the file you downloaded to `/opt/dell/chef/cookbooks/suse-manager-client/files/default/ssl-cert.rpm` on the Administration Server. The package contains the SUSE Manager's CA SSL Public Certificate. The certificate installation has not been automated on purpose, because downloading the certificate manually enables you to check it before copying it.

3. Re-install the barclamp by running the following command:

```
/opt/dell/bin/barclamp_install.rb --rpm suse-manager-client
```

4. Open a browser and point it to the Crowbar Web interface on the Administration Server, for example `http://192.168.124.10/`. Log in as user `crowbar`. The password is `crowbar` by default, if you have not changed it during the installation.

5. Open the barclamp menu by clicking *Barclamps* › *Crowbar*. Click the *SUSE Manager Client* barclamp entry and *Create* to open the proposal.

6. Configure the barclamp by the following attributes. This configuration always applies to all nodes on which the barclamp is deployed. Individual configurations for certain nodes are only supported by creating a separate proposal.

   Activation Key

   > Enter the SUSE Manager activation key for SUSE OpenStack Cloud here. This key must have been generated on the SUSE Manager server.

   SUSE Manager Server Hostname

   > Fully qualified host name of the SUSE Manager server. This name must be resolvable via the DNS server on the Administration Server.

7. Choose the nodes on which the SUSE Manager barclamp should be deployed in the *Node Deployment* section by dragging them to the *suse-manager-client* column. It is recommended to deploy it on all nodes in the SUSE OpenStack Cloud.

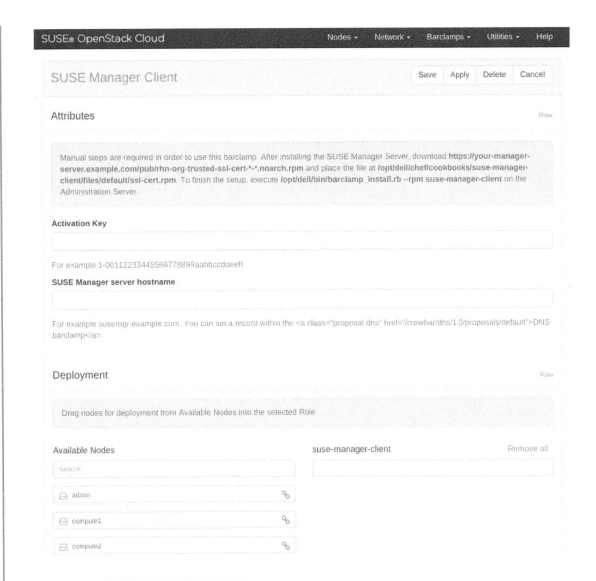

FIGURE 9.8: SUSE MANAGER BARCLAMP

 Warning: Updating Software Packages on Cluster Nodes

Before starting an update for a cluster node, either stop the cluster stack on that node or put the cluster into maintenance mode. If the cluster resource manager on a node is active during the software update, this can lead to unpredictable results like fencing of active nodes. For deatiled instructions refer to http://www.suse.com/documentation/sle-ha-12/book_sleha/data/sec_ha_migration_update.html.

9.4.3   Mounting NFS Shares on a Node

The NFS barclamp allows you to mount NFS share from a remote host on nodes in the cloud. This feature can, for example, be used to provide an image repository for Glance. Note that all nodes which are to mount an NFS share must be able to reach the NFS server. This requires to manually adjust the network configuration.

To deploy the NFS barclamp, proceed as follows. For general instructions on how to edit barclamp proposals refer to *Section 10.1, "Barclamps"*.

1. Open a browser and point it to the Crowbar Web interface on the Administration Server, for example `http://192.168.124.10/`. Log in as user `crowbar`. The password is `crowbar` by default, if you have not changed it during the installation.

2. Open the barclamp menu by clicking *Barclamps › Crowbar*. Click the *NFS Client* barclamp entry and *Create* to open the proposal.

3. Configure the barclamp by the following attributes. Each set of attributes is used to mount a single NFS share.

   Name

   > Unique name for the current configuration. This name is used in the Web interface only to distinguish between different shares.

   NFS Server

   > Fully qualified host name or IP address of the NFS server.

   Export

   > Export name for the share on the NFS server.

   Path

   > Mount point on the target machine.

   Mount Options

   > Mount options that will be used on the node. See **man 8 mount** for general mount options and **man 5 nfs** for a list of NFS-specific options. Note that the general option `nofail` (do not report errors if device does not exist) is automatically set.

4. After having filled in all attributes, click *Add*. If you want to mount more than one share, fill in the data for another NFS mount. Otherwise click *Save* to save the data, or *Apply* to deploy the proposal. Note that you must always click *Add* before saving or applying the barclamp, otherwise the data that was entered will be lost.

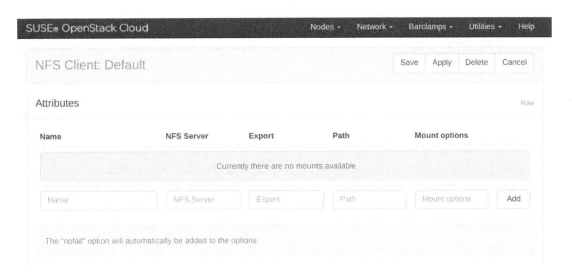

FIGURE 9.9: NFS BARCLAMP

5. Go to the *Node Deployment* section and drag and drop all nodes, on which the NFS shares defined above should be mounted, to the *nfs-client* column. Click *Apply* to deploy the proposal.

The NFS barclamp is the only barclamp that lets you create different proposals, enabling you to mount different NFS shares on different nodes. When you have created an NFS proposal, a special *Edit* is shown in the barclamp overview of the Crowbar Web interface. Click it to either *Edit* an existing proposal or *Create* a new one. Creating a new proposal requires to give it a unique name.

FIGURE 9.10: EDITING AN NFS BARCLAMP PROPOSAL

9.4.4 Using an Externally Managed Ceph Cluster

While deploying Ceph from within SUSE OpenStack Cloud is possible, leveraging an external Ceph cluster is also fully supported. Follow the instructions below to use an external Ceph cluster in SUSE OpenStack Cloud.

9.4.4.1 Requirements

Ceph Release

SUSE OpenStack Cloud uses Ceph clients from the Ceph "Hammer" release. Since other Ceph releases may not fully work with "Hammer" clients, the external Ceph installation must run a "Hammer" release, too. Other releases are not supported.

Network Configuration

The external Ceph cluster needs to be connected to a separate VLAN, which is mapped to the SUSE OpenStack Cloud storage VLAN. See *Section 2.1, "Network"* for more information.

9.4.4.2 Making Ceph Available on the SUSE OpenStack Cloud Nodes

Ceph can be used from the KVM Compute Nodes, with Cinder and with Glance,. The following installation steps need to be executed on each node accessing Ceph:

> **Important: Installation Workflow**
>
> The following steps need to be executed before the barclamps get deployed.

> **Warning: Do Not Deploy the Ceph Barclamp**
>
> If using an external Ceph cluster, you must not deploy the SUSE OpenStack Cloud Ceph barclamp. An external and an internal Ceph cluster cannot be used together.

1. Log in as user `root` to a machine in the Ceph cluster and generate keyring files for Cinder users. Optionally, you can generate keyring files for the Glance users (only needed when using Glance with Ceph/Rados). The keyring file that will be generated for Cinder will also be used on the Compute Nodes. To do so, you need to specify pool names and user names for both services. The default names are:

	Glance	Cinder
User	glance	cinder
Pool	images	volumes

Make a note of user and pool names in case you do not use the default values—you will need this information later, when deploying Glance and Cinder.

2. If you have access to the admin keyring file, copy it together with the Ceph configuration file to the Administration Server. If you cannot access this file, create a keyring:

   a. When you can access the admin keyring file `ceph.client.admin.keyring`, copy it together with `ceph.conf` (both files are usually located in `/etc/ceph`) to a temporary location on the Administration Server, for example `/root/tmp/`.

   b. If you cannot access the admin keyring file create a new keyring file with the following commands. Re-run the commands for Glance, too, if needed. First create a key:

```
ceph auth get-or-create-key client.USERNAME mon "allow r" \
osd 'allow class-read object_prefix rbd_children, allow rwx \
pool=POOLNAME'
```

Replace *USERNAME* and *POOLNAME* with the respective values.
Now use the key to generate the keyring file `/etc/ceph/ceph.client.USERNAME.keyring`:

```
ceph-authtool \
/etc/ceph/ceph.client.USERNAME.keyring \
--create-keyring --name=client.USERNAME> \
--add-key=KEY
```

Replace *USERNAME* with the respective value.

Copy the Ceph configuration file `ceph.conf` (usually located in `/etc/ceph`) and the keyring file(s) generated above to a temporary location on the Administration Server, for example `/root/tmp/`.

3. Log in to the Crowbar Web interface and check whether the nodes which should have access to the Ceph cluster already have an IP address from the storage network. Do so by going to the *Dashboard* and clicking the node name. An *IP address* should be listed for *storage*. Make a note of the *Full name* of each node that has *no* storage network IP address.

4. Log in to the Administration Server as user `root` and run the following command for all nodes you noted down in the previous step:

```
crowbar network allocate_ip "default" NODE "storage" "host"
chef-client
```

NODE needs to be replaced by the node's name.

5. After having executed the command in the previous step for all affected nodes, run the command **chef-client** on the Administration Server.

6. Log in to each affected node as user `root`. See *Q:* for instructions. On each node, do the following:

   a. Manually install nova, cinder (if using cinder) and/or glance (if using glance) packages with the following commands:

   ```
   zypper in openstack-glance
   zypper in openstack-cinder
   zypper in openstack-nova
   ```

   b. Copy the ceph.conf file from the Administration Server to `/etc/ceph`:

   ```
   mkdir -p /etc/ceph
   scp root@admin:/root/tmp/ceph.conf /etc/ceph
   chmod 664 /etc/ceph/ceph.conf
   ```

c. Copy the keyring file(s) to `/etc/ceph`. The exact process depends on whether you have copied the admin keyring file or whether you have created your own keyrings:

    i. If you have copied the admin keyring file, run the following command on the Control Node(s) on which Cinder and Glance will be deployed, and on all KVM Compute Nodes:

```
scp root@admin:/root/tmp/ceph.client.admin.keyring /etc/ceph
chmod 640 /etc/ceph/ceph.client.admin.keyring
```

    ii. If you have created you own keyrings, run the following command on the Control Node on which Cinder will be deployed, and on all KVM Compute Nodes to copy the Cinder keyring:

```
scp root@admin:/root/tmp/ceph.client.cinder.keyring /etc/ceph
chmod 640 /etc/ceph/ceph.client.cinder.keyring
```

Now copy the Glance keyring to the Control Node on which Glance will be deployed:

```
scp root@admin:/root/tmp/ceph.client.glance.keyring /etc/ceph
chmod 640 /etc/ceph/ceph.client.glance.keyring
```

d. Adjust the ownership of the keyring file as follows:

Glance: **chown root.cinder /etc/ceph/ceph.client.cinder.keyring**
Cinder: **chown root.glance /etc/ceph/ceph.client.glance.keyring**
KVM Compute Nodes: **chown root.nova /etc/ceph/ceph.volumes.keyring**

9.4.5 Accessing the Nodes

The nodes can only be accessed via SSH from the Administration Server—it is not possible to connect to them from any other host in the network.

The `root` account *on the nodes* has no password assigned, therefore logging in to a node as `root` @ *node* is only possible via SSH with key authentication. By default, you can only log in with the key of the `root` of the Administration Server (root@ *admin*) via SSH only.

In case you have added additional users to the Administration Server and want to give them permission to log in to the nodes as well, you need to add these user's public SSH keys to `root`'s `authorized_keys` file on all nodes. Proceed as follows:

PROCEDURE 9.1: COPYING SSH KEYS TO ALL NODES

1. If not already existing, generate an SSH key pair for the user that should be able to log in to the nodes with **ssh-keygen**. Alternatively copy an existing public key with **ssh-copy-id**. Refer to the respective man pages for more information.

2. Log in to the Crowbar Web interface available on the Administration Server, for example `http://192.168.124.10/` (user name and default password: `crowbar`).

3. Open the barclamp menu by clicking *Barclamps* › *Crowbar*. Click the *Provisioner* barclamp entry and *Edit* the *Default* proposal.

4. Copy and paste the *public* SSH key of the user into the *Additional SSH Keys* text box. If adding keys for multiple users, note that each key needs to be placed on a new line.

5. Click *Apply* to deploy the keys and save your changes to the proposal.

9.4.6 Enabling SSL

To enable SSL to encrypt communication within the cloud (see *Section 2.3, "SSL Encryption"* for details), the respective certificates need to be available on the nodes running the encrypted services. An SSL certificate is at least required on the Control Node.

To make them available, copy them to the node. Each certificate consists of a pair of files: the certificate file (for example, `signing_cert.pem`) and the key file (for example, `signing_key.pem`). If you use your own certificate authority (CA) for signing, you will also need a certificate file for the CA (for example, `ca.pem`). It is recommended to copy the files to the `/etc` directory using the directory structure outlined below. If you use a dedicated certificate for each service, create directories named after the services (for example, `/etc/keystone`). If sharing the certificates, use a directory such as `/etc/cloud`.

RECOMMENDED LOCATIONS FOR SHARED CERTIFICATES

SSL Certificate File

    /etc/cloud/ssl/certs/signing_cert.pem

SSL Key File

```
/etc/cloud/private/signing_key.pem
```

CA Certificates File

```
/etc/cloud/ssl/certs/ca.pem
```

9.5   Editing Allocated Nodes

All nodes that have been allocated can be decommissioned or re-installed. Click a node's name in the *Node Dashboard* to open a screen with the node details. The following options are available:

Forget

Deletes a node from the pool. If you want to re-use this node again, it needs to be reallocated and re-installed from scratch.

Reinstall

Triggers a reinstallation. The machine stays allocated. If barclamp had been deployed on that machine before, they will be re-applied again after the installation.

Deallocate

Temporarily removes the node from the pool of nodes. After you reallocate the node it will take its former role. Useful for adding additional machines in times of high load or for decommissioning machines in times of low load.

Power Actions > Reboot

Reboots the node.

Power Actions > Shutdown

Shuts the node down.

Power Actions > Power Cycle

Forces a (non-clean) shuts down and a restart afterwards. Only use if a reboot does not work.

Power Actions > Power Off

Forces a (non-clean) node shut down. Only use if a clean shut down does not work.

FIGURE 9.11: NODE INFORMATION

 Warning: Editing Nodes in a Production System

When de-allocating nodes that provide essential services, the complete cloud will become unusable. If you have not disabled redundancy, it is uncritical to disable single storage nodes or single compute nodes. However, disabling Control Node(s) will cause major problems. It will either "kill" certain services (for example Swift) or, at worst the complete cloud (when deallocating the Control Node hosting Neutron). You should also not disable nodes providing Ceph monitoring services or the nodes providing swift ring and proxy services.

10 Deploying the OpenStack Services

After the nodes are installed and configured you can start deploying the OpenStack services to finalize the installation. The services need to be deployed in a given order, because they depend on one another. The *Pacemaker* service for an HA setup is the only exception from this rule—it can be set up at any time. However, when deploying SUSE OpenStack Cloud from scratch, it is recommended to deploy the *Pacemaker* proposal(s) first. Deployment for all services is done from the Crowbar Web interface through recipes, so-called "barclamps".

The services controlling the cloud (including storage management and control services) need to be installed on the Control Node(s) (refer to *Section 1.2, "The Control Node(s)"* for more information). However, you may *not* use your Control Node(s) as a compute node or storage host for Swift or Ceph. Here is a list with services that may *not* be installed on the Control Node(s): *swift-storage*, all Ceph services, *nova-compute-**. These services need to be installed on dedicated nodes.

When deploying an HA setup, the controller nodes are replaced by one or more controller clusters consisting of at least two nodes (three are recommended). Setting up three separate clusters—for data, services, and networking—is recommended. See *Section 2.6, "High Availability"* for more information on requirements and recommendations for an HA setup.

The OpenStack services need to be deployed in the following order. For general instructions on how to edit and deploy barclamp, refer to *Section 10.1, "Barclamps"*. Deploying Pacemaker (only needed for an HA setup), Swift and Ceph is optional; all other services must be deployed.

1. *Deploying Pacemaker (Optional, HA Setup Only)*

2. *Deploying the Database*

3. *Deploying RabbitMQ*

4. *Deploying Keystone*

5. *Deploying Ceph (optional)*

6. *Deploying Swift (optional)*

7. *Deploying Glance*

8. *Deploying Cinder*

9. *Deploying Manila*

10. *Deploying Neutron*

11. *Deploying Nova*

12. *Deploying Horizon (OpenStack Dashboard)*

13. *Deploying Heat (Optional)*

14. *Deploying Ceilometer (Optional)*

15. *Deploying Trove (Optional)*

16. *Deploying Tempest (Optional)*

10.1 Barclamps

The OpenStack services are automatically installed on the nodes by using so-called barclamps—a set of recipes, templates, and installation instructions. A barclamp is configured via a so-called proposal. A proposal contains the configuration of the service(s) associated with the blowlamp and a list of machines onto which the barclamp should be deployed.

All existing barclamps can be accessed from the Crowbar Web interface by clicking *Barclamps*. To create or edit barclamp proposals and deploy them, proceed as follows:

1. Open a browser and point it to the Crowbar Web interface available on the Administration Server, for example `http://192.168.124.10/`. Log in as user `crowbar`. The password is `crowbar` by default, if you have not changed it.
   Click *Barclamps* to open the *All Barclamps* menu. Alternatively you may filter the list to *Crowbar* or *OpenStack* barclamps by choosing the respective option from *Barclamps*. The *Crowbar* barclamps contain general recipes for setting up and configuring all nodes, while the *OpenStack* barclamps are dedicated to OpenStack service deployment and configuration.

2. You can either *Create* a proposal or *Edit* an existing one.
   Most OpenStack barclamps consist of two sections: the *Attributes* section lets you change the configuration, and the *Node Deployment* section lets you choose onto which nodes to deploy the barclamp.

3. To edit the *Attributes* section, change the values via the Web form. Alternatively you can directly edit the configuration file by clicking *Raw*.

Warning: Raw Mode

If you switch between *Raw* mode and Web form (*Custom* mode), make sure to *Save* your changes before switching, otherwise they will be lost.

4. To assign nodes to a role, use the *Deployment* section of the OpenStack barclamp. It shows the *Available Nodes* that you can assign to the roles belonging to the barclamp. If the barclamp contains roles that can also be deployed to a cluster and if you have deployed the Pacemaker barclamp, the *Deployment* section of the barclamp will additionally list *Available Clusters* and of *Available Clusters with Remote Nodes*. The latter are clusters that contain both "normal" nodes and Pacemaker remote nodes. See *Section 2.6.3, "High Availability of the Compute Node(s)"* for the basic details.

   One or more nodes are usually automatically pre-selected for available roles. If this pre-selection does not meet your requirements, click the *Remove* icon next to the role to remove the assignment. Assign a node or cluster of your choice by selecting the respective entry from the list of *Available Nodes, Available Clusters,* or *Available Clusters with Remote Nodes*. Drag it to the desired role and drop it onto the *role name*. Do *not* drop a node or cluster onto the text box—this is used to filter the list of available nodes or clusters!

   If you try to assign clusters or clusters with remote nodes to roles that can only be assigned to individual nodes, the Crowbar Web interface will refuse to accept and show an error message. If you assign a cluster with remote nodes to a role that can only be applied to "normal" (Corosync) nodes, the role will only be applied to the Corosync nodes of that cluster—not to the remote nodes of the same cluster.

5. To save and deploy your edits, click *Apply*. To save your changes without deploying them, click *Save*. To remove the complete proposal, click *Delete*. A proposal that already has been deployed can only be deleted manually, see *Section 10.1.1, "Delete a Proposal That Already Has Been Deployed"* for details.

   If you deploy a proposal onto a node where a previous one is still active, the new proposal will overwrite the old one.

 Note: Wait Until a Proposal has been Deployed

Deploying a proposal might take some time (up to several minutes). It is strongly recommended to always wait until you see the note "Successfully applied the proposal" before proceeding on to the next proposal.

Warning: Barclamp Deployment Failure

In case the deployment of a barclamp fails, make sure to fix the reason that has caused the failure and deploy the barclamp again. Refer to the respective troubleshooting section at *Q & A 12.1.2, "OpenStack Node Deployment"* for help. A deployment failure may leave your node in an inconsistent state.

10.1.1 Delete a Proposal That Already Has Been Deployed

To delete a proposal that already has been deployed, you first need to *Deactivate* it in the Crowbar Web interface. Deactivating a proposal removes the chef role from the nodes, so the routine that installed and set up the services is not executed anymore. After a proposal has been deactivated, you can *Delete* it in the Crowbar Web interface to remove the barclamp configuration data from the server.

Deactivating and deleting a barclamp that already had been deployed does *not* remove packages installed when the barclamp was deployed. Nor does it stop any services that were started during the barclamp deployment. To undo the deployment on the affected node, you need to stop (`systemctl stop` *service*) the respective services and disable (`systemctl disable` *service*) them. Uninstalling packages should not be necessary.

10.1.2 Queuing/Dequeuing Proposals

When a proposal is applied to one or more nodes that are nor yet available for deployment (for example because they are rebooting or have not been fully installed, yet), the proposal will be put in a queue. A message like

```
Successfully queued the proposal until the following become ready:
  d52-54-00-6c-25-44
```

will be shown when having applied the proposal. A new button *Dequeue* will also become available. Use it to cancel the deployment of the proposal by removing it from the queue.

10.2 Deploying Pacemaker (Optional, HA Setup Only)

By setting up one or more clusters by deploying Pacemaker, you can make the SUSE OpenStack Cloud controller functions and the Compute Nodes highly available (see *Section 2.6, "High Availability"* for details). Since it is possible (and recommended) to deploy more than one cluster, a separate proposal needs to be created for each cluster.

Deploying Pacemaker is optional. In case you do not want to deploy it, skip this section and start the node deployment by deploying the database as described in *Section 10.3, "Deploying the Database"*.

 Note: Number of Cluster Nodes

To set up a cluster, at least two nodes are required. If setting up a cluster for storage with replicated storage via DRBD (for example for a cluster for the database and RabbitMQ), exactly two nodes are required. For all other setups an odd number of nodes with a minimum of three nodes is strongly recommended. See *Section 2.6.5, "Cluster Requirements and Recommendations"* for more information.

To create a proposal, go to *Barclamps* > *OpenStack* and click *Edit* for the Pacemaker barclamp. A drop-down box where you can enter a name and a description for the proposal opens. Click *Create* to open the configuration screen for the proposal.

Status	Name	Description	
	Pacemaker	Deploy Pacemaker clusters	Edit
+	data	Created on Mon, 25 Jan 2016 14:10:31 +0100	Create

 Important: Proposal Name

The name you enter for the proposal will be used to generate host names for the virtual IPs of HAProxy. The name uses the following scheme:

```
NAME.cluster-PROPOSAL_NAME.FQDN
```

When *PROPOSAL_NAME* is set to `data`, this results in, for example, `controller.cluster-data.example.com`.

The following options are configurable in the Pacemaker configuration screen:

Transport for Communication

Choose a technology used for cluster communication. You can select between *Multicast (UDP)*, (sending a message to multiple destinations) or *Unicast (UDPU)* (sending a message to a single destination). By default multicast is used.

Policy when cluster does not have quorum

Whenever communication fails between one or more nodes and the rest of the cluster a "cluster partition" occurs. The nodes of a cluster are split in partitions but are still active. They can only communicate with nodes in the same partition and are unaware of the separated nodes. The cluster partition that has the majority of nodes is defined to have "quorum".

This configuration option defines what to do with the cluster partition(s) that do not have the quorum. See http://www.suse.com/documentation/sle-ha-12/book_sleha/data/sec_ha_config_basics_global.html, section *Option no-quorum-policy* for details.

The recommended setting is to choose *Stop*. However, *Ignore* is enforced for two-node clusters to ensure that the remaining node continues to operate normally in case the other node fails. For clusters using shared resources, choosing *freeze* may be used to ensure that these resources continue to be available.

STONITH: Configuration mode for STONITH

"Misbehaving" nodes in a cluster are shut down to prevent it from causing trouble. This mechanism is called STONITH ("Shoot the other node in the head"). STONITH can be configured in a variety of ways, refer to http://www.suse.com/documentation/sle-ha-12/book_sleha/data/cha_ha_fencing.html for details. The following configuration options exist:

Configured manually

STONITH will not be configured when deploying the barclamp. It needs to be configured manually as described in http://www.suse.com/documentation/sle-ha-12/book_sleha/data/cha_ha_fencing.html. For experts only.

Configured with IPMI data from the IPMI barclamp

Using this option automatically sets up STONITH with data received from the IPMI barclamp. Being able to use this option requires that IPMI is configured for all cluster nodes. This should be done by default, when deploying cloud. To check or change the IPMI deployment, go to *Barclamps* › *Crowbar* › *IPMI* › *Edit*. Also make sure the *Enable BMC* option is set to *true* on this barclamp.

 Important: STONITH Devices Must Support IPMI

To configure STONITH with the IPMI data, *all* STONITH devices must support IPMI. Problems with this setup may occur with IPMI implementations that are not strictly standards compliant. In this case it is recommended to set up STONITH with STONITH block devices (SBD).

Configured with STONITH Block Devices (SBD)

This option requires to manually set up shared storage on the cluster nodes before applying the proposal. To do so, proceed as follows:

1. Prepare the shared storage. It needs to be reachable by all nodes and must not use host-based RAID, cLVM2, or DRBD.

2. Install the package `sbd` on all cluster nodes.

3. Initialize SBD device with by running the following command. Make sure to replace `/dev/SBD` with the path to the shared storage device.

```
sbd -d /dev/SBD create
```

Refer to http://www.suse.com/documentation/sle-ha-12/book_sleha/data/sec_ha_storage_protect_fencing.html#pro_ha_storage_protect_sbd_create for details.

After the shared storage has been set up, specify the path using the "by-id" notation (`/dev/disk/by-id/DEVICE`). It is possible to specify multiple paths as a comma-separated list.

Deploying the barclamp will automatically complete the SBD setup on the cluster nodes by starting the SBD daemon and configuring the fencing resource.

Configured with one shared resource for the whole cluster

> All nodes will use the exact same configuration. Specify the *Fencing Agent* to use and enter *Parameters* for the agent.
>
> To get a list of STONITH devices which are supported by the High Availability Extension, run the following command on an already installed cluster nodes: `stonith` `-L`. The list of parameters depends on the respective agent. To view a list of parameters use the following command:
>
> ```
> stonith -t agent -n
> ```

Configured with one resource per node

> All nodes in the cluster use the same *Fencing Agent*, but can be configured with different parameters. This setup is, for example, required when nodes are in different chassis and therefore need different ILO parameters.
>
> To get a list of STONITH devices which are supported by the High Availability Extension, run the following command on an already installed cluster nodes: `stonith` `-L`. The list of parameters depends on the respective agent. To view a list of parameters use the following command:
>
> ```
> stonith -t agent -n
> ```

Configured for nodes running in libvirt

> Use this setting for completely virtualized test installations. This option is not supported.

STONITH: Do not start corosync on boot after fencing

> With STONITH, Pacemaker clusters with two nodes may sometimes hit an issue known as STONITH deathmatch where each node kills the other one, resulting in both nodes rebooting all the time. Another similar issue in Pacemaker clusters is the fencing loop, where a reboot caused by STONITH will not be enough to fix a node and it will be fenced again and again.
>
> This setting can be used to limit these issues. When set to *true*, a node that has not been properly shut down or rebooted will not start the services for Pacemaker on boot, and will wait for action from the SUSE OpenStack Cloud operator. When set to *false*, the services for Pacemaker will always be started on boot. The *Automatic* value is used to have the most appropriate value automatically picked: it will be *true* for two-node clusters (to avoid STONITH deathmatches), and *false* otherwise.

When a node will boot but not start corosync because of this setting, then the node will be displayed with its status set to "`Problem`" (red bullet) in the *Node Dashboard*. To make this node usable again, the following steps need to be performed:

1. Connect to the node via SSH from the Administration Server and run one of **systemctl start pacemaker** or **rm /var/spool/corosync/block_automatic_start**. Waiting for the next periodic of a **chef-client** run, or manually running **chef-client** is also recommended.

2. On the Administration Server, run the following command to update the status of the node specified with *NODE*.

```
crowbar crowbar transition NODE ready
```

Mail Notifications: Enable Mail Notifications

Get notified of cluster node failures via e-mail. If set to *true*, you need to specify which *SMTP Server* to use, a prefix for the mails' subject and sender and recipient addresses. Note that the SMTP server must be accessible by the cluster nodes.

DRBD: Prepare Cluster for DRBD

Set up DRBD for replicated storage on the cluster. This option requires a two-node cluster with a spare hard disk for each node. The disks should have a minimum size of 100 GB. Using DRBD is recommended for making the database and RabbitMQ highly available. For other clusters, set this option to *False*.

HAProxy: Public name for public virtual IP

The public name is the host name that will be used instead of the generated public name (see *Important: Proposal Name*) for the public virtual IP of HAProxy. (This is the case when registering public endpoints, for example). Any name specified here needs to be resolved by a name server placed outside of the SUSE OpenStack Cloud network.

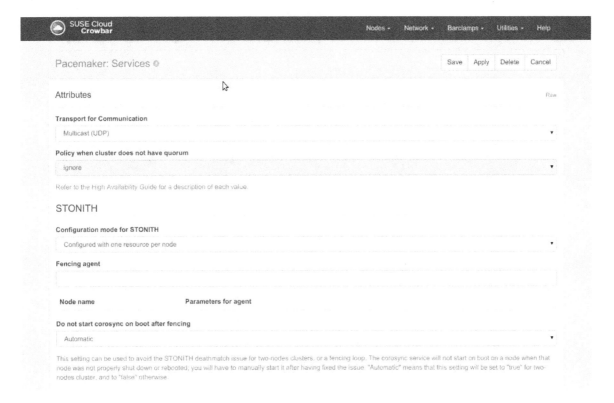

FIGURE 10.1: THE PACEMAKER BARCLAMP

The Pacemaker service consists of the following roles. Deploying the *hawk-server* role is optional:

pacemaker-cluster-member

Deploy this role on all nodes that should become member of the cluster except for the one where *pacemaker-cluster-founder* is deployed.

hawk-server

Deploying this role is optional. If deployed, sets up the Hawk Web interface which lets you monitor the status of the cluster. The Web interface can be accessed via `http://IP-ADDRESS:7630`. Note that the GUI on SUSE OpenStack Cloud can only be used to monitor the cluster status and not to change its configuration.

hawk-server may be deployed on at least one cluster node. It is recommended to deploy it on all cluster nodes.

pacemaker-remote

Deploy this role on all nodes that should become members of the Compute Nodes cluster. They will run as Pacemaker remote nodes that are controlled by the cluster, but do not affect quorum. Instead of the complete cluster stack, only the `pacemaker-remote` service will be installed on this nodes.

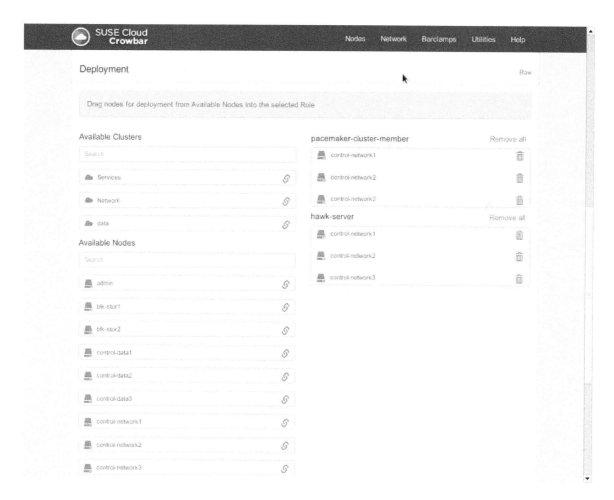

FIGURE 10.2: THE PACEMAKER BARCLAMP: NODE DEPLOYMENT EXAMPLE

After a cluster has been successfully deployed, it is listed under *Available Clusters* in the *Deployment* section and can be used for role deployment like a regular node.

 ## Warning: Deploying Roles on Single Cluster Nodes

When using clusters, roles from other barclamps must never be deployed to single nodes that are already part of a cluster. The only exceptions from this rule are the following roles:

- cinder-volume

- swift-proxy + swift-dispersion

- swift-ring-compute

- swift-storage

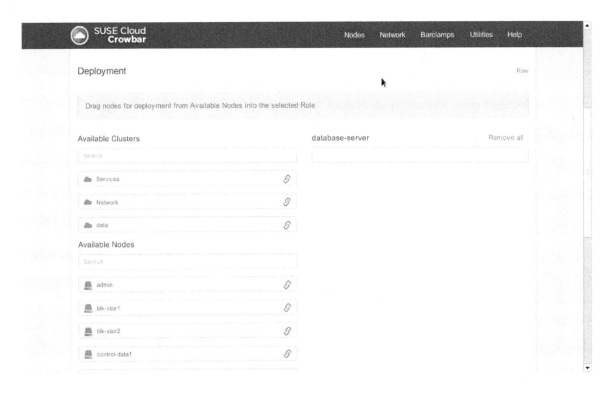

FIGURE 10.3: AVAILABLE CLUSTERS IN THE DEPLOYMENT SECTION

Important: Service Management on the Cluster

After a role has been deployed on a cluster, its services are managed by the HA software. You must *never* manually start or stop an HA-managed service (or configure it to start on boot). Services may only be started or stopped by using the cluster management tools Hawk or the crm shell. See http://www.suse.com/documentation/sle-ha-12/book_sleha/data/sec_ha_config_basics_resources.html for more information.

Note: Testing the Cluster Setup

To check whether all cluster resources are running, either use the Hawk Web interface or run the command `crm_mon -1r`. If it is not the case, clean up the respective resource with `crm resource cleanup` *RESOURCE*, so it gets respawned.

Also make sure that STONITH correctly works before continuing with the SUSE OpenStack Cloud setup. This is especially important when having chosen a STONITH configuration requiring manual setup. To test if STONITH works, log in to a node on the cluster and run the following command:

```
pkill -9 corosync
```

In case STONITH is correctly configured, the node will reboot.

Before testing on a production cluster, plan a maintenance window in case issues should arise.

10.3 Deploying the Database

The very first service that needs to be deployed is the *Database*. The database service is using PostgreSQL and is used by all other services. It must be installed on a Control Node. The Database can be made highly available by deploying it on a cluster.

The only attribute you may change is the maximum number of database connections (*Global Connection Limit*). The default value should usually work—only change it for large deployments in case the log files show database connection failures.

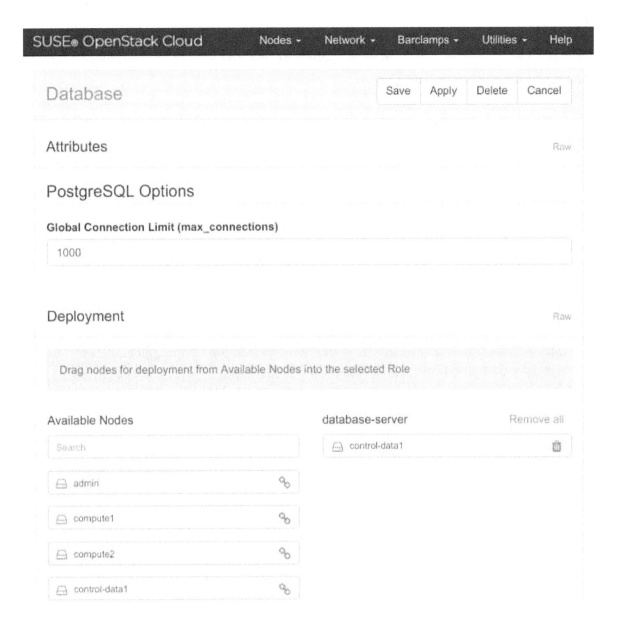

FIGURE 10.4: THE DATABASE BARCLAMP

10.3.1 HA Setup for the Database

To make the database highly available, deploy it on a cluster instead of a single Control Node. This also requires shared storage for the cluster that hosts the database data. To achieve this, either set up a cluster with DRBD support (see *Section 10.2, "Deploying Pacemaker (Optional, HA*

Setup Only)") or use "traditional" shared storage like an NFS share. It is recommended to use a dedicated cluster to deploy the database together with RabbitMQ, since both services require shared storage.

Deploying the database on a cluster makes an additional *High Availability* section available in the *Attributes* section of the proposal. Configure the *Storage Mode* in this section. There are two options:

DRBD

> This option requires a two-node cluster that has been set up with DRBD. Also specify the *Size to Allocate for DRBD Device (in Gigabytes)*. The suggested value of 50 GB should be sufficient.

Shared Storage

> Use a shared block device or an NFS mount for shared storage. Concordantly with the mount command, you need to specify three attributes: *Name of Block Device or NFS Mount Specification* (the mount point), the *Filesystem Type* and the *Mount Options*. Refer to `man 8 mount` for details on file system types and mount options.

Important: NFS Export Options for Shared Storage

If you want to use an NFS share as shared storage for a cluster, export it on the NFS server with the following options:

```
rw,async,insecure,no_subtree_check,no_root_squash
```

In case mounting the NFS share on the cluster nodes fails, change the export options and re-apply the proposal. However, before doing so, you need to clean up the respective resources on the cluster nodes as described in http://www.suse.com/documentation/sle-ha-12/book_sleha/data/sec_ha_config_crm.html#sec_ha_manual_config_cleanup.

Important: Ownership of a Shared NFS Directory

The shared NFS directory that is used for the PostgreSQL database needs to be owned by the same user ID and group ID as of the `postgres` user on the HA database cluster.

To get the IDs log in to one of the HA database cluster machines and issue the following commands:

```
id -g postgres
```

```
getent group postgres | cut -d: -f3
```

The first command returns the numeric user ID, the second one the numeric group ID. Now log in to the NFS server and change the ownership of the shared NFS directory, for example:

```
chown UID.GID /exports/cloud/db
```

Replace *UID* and *GID* by the respective numeric values retrieved above.

✋ Warning: Re-Deploying SUSE OpenStack Cloud with Shared Storage

When re-deploying SUSE OpenStack Cloud and reusing a shared storage hosting database files from a previous installation, the installation may fail, because the old database will be used. Always delete the old database from the shared storage before re-deploying SUSE OpenStack Cloud.

10.4 Deploying RabbitMQ

The RabbitMQ messaging system enables services to communicate with the other nodes via Advanced Message Queue Protocol (AMQP). Deploying it is mandatory. RabbitMQ needs to be installed on a Control Node. RabbitMQ can be made highly available by deploying it on a cluster. It is recommended not to change the default values of the proposal's attributes.

Virtual Host

> Name of the default virtual host to be created and used by the RabbitMQ server (`default_vhost` configuration option in `rabbitmq.config`).

Port

> Port the RabbitMQ server listens on (`tcp_listeners` configuration option in `rabbitmq.config`).

User

> RabbitMQ default user (`default_user` configuration option in `rabbitmq.config`).

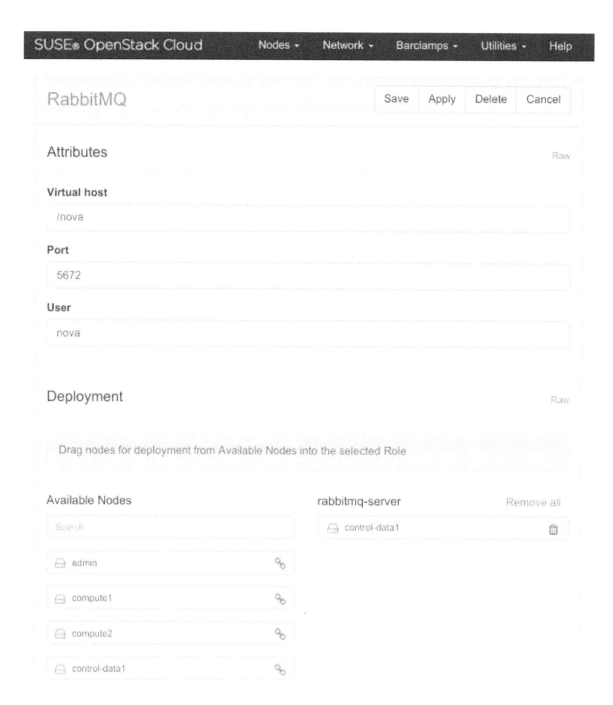

FIGURE 10.5: THE RABBITMQ BARCLAMP

10.4.1 HA Setup for RabbitMQ

To make RabbitMQ highly available, deploy it on a cluster instead of a single Control Node. This also requires shared storage for the cluster that hosts the RabbitMQ data. To achieve this, either set up a cluster with DRBD support (see *Section 10.2, "Deploying Pacemaker (Optional, HA Setup Only)"*) or use "traditional" shared storage like an NFS share. It is recommended to use a dedicated cluster to deploy RabbitMQ together with the database, since both services require shared storage.

Deploying RabbitMQ on a cluster makes an additional *High Availability* section available in the *Attributes* section of the proposal. Configure the *Storage Mode* in this section. There are two options:

DRBD

> This option requires a two-node cluster that has been set up with DRBD. Also specify the *Size to Allocate for DRBD Device (in Gigabytes)*. The suggested value of 50 GB should be sufficient.

Shared Storage

> Use a shared block device or an NFS mount for shared storage. Concordantly with the mount command, you need to specify three attributes: *Name of Block Device or NFS Mount Specification* (the mount point), the *Filesystem Type* and the *Mount Options*.

 Important: NFS Export Options for Shared Storage

> An NFS share that is to be used as a shared storage for a cluster needs to be exported on the NFS server with the following options:

```
rw,async,insecure,no_subtree_check,no_root_squash
```

> In case mounting the NFS share on the cluster nodes fails, change the export options and re-apply the proposal. Before doing so, however, you need to clean up the respective resources on the cluster nodes as described in http://www.suse.com/documentation/sle-ha-12/book_sleha/data/sec_ha_config_crm.html#sec_ha_manual_config_cleanup.

10.5 Deploying Keystone

Keystone is another core component that is used by all other OpenStack services. It provides authentication and authorization services. *Keystone* needs to be installed on a Control Node. Keystone can be made highly available by deploying it on a cluster. You can configure the following parameters of this barclamp:

Algorithm for Token Generation

Set the algorithm used by Keystone to generate the tokens. It is strongly recommended to use `PKI`, since it will reduce network traffic.

Region Name

Allows to customize the region name that crowbar is going to manage.

Default Credentials: Default Tenant

Tenant for the users. Do not change the default value of `openstack`.

Default Credentials: Regular User/Administrator User Name/Password

User name and password for the regular user and the administrator. Both accounts can be used to log in to the SUSE OpenStack Cloud Dashboard to manage Keystone users and access.

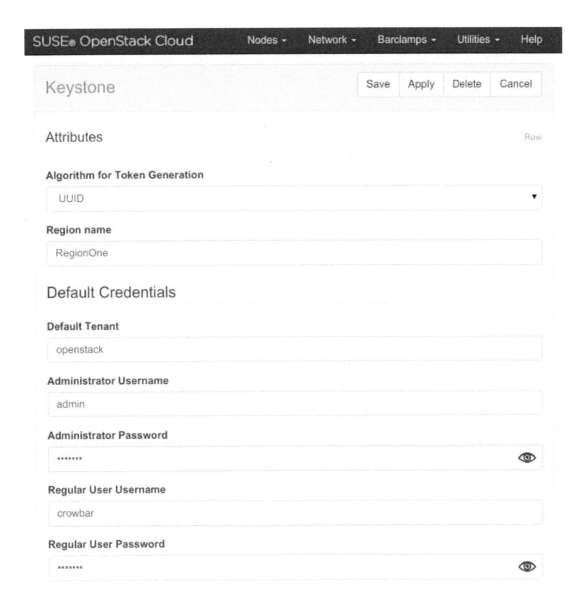

FIGURE 10.6: THE KEYSTONE BARCLAMP

SSL Support: Protocol

When sticking with the default value *HTTP*, public communication will not be encrypted. Choose *HTTPS* to use SSL for encryption. See *Section 2.3, "SSL Encryption"* for background information and *Section 9.4.6, "Enabling SSL"* for installation instructions. The following additional configuration options will become available when choosing *HTTPS*:

Generate (self-signed) certificates

When set to `true`, self-signed certificates are automatically generated and copied to the correct locations. This setting is for testing purposes only and should never be used in production environments!

SSL Certificate File / SSL (Private) Key File

Location of the certificate key pair files.

SSL Certificate is insecure

Set this option to `true` when using self-signed certificates to disable certificate checks. This setting is for testing purposes only and should never be used in production environments!

Require Client Certificate

Set this option to `true` when using your own certificate authority (CA) for signing. Having done so, you also need to specify a path to the *CA Certificates File*. If your certificates are signed by a trusted third party organization, set *Require Client Certificate* to *false*, since the "official" certificate authorities (CA) are already known by the system.

SSL CA Certificates File

Specify the absolute path to the CA certificate here. This option can only be changed if *Require Client Certificate* was set to `true`.

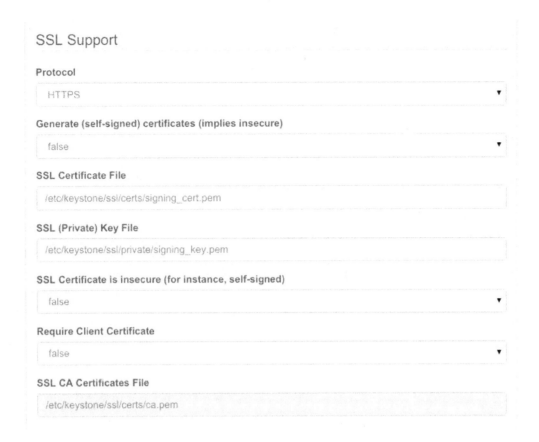

SSL Support

Protocol

HTTPS

Generate (self-signed) certificates (implies insecure)

false

SSL Certificate File

/etc/keystone/ssl/certs/signing_cert.pem

SSL (Private) Key File

/etc/keystone/ssl/private/signing_key.pem

SSL Certificate is insecure (for instance, self-signed)

false

Require Client Certificate

false

SSL CA Certificates File

/etc/keystone/ssl/certs/ca.pem

FIGURE 10.7: THE SSL DIALOG

10.5.1 LDAP Authentication with Keystone

By default Keystone uses an SQL database back-end store for authentication. LDAP can be used in addition to the default or as an alternative. Using LDAP requires the Control Node on which Keystone is installed to be able to contact the LDAP server. See *Appendix D, The Network Barclamp Template File* for instructions on how to adjust the network setup.

10.5.1.1 Using LDAP for Authentication

To configure LDAP as an alternative to the SQL database back-end store, you need to open the Keystone barclamp *Attribute* configuration in *Raw* mode. Search for the *ldap* section.

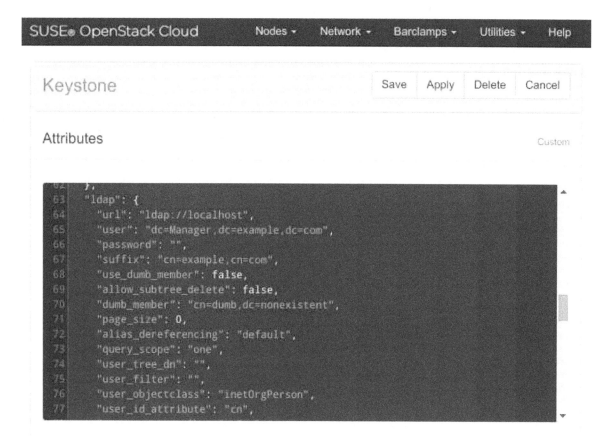

FIGURE 10.8: THE KEYSTONE BARCLAMP: RAW MODE

Adjust the settings according to your LDAP setup. The default configuration does not include all attributes that can be set—a complete list of options is available in the file `/opt/dell/chef/data_bags/crowbar/bc-template-keystone.schema` on the Administration Server (search for `ldap`). There are three types of attribute values: strings (for example, the value for `url:"ldap://localhost"`), bool (for example, the value for `use_dumb_member: false`) and integer (for example, the value for `page_size: 0`). Attribute names and string values always need to be quoted with double quotes; bool and integer values must not be quoted.

 Important: Using LDAP over SSL (ldaps) Is Recommended

In a production environment, it is recommended to use LDAP over SSL (ldaps), otherwise passwords will be transferred as plain text.

10.5.1.2 Using Hybrid Authentication

The Hybrid LDAP back-end allows to create a mixed LDAP/SQL setup. This is especially useful when an existing LDAP server should be used to authenticate cloud users. The system and service users (administrators and operators) needed to set up and manage SUSE OpenStack Cloud will be managed in the local SQL database. Assignments of users to projects and roles will also be stored in the local database.

In this scenario the LDAP Server can be read-only for SUSE OpenStack Cloud installation and no Schema modifications are required. Therefore managing LDAP users from within SUSE OpenStack Cloud is not possible and needs to be done using your established tools for LDAP user management. All user that are create with the Keystone command line client or the Horizon Web UI will be stored in the local SQL database.

To configure hybrid authentication, proceed as follows:

1. Open the Keystone barclamp *Attribute* configuration in *Raw* mode (see *Figure 10.8, "The Keystone Barclamp: Raw Mode"*).

2. Set the identity and assignment drivers to the hybrid back-end:

```
"identity": {
    "driver": "keystone.identity.backends.hybrid.Identity"
},
"assignment": {
    "driver": "keystone.assignment.backends.hybrid.Assignment"
}
```

3. Adjust the settings according to your LDAP setup in the *ldap* section. Since the LDAP back-end is only used to acquire information on users (but not on projects and roles), only the user-related settings matter here. See the following example of settings that may need to be adjusted:

```
"ldap": {
  "url": "ldap://localhost",
  "user": "",
  "password": "",
  "suffix": "cn=example,cn=com",
  "user_tree_dn": "cn=example,cn=com",
```

```
            "query_scope": "one",
            "user_id_attribute": "cn",
            "user_enabled_emulation_dn": "",
            "tls_req_cert": "demand",
            "user_attribute_ignore": "tenant_id,tenants",
            "user_objectclass": "inetOrgPerson",
            "user_mail_attribute": "mail",
            "user_filter": "",
            "use_tls": false,
            "user_allow_create": false,
            "user_pass_attribute": "userPassword",
            "user_enabled_attribute": "enabled",
            "user_enabled_default": "True",
            "page_size": 0,
            "tls_cacertdir": "",
            "tls_cacertfile": "",
            "user_enabled_mask": 0,
            "user_allow_update": true,
            "group_allow_update": true,
            "user_enabled_emulation": false,
            "user_name_attribute": "cn"
        }
```

To access the LDAP server anonymously, leave the values for *user* and *password* empty.

10.5.2   HA Setup for Keystone

Making Keystone highly available requires no special configuration—it is sufficient to deploy it on a cluster.

10.6   Deploying Ceph (optional)

Ceph adds a redundant block storage service to SUSE OpenStack Cloud. It lets you store persistent devices that can be mounted from instances. It offers high data security by storing the data redundantly on a pool of Storage Nodes—therefore Ceph needs to be installed on at least three dedicated nodes. All Ceph nodes need to run SLES 12. Starting with SUSE OpenStack Cloud 5, deploying Ceph on SLES 11 SP3 nodes is no longer possible. For detailed information on how to provide the required repositories, refer to *Section 5.2, "Update and Pool Repositories"*. For Ceph at least four nodes are required. If deploying the optional Calamari server for Ceph management and monitoring, an additional node is required.

For more information on the Ceph project, visit http://ceph.com/.

The Ceph barclamp has the following configuration options:

Disk Selection Method

Choose whether to only use the first available disk or all available disks. "Available disks" are all disks currently not used by the system. Note that one disk (usually `/dev/sda`) of every block storage node is already used for the operating system and is not available for Ceph.

Number of Replicas of an Object

For data security, stored objects are not only stored once, but redundantly. Specify the number of copies that should be stored for each object with this setting. The number includes the object itself. If you for example want the object plus two copies, specify 3.

SSL Support for RadosGW

Choose whether to encrypt public communication (*HTTPS*) or not (*HTTP*). If choosing *HTTPS*, you need to specify the locations for the certificate key pair files.

Calamari Credentials

Calamari is a Web front-end for managing and analyzing the Ceph cluster. Provide administrator credentials (user name, password, e-mail address) in this section. When Ceph has bee deployed you can log in to Calamari with these credentials. Deploying Calamari is optional—leave these text boxes empty when not deploying Calamari.

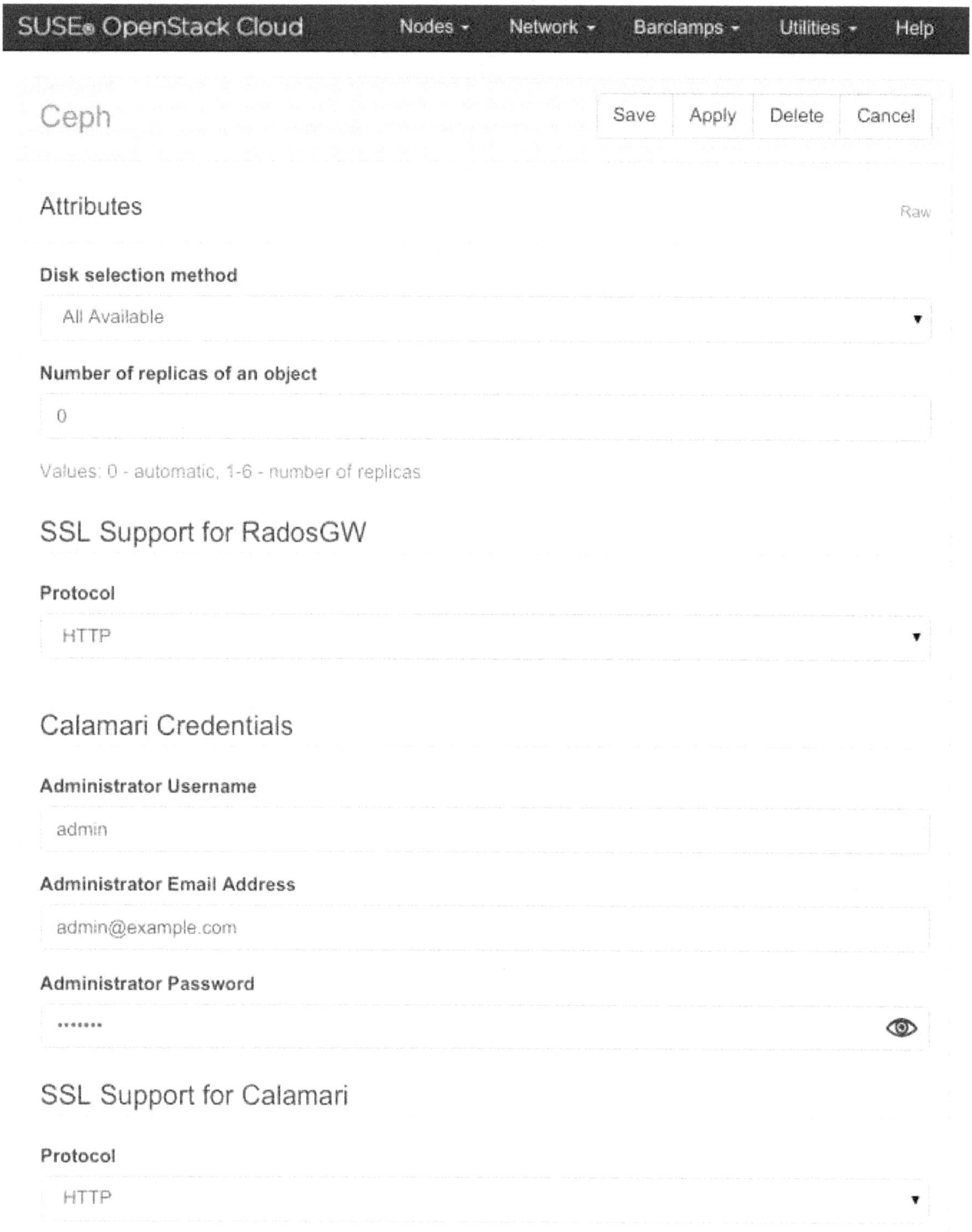

Ceph

Save   Apply   Delete   Cancel

Attributes

Raw

Disk selection method

All Available ▾

Number of replicas of an object

0

Values: 0 - automatic, 1-6 - number of replicas

SSL Support for RadosGW

Protocol

HTTP ▾

Calamari Credentials

Administrator Username

admin

Administrator Email Address

admin@example.com

Administrator Password

•••••••

SSL Support for Calamari

Protocol

HTTP ▾

FIGURE 10.9: THE CEPH BARCLAMP

The Ceph service consists of the following different roles:

ceph-osd

The virtual block storage service. Install this role on all dedicated Ceph Storage Nodes (at least three), but not on any other node.

ceph-mon

Cluster monitor daemon for the Ceph distributed file system. *ceph-mon* needs to be installed on three or five Storage Nodes running *ceph-osd*.

ceph-calamari

Sets up the Calamari Web interface which lets you manage the Ceph cluster. Deploying it is optional. The Web interface can be accessed via http://*IP-ADDRESS*/ (where *IP-ADDRESS* is the address of the machine where *ceph-calamari* is deployed on). *ceph-calamari* needs to be installed on a dedicated node—it is *not* possible to install it on a nodes running other services.

ceph-radosgw

The HTTP REST gateway for Ceph. Install it on a Storage Node running *ceph-osd*.

Important: Ceph Needs Dedicated Nodes

Never deploy on a node that runs non-Ceph OpenStack services. The only services that may be deployed together on a Ceph node, are *ceph-osd*, *ceph-mon* and *ceph-radosgw*. All Ceph nodes need to run SLES 12—starting with SUSE OpenStack Cloud 5, deploying Ceph on SLES 11 SP3 nodes is no longer possible.

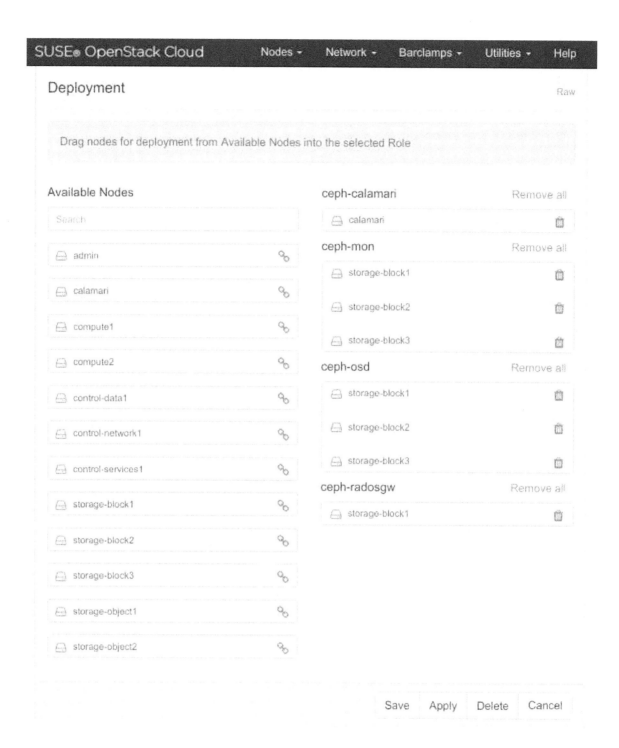

FIGURE 10.10: THE CEPH BARCLAMP: NODE DEPLOYMENT EXAMPLE

10.6.1   HA Setup for Ceph

Ceph is HA-enabled by design, so there is no need for a special HA setup.

10.7   Deploying Swift (optional)

Swift adds an object storage service to SUSE OpenStack Cloud that lets you store single files such as images or snapshots. It offers high data security by storing the data redundantly on a pool of Storage Nodes—therefore Swift needs to be installed on at least two dedicated nodes.

To be able to properly configure Swift it is important to understand how it places the data. Data is always stored redundantly within the hierarchy. The Swift hierarchy in SUSE OpenStack Cloud is formed out of zones, nodes, hard disks, and logical partitions. Zones are physically separated clusters, for example different server rooms each with its own power supply and network segment. A failure of one zone must not affect another zone. The next level in the hierarchy are the individual Swift storage nodes (on which *swift-storage* has been deployed) followed by the hard disks. Logical partitions come last.

Swift automatically places three copies of each object on the highest hierarchy level possible. If three zones are available, the each copy of the object will be placed in a different zone. In a one zone setup with more than two nodes, the object copies will each be stored on a different node. In a one zone setup with two nodes, the copies will be distributed on different hard disks. If no other hierarchy element fits, logical partitions are used.

The following attributes can be set to configure Swift:

Allow Public Containers

Allows to enable public access to containers if set to `true`.

Enable Object Versioning

If set to true, a copy of the current version is archived, each time an object is updated.

Zones

Number of zones (see above). If you do not have different independent installations of storage nodes, set the number of zones to `1`.

Create 2^X Logical Partitions

Partition power. The number entered here is used to compute the number of logical partitions to be created in the cluster. The number you enter is used as a power of 2 (2^X).

It is recommended to use a minimum of 100 partitions per disk. To measure the partition power for your setup, do the following: Multiply the number of disks from all Swift nodes with 100 and then round up to the nearest power of two. Keep in mind that the first disk of each node is not used by Swift, but rather for the operating system.

Example: 10 Swift nodes with 5 hard disks each. Four hard disks on each node are used for Swift, so there is a total of forty disks. Multiplied by 100 gives 4000. The nearest power of two, 4096, equals 2^12. So the partition power that needs to be entered is 12.

 Important: Value Cannot be Changed After the Proposal Has Been Deployed

Changing the number of logical partition after Swift has been deployed is not supported. Therefore the value for the partition power should be calculated from the maximum number of partitions this cloud installation is likely going to need at any point in time.

Minimum Hours before Partition is reassigned

This option sets the number of hours before a logical partition is considered for relocation. 24 is the recommended value.

Replicas

The number of copies generated for each object. Set this value to 3, the tested and recommended value.

Replication interval (in seconds)

Time (in seconds) after which to start a new replication process.

Debug

Shows debugging output in the log files when set to `true`.

SSL Support: Protocol

Choose whether to encrypt public communication (*HTTPS*) or not (*HTTP*). If choosing *HTTPS*, you have two choices. You can either *Generate (self-signed) certificates* or provide the locations for the certificate key pair files. Using self-signed certificates is for testing purposes only and should never be used in production environments!

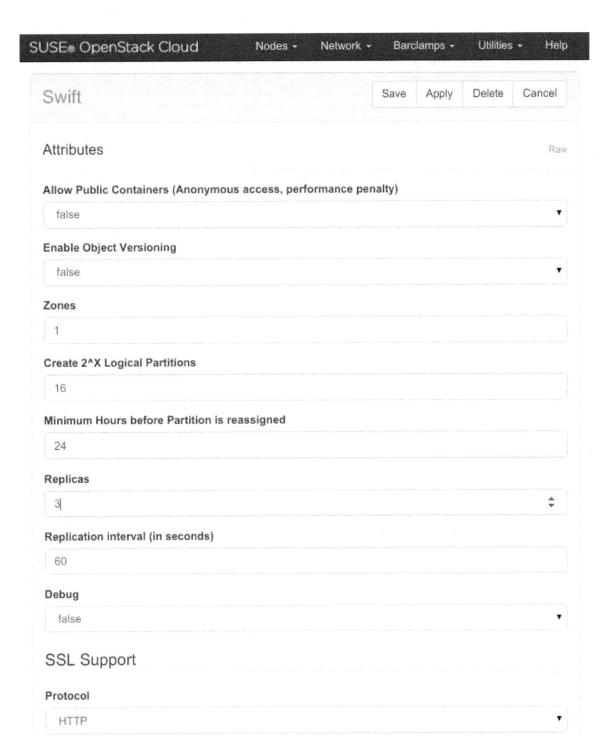

FIGURE 10.11: THE SWIFT BARCLAMP

Apart from the general configuration described above, the Swift barclamp lets you also activate and configure *Additional Middlewares*. The features these middlewares provide can be used via the Swift command line client only. The Ratelimit and S3 middlewares certainly provide for the most interesting features, whereas it is recommended to only enable further middlewares for specific use-cases.

S3 Middleware

Provides an S3 compatible API on top of Swift.

StaticWeb

Enables to serve container data as a static Web site with an index file and optional file listings. See http://docs.openstack.org/developer/swift/middleware.html#staticweb for details. This middleware requires to set *Allow Public Containers* to `true`.

TempURL

Enables to create URLs to provide time limited access to objects. See http://docs.openstack.org/developer/swift/middleware.html#tempurl for details.

FormPOST

Enables to upload files to a container via Web form. See http://docs.openstack.org/developer/swift/middleware.html#formpost for details.

Bulk

Enables the possibility to extract tar files into a swift account and to delete multiple objects or containers with a single request. See http://docs.openstack.org/developer/swift/middleware.html#module-swift.common.middleware.bulk for details.

Cross Domain

Allows to interact with the Swift API via Flash, Java and Silverlight from an external network. See http://docs.openstack.org/developer/swift/middleware.html#module-swift.common.middleware.crossdomain for details.

Domain Remap

Translates container and account parts of a domain to path parameters that the Swift proxy server understands. Can be used to create short URLs that are easy to remember, for example by rewriting `home.tux.example.com/$ROOT/exampleuser;/home/my-file` to `home.tux.example.com/myfile`. See http://docs.openstack.org/developer/swift/middleware.html#module-swift.common.middleware.domain_remap for details.

Ratelimit

Ratelimit enables you to throttle resources such as requests per minute to provide denial of service protection. See http://docs.openstack.org/developer/swift/middleware.html#module-swift.common.middleware.ratelimit for details.

The Swift service consists of four different roles. Deploying *swift-dispersion* is optional:

swift-storage

The virtual object storage service. Install this role on all dedicated Swift Storage Nodes (at least two), but not on any other node.

 Warning: swift-storage Needs Dedicated Machines

Never install the swift-storage service on a node that runs other OpenStack services.

swift-ring-compute

The ring maintains the information about the location of objects, replicas, and devices. It can be compared to an index, that is used by various OpenStack services to look up the physical location of objects. *swift-ring-compute* must only be installed on a single node; it is recommended to use a Control Node.

swift-proxy

The Swift proxy server takes care of routing requests to Swift. Installing a single instance of *swift-proxy* on a Control Node is recommended. The *swift-proxy* role can be made highly available by deploying it on a cluster.

swift-dispersion

Deploying *swift-dispersion* is optional. The Swift dispersion tools can be used to test the health of the cluster. It creates a heap of dummy objects (using 1% of the total space available). The state of these objects can be queried using the swift-dispersion-report query. *swift-dispersion* needs to be installed on a Control Node.

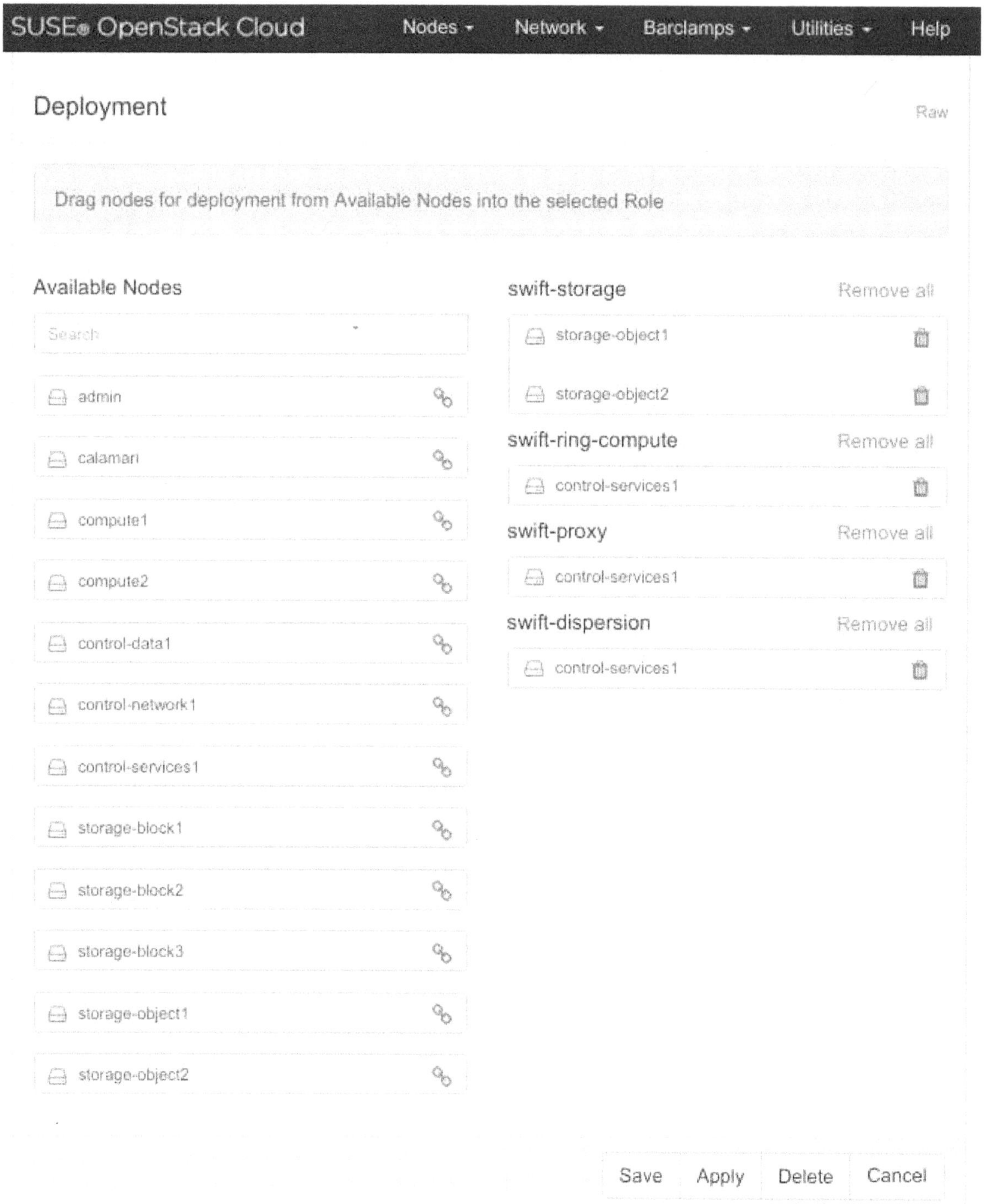

SUSE® OpenStack Cloud
Nodes
Network
Barclamps
Utilities
Help
Deployment
Raw
Drag nodes for deployment from Available Nodes into the selected Role
Available Nodes
Search
admin
calamari
compute1
compute2
control-data1
control-network1
control-services1
storage-block1
storage-block2
storage-block3
storage-object1
storage-object2
swift-storage
Remove all
storage-object1
storage-object2
swift-ring-compute
Remove all
control-services1
swift-proxy
Remove all
control-services1
swift-dispersion
Remove all
control-services1
Save
Apply
Delete
Cancel

FIGURE 10.12: THE SWIFT BARCLAMP: NODE DEPLOYMENT EXAMPLE

10.7.1 HA Setup for Swift

Swift replicates by design, so there is no need for a special HA setup. Make sure to fulfill the requirements listed in *Section 2.6.4.1, "Swift—Avoiding Points of Failure"*.

10.8 Deploying Glance

Glance provides discovery, registration, and delivery services for virtual disk images. An image is needed to start an instance—it is its pre-installed root-partition. All images you want to use in your cloud to boot instances from, are provided by Glance. Glance must be deployed onto a Control Node. Glance can be made highly available by deploying it on a cluster.

There are a lot of options to configure Glance. The most important ones are explained below—for a complete reference refer to http://github.com/crowbar/crowbar/wiki/Glance--barclamp.

Image Storage: Default Storage Store

> Choose whether to use Swift or Ceph (*Rados*) to store the images. If you have deployed neither of these services, the images can alternatively be stored in an image file on the Control Node (*File*). If you have deployed Swift or Ceph, it is recommended to use it for Glance as well.
>
> If using VMware as a hypervisor, it is recommended to use it for storing images, too (*VMWare*). This will make starting VMware instances much faster.
>
> Depending on the storage back-end, there are additional configuration options available:

File Store Parameters

Image Store Directory

> Specify the directory to host the image file. The directory specified here can also be an NFS share. See *Section 9.4.3, "Mounting NFS Shares on a Node"* for more information.

Swift Store Parameters

Swift Container

> Set the name of the container to use for the images in Swift.

RADOS Store Parameters

RADOS User for CephX Authentication

If using a SUSE OpenStack Cloud internal Ceph setup, the user you specify here is created in case it does not exist. If using an external Ceph cluster, specify the user you have set up for Glance (see *Section 9.4.4, "Using an Externally Managed Ceph Cluster"* for more information).

RADOS Pool for Glance images

If using a SUSE OpenStack Cloud internal Ceph setup, the pool you specify here is created in case it does not exist. If using an external Ceph cluster, specify the pool you have set up for Glance (see *Section 9.4.4, "Using an Externally Managed Ceph Cluster"* for more information).

VMWare Store Parameters

vCenter Host/IP Address

Name or IP address of the vCenter server.

vCenter Username / vCenter Password

vCenter login credentials.

Datastores for Storing Images

A comma-separated list of datastores specified in the format: *DATACENTER_NAME* : *DATASTORE_NAME*

Path on the datastore, where the glance images will be stored

Specify an absolute path here.

SSL Support: Protocol

Choose whether to encrypt public communication (*HTTPS*) or not (*HTTP*). If choosing *HTTPS*, refer to *SSL Support: Protocol* for configuration details.

Caching

Enable and configure image caching in this section. By default, image caching is disabled. Learn more about Glance's caching feature at http://docs.openstack.org/developer/glance/cache.html.

Logging: Verbose Logging

Shows debugging output in the log files when set to *true*.

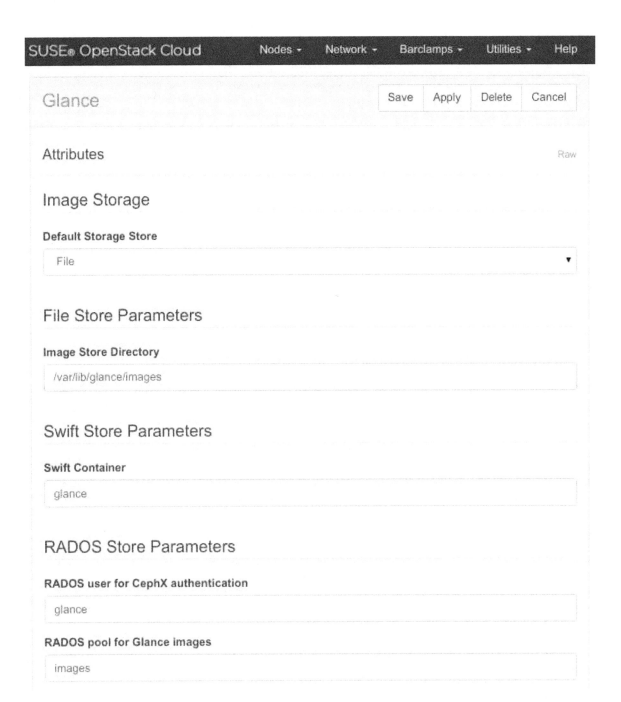

FIGURE 10.13: THE GLANCE BARCLAMP

10.8.1 HA Setup for Glance

Glance can be made highly available by deploying it on a cluster. It is also strongly recommended to do so for the image data, too. The recommended way to achieve this is to use Swift or an external Ceph cluster for the image repository. If using a directory on the node instead (file storage back-end), you should set up shared storage on the cluster for it.

10.9 Deploying Cinder

Cinder, the successor of Nova Volume, provides volume block storage. It adds persistent storage to an instance that will persist until deleted (contrary to ephemeral volumes that will only persist while the instance is running).

Cinder can provide volume storage by using different back-ends such as local file, one or more local disks, Ceph (RADOS), VMware or network storage solutions from EMC, EqualLogic, Fujitsu or NetApp. Since SUSE OpenStack Cloud 5, Cinder supports using several back-ends simultaneously. It is also possible to deploy the same network storage back-end multiple times and therefore use different installations at the same time.

The attributes that can be set to configure Cinder depend on the back-end. The only general option is *SSL Support: Protocol* (see *SSL Support: Protocol* for configuration details).

 Tip: Adding or Changing a Back-End

> When first opening the Cinder barclamp, the default proposal—*Raw Devices*— is already available for configuration. To optionally add a back-end, go to the section *Add New Cinder Back-End* and choose a *Type Of Volume* from the drop-down box. Optionally, specify the *Name for the Backend*. This is recommended when deploying the same volume type more than once. Existing back-end configurations (including the default one) can be deleted by clicking the trashcan icon if no longer needed. Note that at least one back-end must be configured.

Raw devices (local disks)

Disk Selection Method

Choose whether to only use the *First Available* disk or *All Available* disks. "Available disks" are all disks, currently not used by the system. Note that one disk (usually `/dev/sda`) of every block storage node is already used for the operating system and is not available for Cinder.

Name of Volume

Specify a name for the Cinder volume.

EMC (EMC² Storage)

IP address of the ECOM server / Port of the ECOM server

IP address and Port of the ECOM server.

Unisphere for VMAX Masking View

For VMAX, the user needs to create an initial setup on the Unisphere for VMAX server first. It needs to contain an initiator group, a storage group and a port group and needs to be put in a masking view. This masking view needs to be specified here.

User Name / Password for accessing the ECOM server

Login credentials for the ECOM server.

Thin pool where user wants to create volume from

Only thin LUNs are supported by the plugin. Thin pools can be created using Unisphere for VMAX and VNX.

For more information on the EMC driver refer to the OpenStack documentation at http://docs.openstack.org/liberty/config-reference/content/emc-vmax-driver.html.

EqualLogic

EqualLogic drivers are included as a technology preview and are not supported.

Fujitsu ETERNUS DX

Connection Protocol

Select the protocol used to connect, either *FibreChannel* or *iSCSI*.

IP / Port for SMI-S

IP address and port of the ETERNUS SMI-S Server.

Username / Password for SMI-S

Login credentials for the ETERNUS SMI-S Server.

Snapshot (Thick/RAID Group) Pool Name

Storage pool (RAID group) in which the volumes are created. Make sure to have created that RAID group on the server in advance. If a RAID group that does not exist is specified, the RAID group is created by using unused disk drives. The RAID level is automatically determined by the ETERNUS DX Disk storage system.

NetApp

Storage Family Type/Storage Protocol

SUSE OpenStack Cloud can either use "Data ONTAP" in *7-Mode* or in *Clustered Mode*. In *7-Mode* vFiler will be configured, in *Clustered Mode* vServer will be configured. The *Storage Protocoll* can either be set to *iSCSI* or *NFS*. Choose the driver and the protocol your NetApp is licensed for.

Server host name

The management IP address for the 7-Mode storage controller or the cluster management IP address for the clustered Data ONTAP.

Transport Type

Transport protocol for communicating with the storage controller or clustered Data ONTAP. Supported protocols are HTTP and HTTPS. Choose the protocol your NetApp is licensed for.

Server port

The port to use for communication. Port 80 is usually used for HTTP, 443 for HTTPS.

User Name/Password for Accessing NetApp

Login credentials.

The vFiler Unit Name for provisioning OpenStack volumes (netapp_vfiler)

The vFiler unit to be used for provisioning of OpenStack volumes. This setting is only available in *7-Mode*.

Restrict provisioning on iSCSI to these volumes (netapp_volume_list)

Provide a list of comma-separated volumes names to be used for provisioning. This setting is only available when using iSCSI as storage protocol.

Name of the Virtual Storage Server ((netapp_vserver)

Host name of the Virtual Storage Server. This setting is only available in *Clustered Mode* when using NFS as storage protocol.

List of Netapp NFS Exports

Provide a list of NFS Exports from the Virtual Storage Server. Specify one entry per line in the form of `host name:/volume/path mount-options`. Specifying mount options is optional. This setting is only available when using NFS as storage protocol.

RADOS (Ceph)

Use Ceph Deployed by Crowbar

Select *true* if you have deployed Ceph with SUSE OpenStack Cloud. In case you are using an external Ceph cluster (see *Section 9.4.4, "Using an Externally Managed Ceph Cluster"* for setup instructions), select *false*.

Path to Ceph Configuration File

This configuration option is only available, if using an external Ceph cluster. Specify the path to the `ceph.conf` file—the default value (`/etc/ceph/ceph.conf`) should be fitting if you have followed the setup instructions in *Section 9.4.4, "Using an Externally Managed Ceph Cluster"*.

Path to Ceph Admin Keyring

This configuration option is only available, if using an external Ceph cluster. If you have had access to the admin keyring file, the path is `/etc/ceph/ceph.client.admin.keyring`. If you have created your own keyring, use `/etc/ceph/ceph.client.cinder.keyring`. See *Section 9.4.4, "Using an Externally Managed Ceph Cluster"* for more information.

RADOS pool for Cinder volumes

Name of the pool used to store the Cinder volumes.

RADOS user (Set Only if Using CephX authentication)

Ceph user name.

VMware Parameters

vCenter Host/IP Address

Host name or IP address of the vCenter server.

vCenter Username / vCenter Password

vCenter login credentials.

vCenter Cluster Names for Volumes

Provide a comma-separated list of cluster names.

Folder for Volumes

Path to the directory used to store the Cinder volumes.

CA file for verifying the vCenter certificate

Absolute path to the vCenter CA certificate.

vCenter SSL Certificate is insecure (for instance, self-signed)

Default value: `false` (the CA truststore is used for verification). Set this option to `true` when using self-signed certificates to disable certificate checks. This setting is for testing purposes only and must not be used in production environments!

Local file

Volume File Name

Absolute path to the file to be used for block storage.

Maximum File Size (GB)

Maximum size of the volume file. Make sure not to overcommit the size, since it will result in data loss.

Name of Volume

Specify a name for the Cinder volume.

Note: Using *Local File* for Block Storage

Using a file for block storage is not recommended for production systems, because of performance and data security reasons.

Other driver

Lets you manually pick and configure a driver. Only use this option for testing purposes, it is not supported.

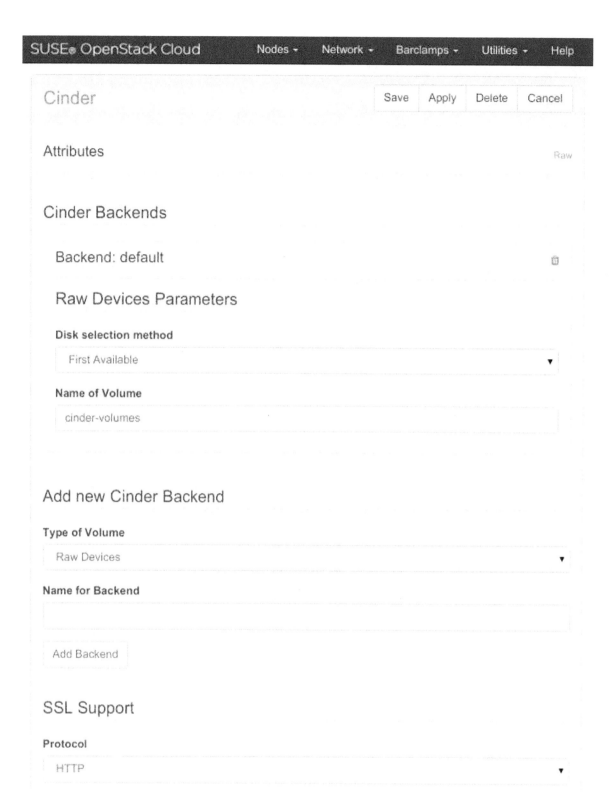

FIGURE 10.14: THE CINDER BARCLAMP

The Cinder service consists of two different roles:

cinder-controller

The Cinder controller provides the scheduler and the API. Installing *cinder-controller* on a Control Node is recommended.

cinder-volume

The virtual block storage service. It can be installed on a Control Node. However, it is recommended to deploy it on one or more dedicated nodes supplied with sufficient networking capacity, since it will generate a lot of network traffic.

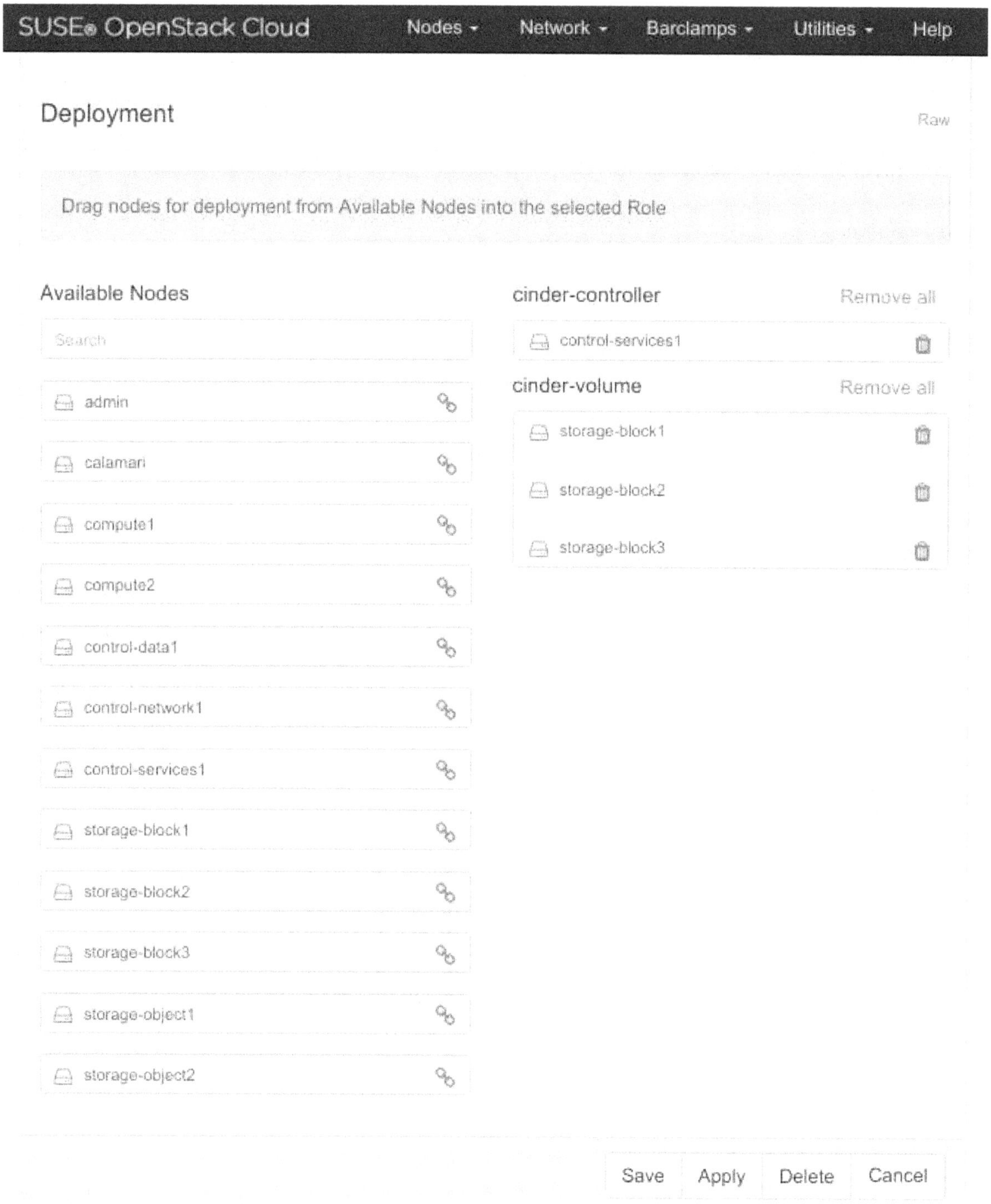
SUSE OpenStack Cloud
Nodes
Network
Barclamps
Utilities
Help
Deployment
Raw
Drag nodes for deployment from Available Nodes into the selected Role
Available Nodes
Search
admin
calamari
compute1
compute2
control-data1
control-network1
control-services1
storage-block1
storage-block2
storage-block3
storage-object1
storage-object2
cinder-controller
Remove all
control-services1
cinder-volume
Remove all
storage-block1
storage-block2
storage-block3
Save
Apply
Delete
Cancel

FIGURE 10.15: THE CINDER BARCLAMP: NODE DEPLOYMENT EXAMPLE

10.9.1   HA Setup for Cinder

While the *cinder-controller* role can be deployed on a cluster, deploying *cinder-volume* on a cluster is not supported. Therefore it is generally recommended to deploy *cinder-volume* on several nodes—this ensures the service continues to be available even when a node fails. In addition with Ceph or a network storage solution, such a setup minimizes the potential downtime.

In case using Ceph or a network storage is no option, you need to set up a shared storage directory (for example, with NFS), mount it on all cinder volume nodes and use the *Local File* back-end with this shared directory. Using *Raw Devices* is not an option, since local disks cannot be shared.

10.10   Deploying Manila

Manila provides coordinated access to shared or distributed file systems, similar to what Cinder does for block storage. These file systems can be shared between instances in SUSE OpenStack Cloud.

Manila uses different back-ends. As of SUSE OpenStack Cloud 6 the only back-end that is currently supported is the *NetApp Driver*. Two more back-end options, *Generic Driver* and *Other Driver* are available for testing purposes and are not supported.

When first opening the Manila barclamp, the default proposal *Generic Driver* is already available for configuration. To replace it, first delete it by clicking the trashcan icon and then choose a different back-end in the section *Add new Manila Backend*. Select a *Type of Share* and—optionally—provide a *Name for Backend*. Activate the back-end with *Add Backend*. Note that at least one back-end must be configured.

The attributes that can be set to configure Cinder depend on the back-end:

Back-end: Generic

The generic driver is included as a technology preview and is not supported.

Back-end: Netapp

Name of the Virtual Storage Server (vserver)
> Host name of the Virtual Storage Server.

Server Host Name

The name or IP address for the storage controller or the cluster.

Server Port

The port to use for communication. Port 80 is usually used for HTTP, 443 for HTTPS.

User name/Password for Accessing NetApp

Login credentials.

Transport Type

Transport protocol for communicating with the storage controller or cluster. Supported protocols are HTTP and HTTPS. Choose the protocol your NetApp is licensed for.

Back-end: Manual

Lets you manually pick and configure a driver. Only use this option for testing purposes, it is not supported.

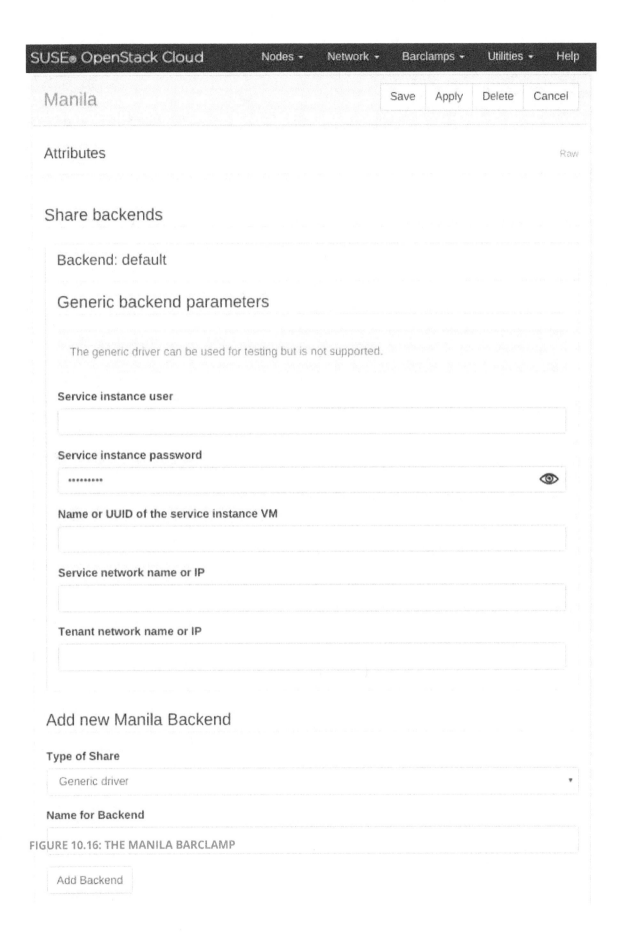

FIGURE 10.16: THE MANILA BARCLAMP

The Manila service consists of two different roles:

manila-server

> The Manila server provides the scheduler and the API. Installing it on a Control Node is recommended.

manila-share

> The shared storage service. It can be installed on a Control Node, but it is recommended to deploy it on one or more dedicated nodes supplied with sufficient disk space and networking capacity, since it will generate a lot of network traffic.

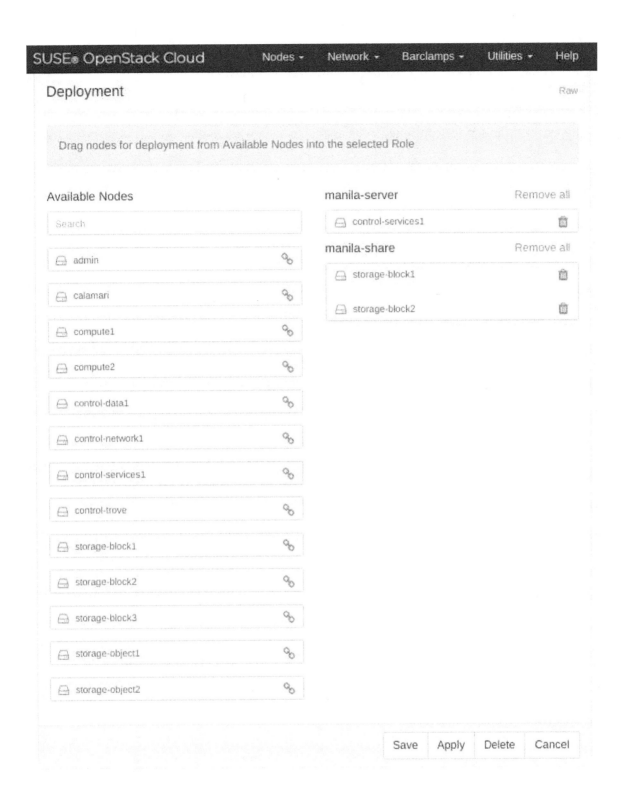

FIGURE 10.17: THE MANILA BARCLAMP: NODE DEPLOYMENT EXAMPLE

10.10.1　HA Setup for Manila

While the *manila-server* role can be deployed on a cluster, deploying *manila-share* on a cluster is not supported. Therefore it is generally recommended to deploy *manila-share* on several nodes —this ensures the service continues to be available even when a node fails.

10.11　Deploying Neutron

Neutron provides network connectivity between interface devices managed by other OpenStack services (most likely Nova). The service works by enabling users to create their own networks and then attach interfaces to them.

Neutron must be deployed on a Control Node. You first need to choose a core plug-in—*ml2* or *vmware*. Depending on your choice, more configuration options will become available.

The *vmware* option lets you use an existing VMWare NSX installation. Using this plugin is not a prerequisite for the VMWare vSphere hypervisor support. However, it is needed when wanting to have security groups supported on VMWare compute nodes. For all other scenarios, choose *ml2*.

The only global option that can be configured is *SSL Support*. Choose whether to encrypt public communication (*HTTPS*) or not (*HTTP*). If choosing *HTTPS*, refer to *SSL Support: Protocol* for configuration details.

ml2 (Modular Layer 2)

Modular Layer 2 Mechanism Drivers

  Select which mechanism driver(s) shall be enabled for the ml2 plugin. It is possible to select more than one driver by holding the `Ctrl` key while clicking. Choices are:

  openvswitch. Supports GRE, VLAN and VLANX networks (to be configured via the *Modular Layer 2 type drivers* setting).

  linuxbridge. Supports VLANs only. Requires to specify the *Maximum Number of VLANs*.

  cisco_nexus. Enables Neutron to dynamically adjust the VLAN settings of the ports of an existing Cisco Nexus switch when instances are launched. It also requires *openvswitch* which will automatically be selected. With *Modular Layer 2 type drivers*, *vlan* must be added.

This option also requires to specify the *Cisco Switch Credentials*. See *Appendix H, Using Cisco Nexus Switches with Neutron* for details.

Use Distributed Virtual Router Setup

With the default setup, all intra-Compute Node traffic flows through the network Control Node. The same is true for all traffic from floating IPs. In large deployments the network Control Node can therefore quickly become a bottleneck. When this option is set to *true*, network agents will be installed on all compute nodes. This will de-centralize the network traffic, since Compute Nodes will be able to directly "talk" to each other. Distributed Virtual Routers (DVR) require the *openvswitch* driver and will not work with the *linuxbridge* driver. HyperV Compute Nodes will not be supported—network traffic for these nodes will be routed via the Control Node on which *neutron-network* is deployed. For details on DVR refer to https://wiki.openstack.org/wiki/Neutron/DVR.

Modular Layer 2 Type Drivers

This option is only available when having chosen the *openvswitch* or the *cisco_nexus* mechanism drivers. Options are *vlan*, *gre* and *vxlan*. It is possible to select more than one driver by holding the `Ctrl` key while clicking.

 Important: Drivers for HyperV Compute Nodes

HyperV Compute Nodes do not support *gre* and *vxlan*. If your environment includes a heterogenous mix of Compute Nodes incluing HyperV nodes, make sure to select *vlan*. This can be done in addition to the other drivers.

When multiple type drivers are enabled, you need to select the *Default Type Driver for Provider Network*, that will be used for newly created provider networks. This also includes the `nova_fixed` network, that will be created when applying the Neutron proposal. When manually creating provider networks with the **neutron** command, the default can be overwritten with the `--provider:network_type` *type* switch. You will also need to set a *Default Type Driver for Tenant Network*. It is not possible to change this default when manually creating tenant networks with the **neutron** command. The non-default type driver will only be used as a fallback.

Depending on your choice of the type driver, more configuration options become available.

gre. Having chosen *gre*, you also need to specify the start and end of the tunnel ID range.

vlan. The option *vlan* requires you to specify the *Maximum number of VLANs*.

vxlan. Having chosen *vxlan,* you also need to specify the start and end of the VNI range.

vmware

This plug-in requires to configure access to the VMWare NSX service.

VMWare NSX User Name/Password

Login credentials for the VMWare NSX server. The user needs to have administrator permissions on the NSX server.

VMWare NSX Controllers

Enter the IP address and the port number (*IP-ADDRESS*:*PORT*) of the controller API endpoint. If the port number is omitted, port 443 will be used. You may also enter multiple API endpoints (comma-separated), provided they all belong to the same controller cluster. When multiple API endpoints are specified, the plugin will load balance requests on the various API endpoints.

UUID of the NSX Transport Zone/Gateway Service

The UUIDs for the transport zone and the gateway service can be obtained from the NSX server. They will be used when networks are created.

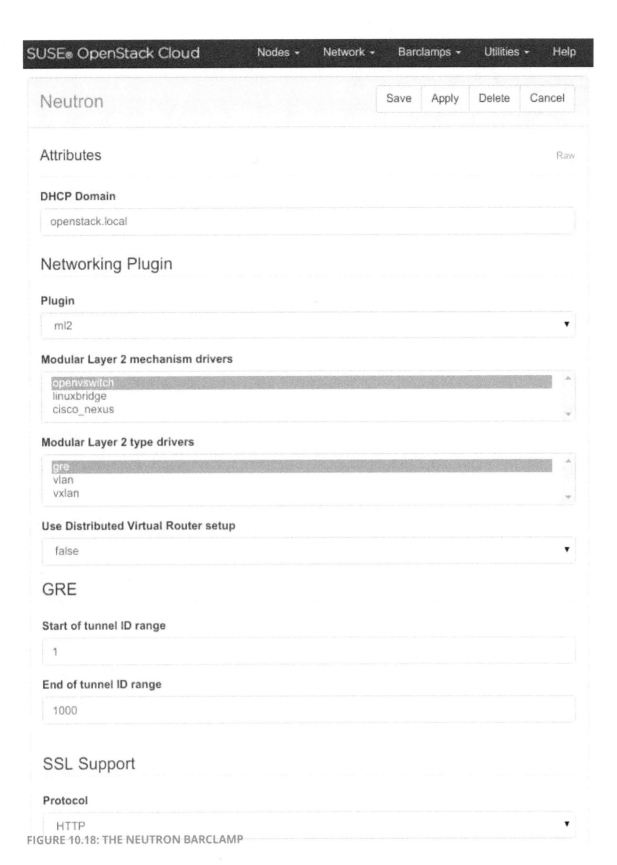

FIGURE 10.18: THE NEUTRON BARCLAMP

The Neutron service consists of two different roles:

neutron-server

> *neutron-server* provides the scheduler and the API. It needs to be installed on a Control Node.

neutron-network

> This service runs the various agents that manage the network traffic of all the cloud instances. It acts as the DHCP and DNS server and as a gateway for all cloud instances. It is recommend to deploy this role on a dedicated node supplied with sufficient network capacity.

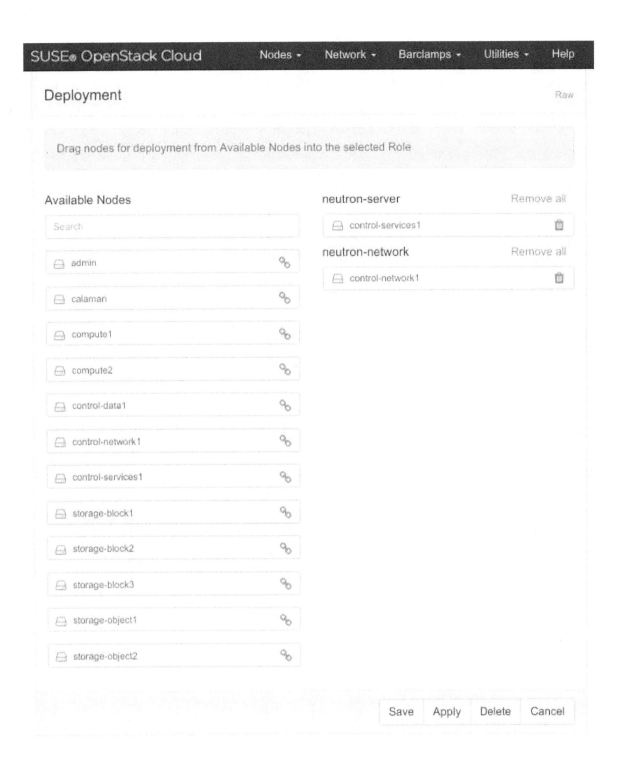

FIGURE 10.19: THE NEUTRON BARCLAMP

10.11.1　HA Setup for Neutron

Neutron can be made highly available by deploying *neutron-server* and *neutron-network* on a cluster. While *neutron-server* may be deployed on a cluster shared with other services, it is strongly recommended to use a dedicated cluster solely for the *neutron-network* role.

10.12　Deploying Nova

Nova provides key services for managing the SUSE OpenStack Cloud, sets up the Compute Nodes. SUSE OpenStack Cloud currently supports KVM, Xen and Microsoft Hyper V and VMWare vSphere. The unsupported QEMU option is included to enable test setups with virtualized nodes. The following attributes can be configured for Nova:

Scheduler Options: Virtual RAM to Physical RAM allocation ratio

Set the "overcommit ratio" for RAM for instances on the Compute Nodes. A ratio of `1.0` means no overcommitment. Changing this value is not recommended.

Scheduler Options: Virtual CPU to Physical CPU allocation ratio

Set the "overcommit ratio" for CPUs for instances on the Compute Nodes. A ratio of `1.0` means no overcommitment.

Live Migration Support: Enable Libvirt Migration

Allows to move KVM and Xen instances to a different Compute Node running the same hypervisor (cross hypervisor migrations are not supported). Useful when a Compute Node needs to be shut down or rebooted for maintenance or when the load of the Compute Node is very high. Instances can be moved while running (Live Migration).

 Warning: Libvirt Migration and Security

Enabling the libvirt migration option will open a TCP port on the Compute Nodes that allows access to all instances from all machines in the admin network. Ensure that only authorized machines have access to the admin network when enabling this option.

Live Migration Support: Setup Shared Storage

Sets up a directory `/var/lib/nova/instances` on the Control Node on which *nova-controller* is running. This directory is exported via NFS to all compute nodes and will host a copy of the root disk of *all* Xen instances. This setup is required for live migration of

Xen instances (but not for KVM) and is used to provide central handling of instance data. Enabling this option is only recommended if Xen live migration is required—otherwise it should be disabled.

 Warning: Do Not Set Up Shared Storage When instances are Running

Setting up shared storage in a SUSE OpenStack Cloud where instances are running will result in connection losses to all running instances. It is strongly recommended to set up shared storage when deploying SUSE OpenStack Cloud. If it needs to be done at a later stage, make sure to shut down all instances prior to the change.

KVM Options: Enable Kernel Samepage Merging

Kernel SamePage Merging (KSM) is a Linux Kernel feature which merges identical memory pages from multiple running processes into one memory region. Enabling it optimizes memory usage on the Compute Nodes when using the KVM hypervisor at the cost of slightly increasing CPU usage.

VMware vCenter Settings

Setting up VMware support is described in a separate section. See *Appendix G, VMware vSphere Installation Instructions*.

SSL Support: Protocol

Choose whether to encrypt public communication (*HTTPS*) or not (*HTTP*). If choosing *HTTPS*, refer to *SSL Support: Protocol* for configuration details.

VNC Settings: Keymap

Change the default VNC keymap for instances. By default, `en-us` is used. Enter the value in lowercase, either as a two character code (such as `de` or `jp`) or, as a five character code such as `de-ch` or `en-uk`, if applicable.

VNC Settings: NoVNC Protocol

After having started an instance you can display its VNC console in the OpenStack Dashboard (Horizon) via the browser using the noVNC implementation. By default this connection is not encrypted and can potentially be eavesdropped.

Enable encrypted communication for noVNC by choosing *HTTPS* and providing the locations for the certificate key pair files.

Logging: Verbose Logging

Shows debugging output in the log files when set to *true*.

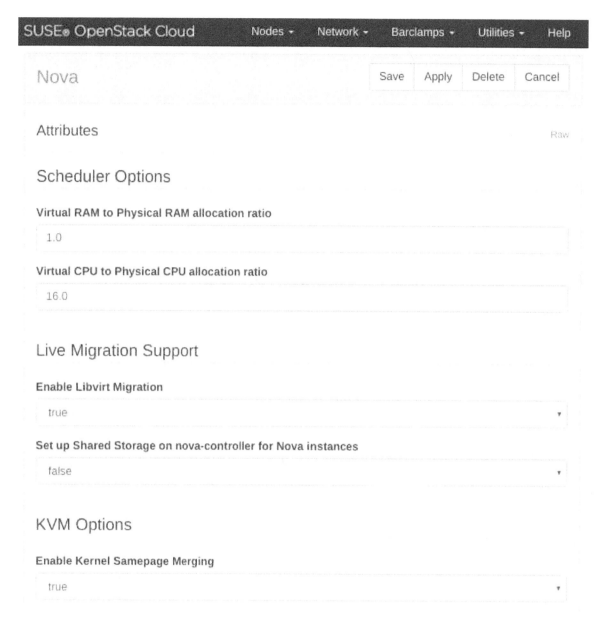

FIGURE 10.20: THE NOVA BARCLAMP

The Nova service consists of eight different roles:

nova-controller

Distributing and scheduling the instances is managed by the *nova-controller*. It also provides networking and messaging services. *nova-controller* needs to be installed on a Control Node.

nova-compute-docker / nova-compute-hyperv / nova-compute-kvm / nova-compute-qemu / nova-compute-vmware / nova-compute-xen / nova-compute-zvm

Provides the hypervisors (Docker, Hyper-V, KVM, QEMU, VMware vSphere, Xen, and z/VM) and tools needed to manage the instances. Only one hypervisor can be deployed on a single compute node. To use different hypervisors in your cloud, deploy different hypervisors to different Compute Nodes. A `nova-compute-*` role needs to be installed on every Compute Node. However, not all hypervisors need to be deployed.

Each image that will be made available in SUSE OpenStack Cloud to start an instance is bound to a hypervisor. Each hypervisor can be deployed on multiple Compute Nodes (except for the VMWare vSphere role, see below). In a multi-hypervisor deployment you should make sure to deploy the `nova-compute-*` roles in a way, that enough compute power is available for each hypervisor.

 ## Note: Re-assigning Hypervisors

Existing `nova-compute-*` nodes can be changed in a productive SUSE OpenStack Cloud without service interruption. You need to "evacuate" the node, re-assign a new `nova-compute` role via the Nova barclamp and *Apply* the change. *nova-compute-vmware* can only be deployed on a single node.

Important: Deploying Hyper-V

`nova-compute-hyperv` can only be deployed to Compute Nodes running either Microsoft Hyper-V Server or Windows Server 2012. Being able to set up such Compute Nodes requires to set up a netboot environment for Windows. Refer to *Appendix F, Setting up a Netboot Environment for Microsoft* Windows* for details.

The default password for Hyper-V Compute Nodes will be "crowbar".

Important: Deploying VMware vSphere (vmware)

VMware vSphere is not supported "natively" by SUSE OpenStack Cloud—it rather delegates requests to an existing vCenter. It requires preparations at the vCenter and post install adjustments of the Compute Node. See *Appendix G, VMware vSphere Installation Instructions* for instructions. *nova-compute-vmware* can only be deployed on a single Compute Node.

Note: Deploying Docker

The ability to use Docker is only included as a technology preview and not supported by SUSE. The following features are known to work:

- Starting and shutting down an instance.

- Resuming a paused instance.

- Taking a snapshot of running instance and starting a new image based on this snapshot.

The following features are known to *not* work:

- Suspend and resume.

- Attaching Cinder volumes.

If you assign the `nova-compute-docker` role to a node, it is recommended to use Btrfs for the respective node to enhance the performance. How to specify a file system for a node is described in *Section 9.2, "Node Installation"*.

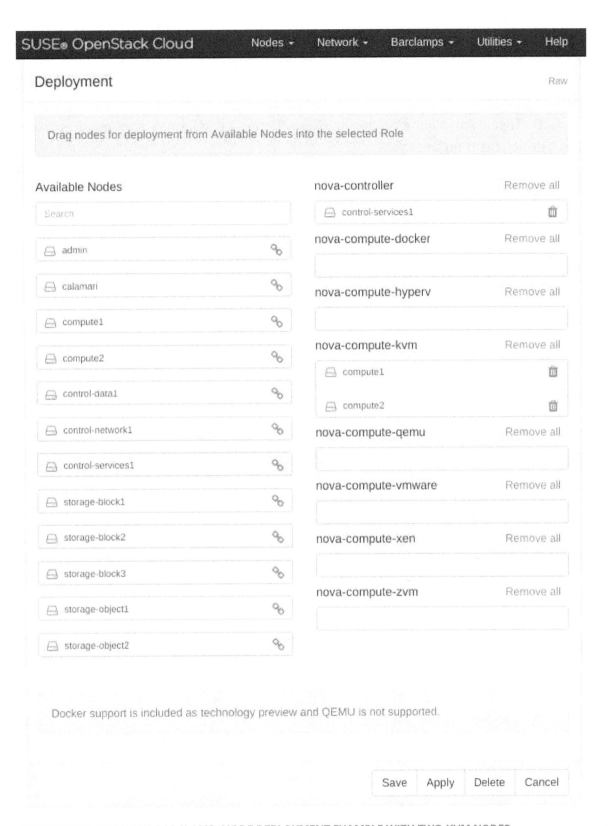

FIGURE 10.21: THE NOVA BARCLAMP: NODE DEPLOYMENT EXAMPLE WITH TWO KVM NODES

10.12.1 HA Setup for Nova

Making *nova-controller* highly available requires no special configuration—it is sufficient to deploy it on a cluster.

To enable High Availability for Compute Nodes, deploy the following roles to one or more clusters with remote nodes:

- nova-compute-kvm

- nova-compute-qemu

- nova-compute-xen

The cluster to which you deploy the roles above can be completely independent of the one to which the role `nova-controller` is deployed.

10.13 Deploying Horizon (OpenStack Dashboard)

The last service that needs to be deployed is Horizon, the OpenStack Dashboard. It provides a Web interface for users to start and stop instances and for administrators to manage users, groups, roles, etc. Horizon should be installed on a Control Node. To make Horizon highly available, deploy it on a cluster.

The following attributes can be configured:

Session Timeout

Timeout (in minutes) after which a user is been logged out automatically. The default value is set to 4 hours (240 minutes).

User Password Validation: Regular expression used for password validation

Specify a regular expression with which to check the password. The default expression (`.{8,}`) tests for a minimum length of 8 characters. The string you enter is interpreted as a Python regular expression (see http://docs.python.org/2.7/library/re.html#module-re for a reference).

User Password Validation: Text to display if the password does not pass validation

Error message that will be displayed in case the password validation fails.

SSL Support: Protocol

Choose whether to encrypt public communication (*HTTPS*) or not (*HTTP*). If choosing *HTTPS*, you have two choices. You can either *Generate (self-signed) certificates* or provide the locations for the certificate key pair files and,—optionally— the certificate chain file. Using self-signed certificates is for testing purposes only and should never be used in production environments!

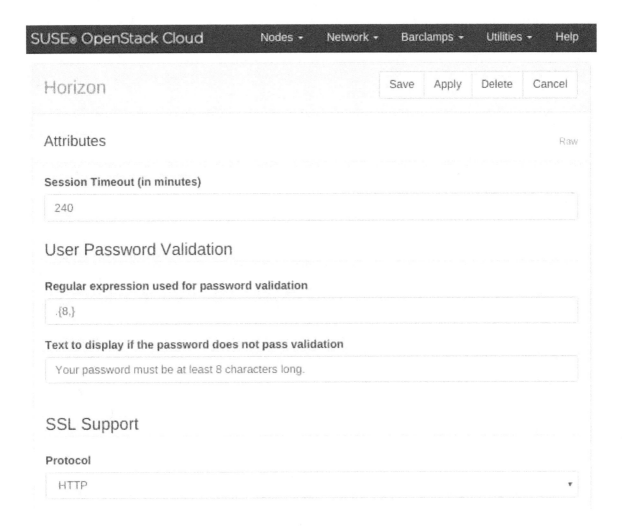

FIGURE 10.22: THE HORIZON BARCLAMP

10.13.1   HA Setup for Horizon

Making Horizon highly available requires no special configuration—it is sufficient to deploy it on a cluster.

10.14 Deploying Heat (Optional)

Heat is a template-based orchestration engine that enables you to, for example, start workloads requiring multiple servers or to automatically restart instances if needed. It also brings auto-scaling to SUSE OpenStack Cloud by automatically starting additional instances if certain criteria are met. For more information about Heat refer to the OpenStack documentation at http://docs.openstack.org/developer/heat/.

Heat should be deployed on a Control Node. To make Heat highly available, deploy it on a cluster.

The following attributes can be configured for Heat:

Verbose Logging

Shows debugging output in the log files when set to *true*.

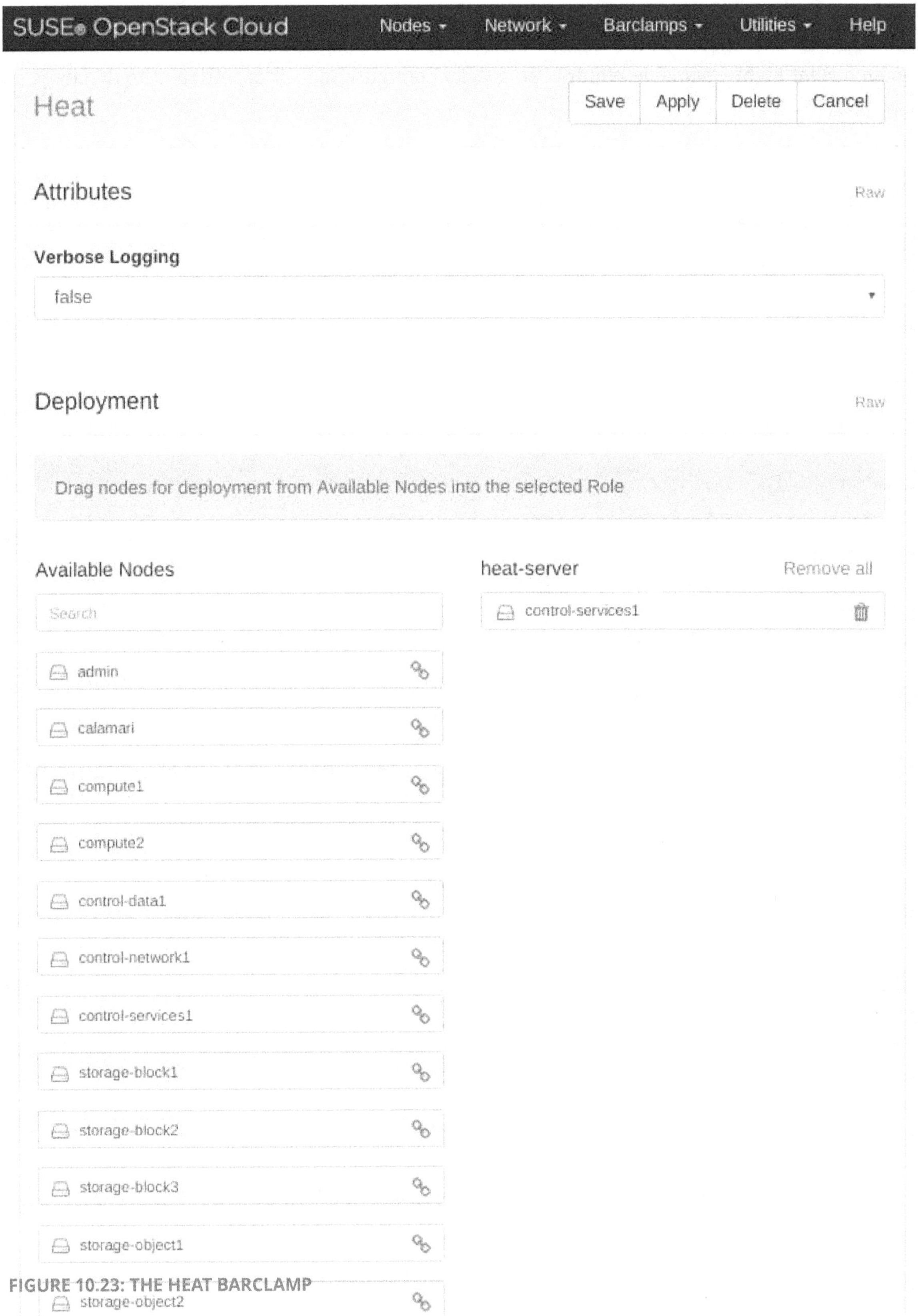
SUSE OpenStack Cloud
Nodes
Network
Barclamps
Utilities
Help
Heat
Save
Apply
Delete
Cancel
Attributes
Raw
Verbose Logging
false
Deployment
Raw
Drag nodes for deployment from Available Nodes into the selected Role
Available Nodes
Search
admin
calamari
compute1
compute2
control-data1
control-network1
control-services1
storage-block1
storage-block2
storage-block3
storage-object1
storage-object2
heat-server
Remove all
control-services1

FIGURE 10.23: THE HEAT BARCLAMP

10.14.1   HA Setup for Heat

Making Heat highly available requires no special configuration—it is sufficient to deploy it on a cluster.

10.15   Deploying Ceilometer (Optional)

Ceilometer collects CPU and networking data from SUSE OpenStack Cloud. This data can be used by a billing system to enable customer billing. Deploying Ceilometer is optional.

For more information about Ceilometer refer to the OpenStack documentation at http://docs.openstack.org/developer/ceilometer/.

 Important: Ceilometer Restrictions

> As of SUSE OpenStack Cloud 6 data measuring is only supported for KVM, Xen and Windows instances. Other hypervisors and SUSE OpenStack Cloud features such as object or block storage will not be measured.

The following attributes can be configured for Ceilometer:

Interval used for CPU/disk/network/other meter updates (in seconds)

> Specify an interval in seconds after which Ceilometer performs an update of the specified meter.

Evaluation interval for threshold alarms (in seconds)

> Set the interval after which to check whether to raise an alarm because a threshold has been exceeded. For performance reasons, do not set a value lower than the default (60s).

Use MongoDB instead of standard database

> Ceilometer collects a huge amount of data, which is written to a database. In a production system it is recommended to use a separate database for Ceilometer rather than the standard database that is also used by the other SUSE OpenStack Cloud services. MongoDB is optimized to write a lot of data. As of SUSE OpenStack Cloud 6, MongoDB is only included as a technology preview and not supported.

How long are metering/event samples kept in the database (in days)

> Specify how long to keep the data. -1 means that samples are kept in the database forever.

Verbose Logging

Shows debugging output in the log files when set to *true*.

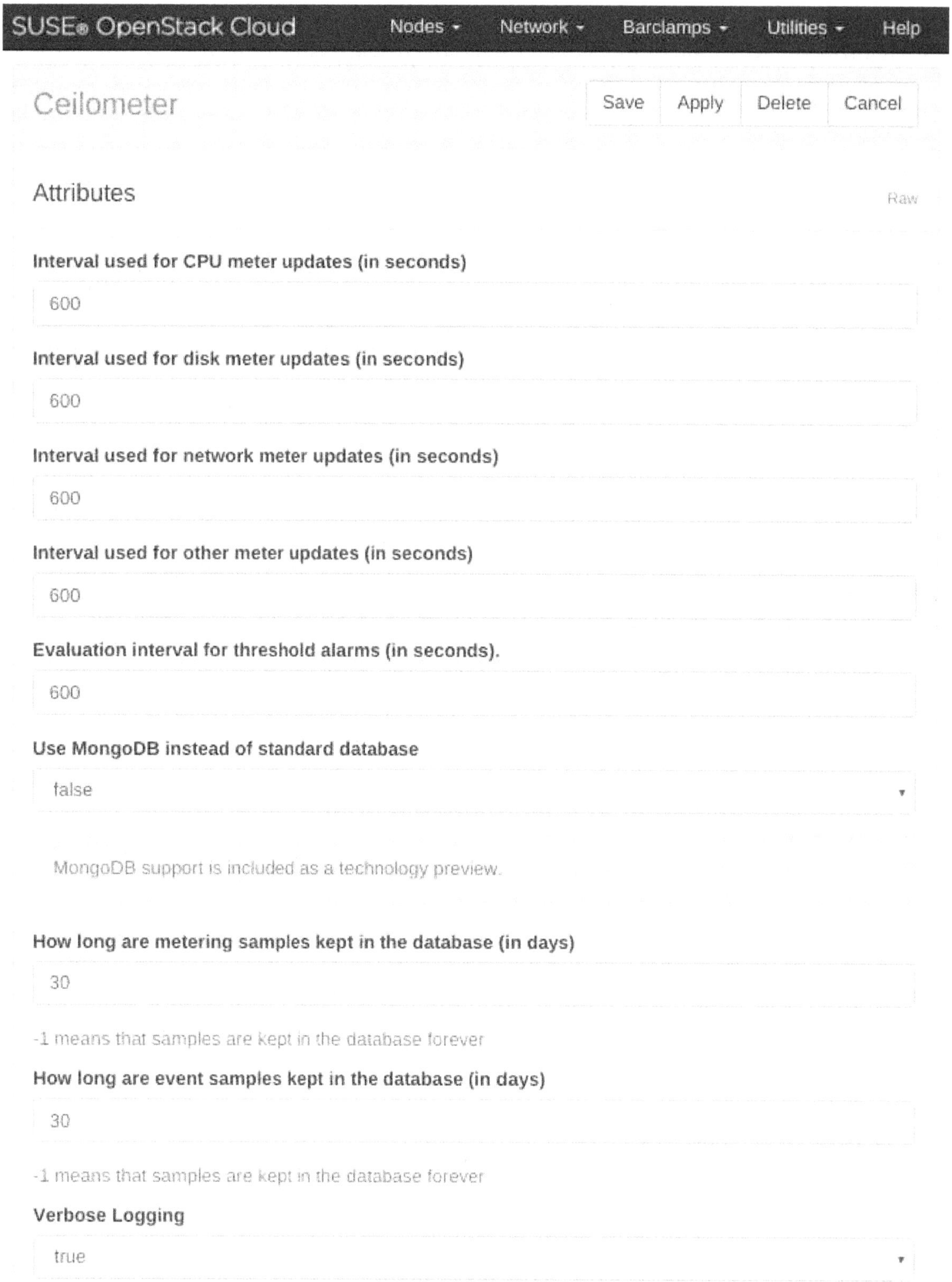
SUSE® OpenStack Cloud
Nodes
Network
Barclamps
Utilities
Help
Ceilometer
Save
Apply
Delete
Cancel
Attributes
Raw
Interval used for CPU meter updates (in seconds)
600
Interval used for disk meter updates (in seconds)
600
Interval used for network meter updates (in seconds)
600
Interval used for other meter updates (in seconds)
600
Evaluation interval for threshold alarms (in seconds).
600
Use MongoDB instead of standard database
false
MongoDB support is included as a technology preview.
How long are metering samples kept in the database (in days)
30
-1 means that samples are kept in the database forever
How long are event samples kept in the database (in days)
30
-1 means that samples are kept in the database forever
Verbose Logging
true

FIGURE 10.24: THE CEILOMETER BARCLAMP

The Ceilometer service consists of five different roles:

ceilometer-server

> The Ceilometer API server role. This role needs to be deployed on a Control Node. Ceilometer collects approximately 200 bytes of data per hour and instance. Unless you have a very huge number of instances, there is no need to install it on a dedicated node.

ceilometer-polling

> The polling agent listens to the message bus to collect data. It needs to be deployed on a Control Node. It can be deployed on the same node as *ceilometer-server*.

ceilometer-agent

> The compute agents collect data from the compute nodes. They need to be deployed on all KVM and Xen compute nodes in your cloud (other hypervisors—except for Hyper-V—are currently not supported).

ceilometer-agent-hyperv

> This compute agents collect data from the compute nodes running on Microsoft Windows. It needs need to be deployed on all Hyper-V Compute Nodes in your cloud.

ceilometer-swift-proxy-middleware

> An agent collecting data from the Swift nodes. This role needs to be deployed on the same node as swift-proxy.

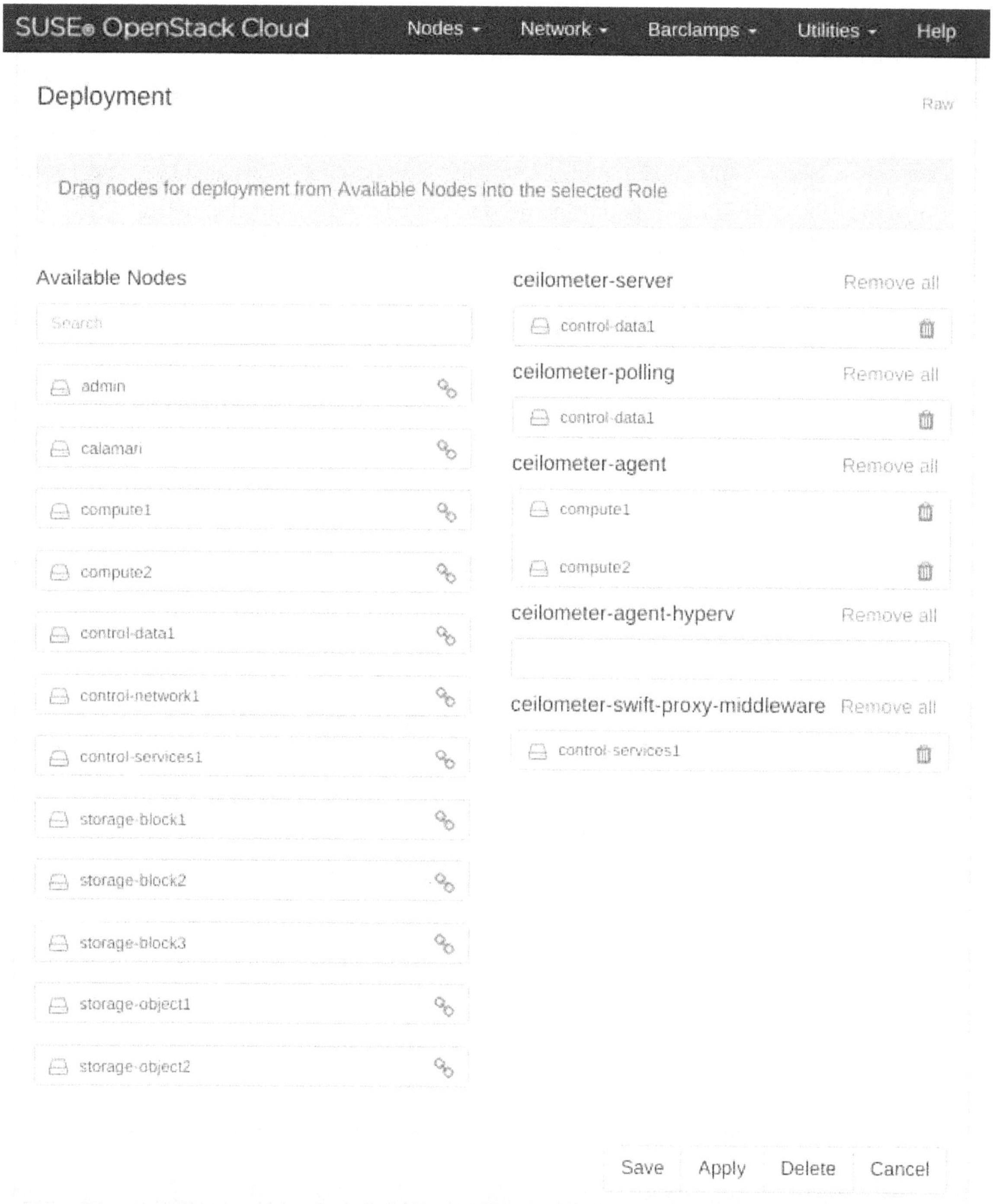
SUSE® OpenStack Cloud
Nodes
Network
Barclamps
Utilities
Help
Deployment
Raw
Drag nodes for deployment from Available Nodes into the selected Role
Available Nodes
Search
admin
calamari
compute1
compute2
control-data1
control-network1
control-services1
storage-block1
storage-block2
storage-block3
storage-object1
storage-object2
ceilometer-server
Remove all
control-data1
ceilometer-polling
Remove all
control-data1
ceilometer-agent
Remove all
compute1
compute2
ceilometer-agent-hyperv
Remove all
ceilometer-swift-proxy-middleware
Remove all
control-services1
Save
Apply
Delete
Cancel

FIGURE 10.25: THE CEILOMETER BARCLAMP: NODE DEPLOYMENT

10.15.1   HA Setup for Ceilometer

Making Ceilometer highly available requires no special configuration—it is sufficient to deploy the roles *ceilometer-server* and *ceilometer-polling* on a cluster. The cluster needs to consist of an odd number of nodes, otherwise the Ceilometer deployment will fail.

10.16   Deploying Trove (Optional)

Trove is a Database-as-a-Service for SUSE OpenStack Cloud. It provides database instances which can be used by all instances. With Trove being deployed, SUSE OpenStack Cloud users no longer need to deploy and maintain their own database applications. For more information about Trove; refer to the OpenStack documentation at http://docs.openstack.org/developer/trove/.

> **Important: Technology Preview**
>
> Trove is only included as a technology preview and not supported.

Trove should be deployed on a dedicated Control Node.

The following attributes can be configured for Trove:

Enable Trove Volume Support

When enabled, Trove will use a Cinder volume to store the data.

Logging: Verbose

Increases the amount of information that is written to the log files when set to *true*.

Logging: Debug

Shows debugging output in the log files when set to *true*.

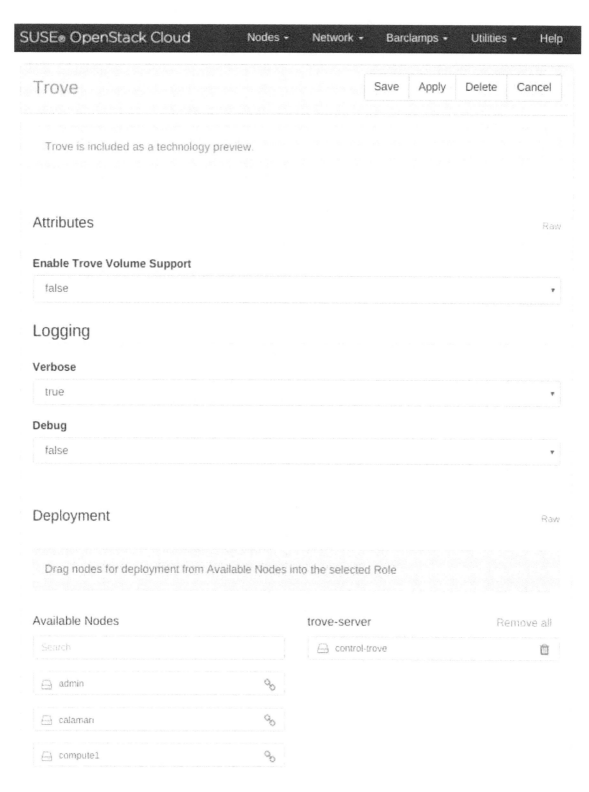

FIGURE 10.26: THE TROVE BARCLAMP

10.16.1　HA Setup for Trove

An HA Setup for Trove is currently not supported.

10.17　Deploying Tempest (Optional)

Tempest is an integration test suite for SUSE OpenStack Cloud written in Python. It contains multiple integration tests for validating your SUSE OpenStack Cloud deployment. For more information about Tempest refer to the OpenStack documentation at http://docs.openstack.org/developer/tempest/.

 Important: Technology Preview

Tempest is only included as a technology preview and not supported.

Tempest may be used for testing whether the intended setup will run without problems. It should not be used in a production environment.

Tempest should be deployed on a Control Node.

The following attributes can be configured for Tempest:

Choose User name / Password

Credentials for a regular user. If the user does not exist, it will be created.

Choose Tenant

Tenant to be used by Tempest. If it does not exist, it will be created. It is safe to stick with the default value.

Choose Tempest Admin User name/Password

Credentials for an admin user. If the user does not exist, it will be created.

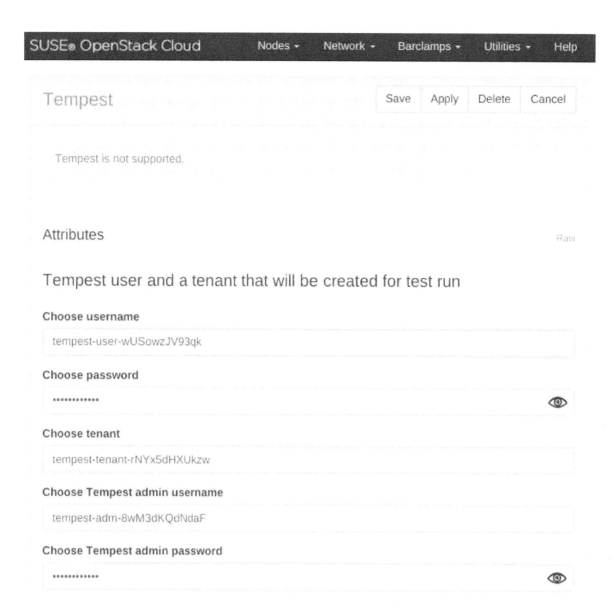

FIGURE 10.27: THE TEMPEST BARCLAMP

 Tip: Running Tests

To run tests with Tempest, log in to the Control Node on which Tempest was deployed. Change into the directory `/var/lib/openstack-tempest-test`. To get an overview of available commands, run:

```
./run_tempest.sh --help
```

To serially invoke a subset of all tests ("the gating smoketests") to help validate the working functionality of your local cloud instance, run the following command. It will save the output to a log file tempest_*CURRENT_DATE*.log.

```
./run_tempest.sh --no-virtual-env -serial --smoke 2>&1 \
| tee "tempest_$(date +%Y-%m-%d_%H%M%S).log"
```

10.17.1   HA Setup for Tempest

Tempest cannot be made highly available.

10.18   How to Proceed

With a successful deployment of the OpenStack Dashboard, the SUSE OpenStack Cloud installation is finished. To be able to test your setup by starting an instance one last step remains to be done—uploading an image to the Glance service. Refer to the *Supplement to Admin User Guide and End User Guide,* chapter *Manage images* for instructions. Images for SUSE OpenStack Cloud can be built in SUSE Studio. Refer to the *Supplement to Admin User Guide and End User Guide,* section *Building Images with SUSE Studio.*

Now you can hand over to the cloud administrator to set up users, roles, flavors, etc.—refer to the *Admin User Guide* for details. The default credentials for the OpenStack Dashboard are user name admin and password crowbar.

IV Maintenance and Support

11 SUSE OpenStack Cloud Maintenance

11.1 Keeping the Nodes Up-to-date

Keeping the nodes in SUSE OpenStack Cloud up-to-date requires an appropriate setup of the update and pool repositories and the deployment of either the *Updater* barclamp or the SUSE Manager barclamp. For details, see *Section 5.2, "Update and Pool Repositories"*, *Section 9.4.1, "Deploying Node Updates with the Updater Barclamp"*, and *Section 9.4.2, "Configuring Node Updates with the SUSE Manager Client Barclamp"*.

If one of those barclamps is deployed, patches are installed on the nodes. Installing patches that do not require a reboot of a node does not come with any service interruption. If a patch (for example, a kernel update) requires a reboot after the installation, services running on the machine that is rebooted will not be available within SUSE OpenStack Cloud. Therefore it is strongly recommended to install those patches during a maintenance window.

 Note: No Maintenance Mode

As of SUSE OpenStack Cloud 6 it is not possible to put SUSE OpenStack Cloud into "Maintenance Mode".

CONSEQUENCES WHEN REBOOTING NODES

Administration Server

While the Administration Server is offline, it is not possible to deploy new nodes. However, rebooting the Administration Server has no effect on starting instances or on instances already running.

Control Nodes

The consequences a reboot of a Control Node has, depends on the services running on that node:

Database, Keystone, RabbitMQ, Glance, Nova: No new instances can be started.

Swift: No object storage data is available. If Glance uses Swift, it will not be possible to start new instances.

Cinder, Ceph: No block storage data is available.

Neutron: No new instances can be started. On running instances the network will be unavailable.

Horizon. Horizon will be unavailable. Starting and managing instances can be done with the command line tools.

Compute Nodes

Whenever a Compute Node is rebooted, all instances running on that particular node will be shut down and must be manually restarted. Therefore it is recommended to "evacuate" the node by migrating instances to another node, before rebooting it.

11.2 Service Order on SUSE OpenStack Cloud Start-up or Shutdown

In case you need to restart your complete SUSE OpenStack Cloud (after a complete shut down or a power outage), the services need to started in the following order:

1. Control Node/Cluster on which the Database is deployed

2. Control Node/Cluster on which RabbitMQ is deployed

3. Control Node/Cluster on which Keystone is deployed

4. Any remaining Control Node/Cluster. The following additional rules apply:

   * The Control Node/Cluster on which the `neutron-server` role is deployed needs to be started before starting the node/cluster on which the `neutron-l3` role is deployed.

   * The Control Node/Cluster on which the `nova-controller` role is deployed needs to be started before starting the node/cluster on which Heat is deployed.

5. Compute Nodes

If multiple roles are deployed on a single Control Node, the services are automatically started in the correct order on that node. If you have more than one node on which multiple roles are installed, make sure they are started in a way that the order listed above is met as best as possible.

If you need to shut down SUSE OpenStack Cloud, the services need to be terminated in reverse order than on start-up:

1. Compute Nodes

2. Control Node/Cluster on which Heat is deployed

3. Control Node/Cluster on which the `nova-controller` role is deployed

4. Control Node/Cluster on which the `neutron-l3` role is deployed

5. All Control Node(s)/Cluster(s) on which neither of the following services is deployed: Database, RabbitMQ, and Keystone.

6. Control Node/Cluster on which Keystone is deployed

7. Control Node/Cluster on which RabbitMQ is deployed

8. Control Node/Cluster on which the Database is deployed

11.3   Upgrading from SUSE OpenStack Cloud 5 to SUSE OpenStack Cloud 6

Upgrading from SUSE OpenStack Cloud 5 to SUSE OpenStack Cloud 6 is done via a Web interface guiding you through the process. The process consists of four phases:

1. Saving the configuration data of your SUSE OpenStack Cloud 5 installation in a data dump.

2. Re-Installing and setting up the Administration Server with SUSE OpenStack Cloud 6.

3. Upgrading the all nodes to SUSE Linux Enterprise Server 12 SP1 and SUSE OpenStack Cloud 6.

4. Re-applying the barclamps.

11.3.1 Requirements

Before you start upgrading SUSE OpenStack Cloud, make sure the following requirements are met:

- The Administration Server needs to have the latest SUSE OpenStack Cloud 5 updates installed. One of these updates will add the new upgrade routine to the Crowbar Web interface.

- All other nodes need to have the latest SUSE OpenStack Cloud 5 updates *and* the latest SLES updates. If this is not the case, refer to *Section 9.4.1, "Deploying Node Updates with the Updater Barclamp"* for instructions.

- All allocated nodes need to be turned on.

- During the upgrade of the Control Nodes and the Compute Nodes the instances need to be shut down. However it is not necessary to do so at the beginning of the upgrade procedure. This step can be postponed until after the Administration Server has been upgraded to SUSE OpenStack Cloud 6 to keep the downtime as short as possible.

 Important: Instance Running on HyperV Nodes Will Not "Survive" an Upgrade

As of SUSE OpenStack Cloud 6, HyperV Nodes need to be re-installed after the upgrade procedure. This re-installation will overwrite the instance's data and therefore they will be lost. KVM, VMware and Xen instances are not affected.

 Tip: Back Up the Administration Server

It is strongly recommended to create a backup of the Administration Server before starting the upgrade procedure, to be able to restore the server in case the upgrade fails. Refer to the chapter Backing Up and Restoring the Administration Server [http://www.suse.com/documentation/suse-cloud-5/book_cloud_deploy/data/sec_depl_maintenance_backup_admin.html] in the SUSE Cloud 5 documentation for instructions.

11.3.2 The Upgrade Procedure

To start the upgrade procedure, proceed as follows:

PROCEDURE 11.1: UPGRADE PART 1: CREATE THE UPGRADE DATA

1. Open a browser and point it to the Crowbar Web interface, for example http://192.168.124.10/. Log in as user crowbar. The password is `crowbar`, if you have not changed the default.

2. Open *Utilities* › *Upgrade to Cloud 6.*

3. Follow the instructions in the Web interface to create and save the upgrade data. Part 1 of the upgrade procedure is finished when you have saved the data.

    Important: Location for Saving the Upgrade Data

   Make sure to save the upgrade data to a location that can be accessed from the Administration Server after having re-installed it. Do not save it on the Administration Server itself, since it might get overwritten when re-installing the machine.

When the upgrade data has been saved, the Administration Server needs to be re-installed with SUSE OpenStack Cloud 6 on SUSE Linux Enterprise Server 12 SP1:

PROCEDURE 11.2: PART 2: RE-INSTALLING THE ADMINISTRATION SERVER

1. Check the network configuration of the Administration Server with the command `ifconfig`. Note the MAC address and the IP address of the interface named `eth0`. Also note the IP addresses and ranges of all SUSE OpenStack Cloud networks. You can either find them in `/etc/crowbar/network.json` or when checking the *Networks* section in YaST Crowbar (see *Section 7.2, "Networks"* for details).

    Warning: No Parallel Setup

   It is *not* possible to set up a second machine, install SUSE OpenStack Cloud 6 and then switch the old machine with the new one. The MAC address of the network interfaces need to be the same before and after the upgrade.

2. Reboot the Administration Server from a SUSE Linux Enterprise Server 12 SP1 installation source and install the operating system plus SUSE OpenStack Cloud 6 as an add-on products. For details, see *Chapter 3, Installing the Administration Server*.

Tip: Deleting Unused Mirror Data

SUSE OpenStack Cloud 6 does not use any of the repositories that were required for SUSE OpenStack Cloud 5. In case you have mirrored repositories to the Administration Server and /srv resides on a separate partition, it is safe to format this partition to free space for the new repositories.

3. Optional: If you have installed a local SMT server, configure it as described in *Section 4.2, "SMT Configuration"*. Make sure the repositories are set up and mirrored as described in *Section 4.3, "Setting up Repository Mirroring on the SMT Server"*.

4. Make sure all required repositories are made available as described in *Chapter 5, Software Repository Setup*.

5. Configure the network of the Administration Server as described in *Chapter 6, Service Configuration: Administration Server Network Configuration*. Make sure to use the exact same settings as in the previous installation.

6. Configure SUSE OpenStack Cloud with YaST Crowbar as described in *Chapter 7, Crowbar Setup*. Make sure to configure the exact same network settings for Crowbar as in the previous installation.

7. The Administration Server setup is finished as soon as you have finished the configuration with YaST Crowbar. Do *not* start the regular SUSE OpenStack Cloud Crowbar installation!

When the Administration Server has been set up and configured, return to the upgrade Web interface to upgrade all nodes in SUSE OpenStack Cloud:

PROCEDURE 11.3: PART 3: UPGRADING THE NODES

1. Open a browser and point it to the Crowbar Web interface available on the Administration Server, for example `http://192.168.124.10/`.

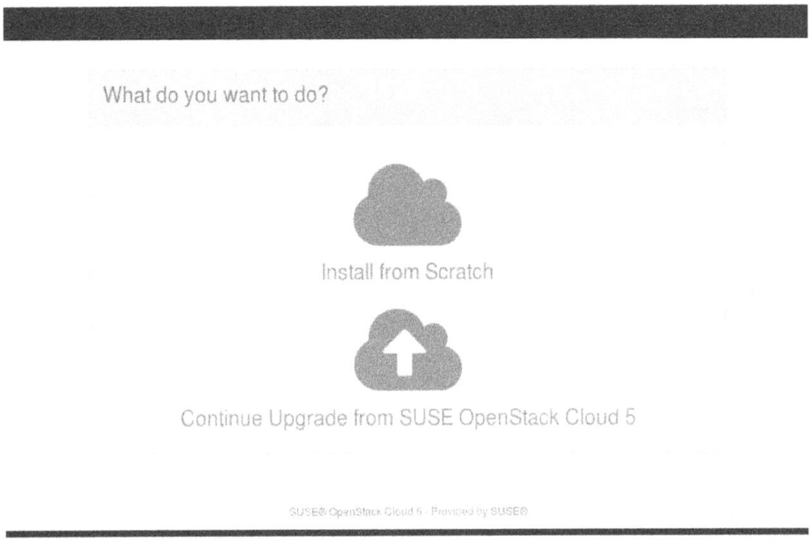

What do you want to do?

Install from Scratch

Continue Upgrade from SUSE OpenStack Cloud 5

SUSE® OpenStack Cloud 6 - Provided by SUSE®

FIGURE 11.1: THE SUSE OPENSTACK CLOUD INSTALLER

2. Choose *Continue Upgrade from SUSE OpenStack Cloud 5* and start the upgrade process by uploading the upgrade data downloaded in Part 1 of the upgrade procedure. Follow the on-screen instruction to finish the upgrade process. Depending on the amount of nodes in your installation this will take up to several hours.

 Note: Login Credentials

During the upgrade procedure you will be asked to provide login credentials for the Crowbar Web interface two times. First time you need to provide the default login credentials (`crowbar/crowbar`. On the second occasion you need to specify the ones you used with Cloud 5. These credentials are also the ones you need to provide for subsequent logins to the Crowbar Web interface.

When all nodes have been upgraded, the barclamps need to be re-applied:

PROCEDURE 11.4: PART 4: RE-APPLYING THE BARCLAMPS

1. Go to the Dashboard on the Crowbar Web interface *Nodes › Dashboard* and check whether all nodes have been successfully updated—all nodes should be listed in state *Ready*, indicated by a green dot.

2. If nodes have not been upgraded successfully, they are marked with a yellow or gray dot. Log in to those nodes (see *Q:*) and check the log files (see *Appendix A, Log Files* for reasons. Fix the issues and reboot the node to restart the upgrade process. For more information also refer to *Q:*.

3. When all nodes have bee upgraded successfully re-apply the barclamps. Go to *Barclamps › All Barclamps* and apply the barclamps in the given order. For each barclamp the service configuration and the deployment configuration is the same as on SUSE OpenStack Cloud 5, since it was restored from the data dump.

4. When all barclamp have been successfully deployed, you can restart the instances on the Compute Nodes.

11.4   Upgrading to an HA Setup

When making an existing SUSE OpenStack Cloud deployment highly available (by setting up HA clusters and moving roles to these clusters), there are a few issues to pay attention to. To make existing services highly available, proceed as follows. Note that moving to an HA setup cannot be done without SUSE OpenStack Cloud service interruption, because it requires OpenStack services to be restarted.

> **❗ Important: Teaming Network Mode is Required for HA**
>
> Teaming network mode is required for an HA setup of SUSE OpenStack Cloud. If you are planning to move your cloud to an HA setup at a later point in time, make sure to deploy SUSE OpenStack Cloud with teaming network mode from the beginning. Otherwise a migration to an HA setup is not supported.

1. Make sure to have read the sections *Section 1.5, "HA Setup"* and *Section 2.6, "High Availability"* of this manual and taken any appropriate action.

2. Make the HA repositories available on the Administration Server as described in *Section 5.2, "Update and Pool Repositories"*. Run the command **chef-client** afterwards.

3. Set up your cluster(s) as described in *Section 10.2, "Deploying Pacemaker (Optional, HA Setup Only)"*.

4. To move a particular role from a regular control node to a cluster, you need to stop the associated service(s) before re-deploying the role on a cluster:

   a. Log in to each node on which the role is deployed and stop its associated service(s) (a role can have multiple services). Do so by running the service's start/stop script with the stop argument, for example:

   ```
   rcopenstack-keystone stop
   ```

   See *Appendix C, Roles and Services in SUSE OpenStack Cloud* for a list of roles, services and start/stop scripts.

   b. The following roles need additional treatment:

   database-server (Database barclamp)

   1. Stop the database on the node the Database barclamp is deployed with the command:

   ```
   rcpostgresql stop
   ```

   2. Copy /var/lib/pgsql to a temporary location on the node, for example:

   ```
   cp -ax /var/lib/pgsql /tmp
   ```

   3. Redeploy the Database barclamp to the cluster. The original node may also be part of this cluster.

   4. Log in to a cluster node and run the following command to determine which cluster node runs the postgresql service:

   ```
   crm_mon -1
   ```

   5. Log in to the cluster node running postgresql.

   6. Stop the postgresql service:

   ```
   crm resource stop postgresql
   ```

7. Copy the data backed up earlier to the cluster node:

```
rsync -av --delete
            NODE_WITH_BACKUP:/tmp/pgsql/ /var/lib/pgsql/
```

8. Restart the `postgresql` service:

```
crm resource start postgresql
```

Copy the content of `/var/lib/pgsql/data/` from the original database node to the cluster node with DRBD or shared storage.

keystone-server (Keystone barclamp)

If using Keystone with PKI tokens, the PKI keys on all nodes need to be regenerated. This can be achieved by removing the contents of `/var/cache/*/keystone-signing/` on the nodes. Use a command similar to the following on the Administration Server as `root`:

```
for NODE in NODE1
        NODE2 NODE3; do
  ssh $NODE rm /var/cache/*/keystone-signing/*
done
```

5. Go to the barclamp featuring the role you want to move to the cluster. From the left side of the *Deployment* section, remove the node the role is currently running on. Replace it with a cluster from the *Available Clusters* section. Then apply the proposal and verify that application succeeded via the Crowbar Web interface. You can also check the cluster status via Hawk or the **crm** / **crm_mon** CLI tools.

6. Repeat these steps for all roles you want to move to cluster. See *Section 2.6.2.1, "Control Node(s)—Avoiding Points of Failure"* for a list of services with HA support.

> **❗ Important: SSL Certificates**
>
> Moving to an HA setup also requires to create SSL certificates for nodes in the cluster that run services using SSL. Certificates need to be issued for the generated names (see *Important: Proposal Name*) and for all public names you have configured in the cluster.

> **!** Important: Service Management on the Cluster
>
> After a role has been deployed on a cluster, its services are managed by the HA software. You must *never* manually start or stop an HA-managed service or configure it to start on boot. Services may only be started or stopped by using the cluster management tools Hawk or the crm shell. See http://www.suse.com/documentation/sle-ha-12/book_sleha/data/sec_ha_config_basics_resources.html for more information.

11.5 Backing Up and Restoring the Administration Server

Backing Up and Restoring the Administration Server can either be done via the Crowbar Web interface or on the Administration Server's command line via the **crowbarctl backup** command. Both tools provide the same functionality.

11.5.1 Backup and Restore via the Crowbar Web interface

To use the Web interface for backing up and restoring the Administration Server, go to the Crowbar Web interface on the Administration Server, for example `http://192.168.124.10/`. Log in as user `crowbar`. The password is `crowbar` by default, if you have not changed it. Go to *Utilities › Backup & Restore*.

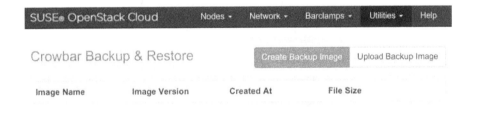

FIGURE 11.2: BACKUP AND RESTORE: INITIAL PAGE VIEW

To create a backup, click the respective button. Provide a descriptive name (allowed characters are letters, numbers, dashes and underscores) and confirm with *Create Backup*. Alternatively, you can upload a backup, for example from a previous installation.

Existing backups are listed with name and creation date. For each backup, three actions are available:

Download

Download a copy of the backup file. The TAR archive you receive with this download can be uploaded again via *Upload Backup Image*.

Restore

Restore the backup.

Delete

Delete the backup.

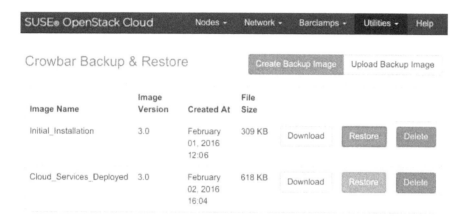

FIGURE 11.3: BACKUP AND RESTORE: LIST OF BACKUPS

11.5.2 Backup and Restore via the Command Line

Backing up and restoring the Administration Server from the command line can be done with the command `crowbarctl backup`. For getting general help, run the command `crowbarctl --help backup`, help on a subcommand is available by running `crowbarctl SUBCOMMAND --help`. The following commands for creating and managing backups exist:

`crowbarctl backup create NAME`

Create a new backup named `NAME`. It will be stored at `/var/lib/crowbar/backup`.

`crowbarctl backup [--yes] NAME`

Restore the backup named `NAME`. You will be asked for confirmation before any existing proposals will get overwritten. If using the option `--yes`, confirmations are tuned off and the restore is forced.

crowbarctl backup delete *NAME*

> Delete the backup named *NAME*.

crowbarctl backup download *NAME [FILE]*

> Download the backup named *NAME*. If you specify the optional *[FILE]*, the download is written to the specified file. Otherwise it is saved to the current working directory with an automatically generated file name. If specifying - for *[FILE]*, the output is written to STDOUT.

crowbarctl backup list

> List existing backups. You can optionally specify different output formats and filters—refer to **crowbarctl backup list --help** for details.

crowbarctl backup upload *FILE*

> Upload a backup from *FILE*.

12 Troubleshooting and Support

Find solutions for the most common pitfalls and technical details on how to create a support request for SUSE OpenStack Cloud here.

12.1 FAQ

If your problem is not mentioned here, checking the log files on either the Administration Server or the OpenStack nodes may help. A list of log files is available at *Appendix A, Log Files*.

12.1.1 Admin Node Deployment

Q: What to do when **install-suse-cloud** fails?

A: Check the script's log file at `/var/log/crowbar/install.log` for error messages.

Q: What to do if **install-suse-cloud** fails while deploying the IPMI/BMC network?

A: As of SUSE OpenStack Cloud 6, it is assumed that each machine can be accessed directly via IPMI/BMC. However, this is not the case on certain blade hardware, where several nodes are accessed via a common adapter. Such a hardware setup causes an error on deploying the IPMI/BMC network. You need to disable the IPMI deployment running the following command:

```
/opt/dell/bin/json-edit -r -a "attributes.ipmi.bmc_enable" \
-v "false" /opt/dell/chef/data_bags/crowbar/bc-template-ipmi.json
```

Re-run **install-suse-cloud** after having disabled the IPMI deployment.

Q: Why am I not able to reach the Administration Server from outside the admin network via the bastion network?

A: If **route** -n shows no gateway for the bastion network, check the value of the following entries in `/etc/crowbar/network.json`: `"router_pref":` and `"router_pref":`. Make sure the value for the bastion network's `"router_pref":` is set to a *lower* value than `"router_pref":` for the admin network.

If the router preference is set correctly, **route** -n shows a gateway for the bastion network. In case the Administration Server is still not accessible via its admin network address (for example, 192.168.124.10), you need to disable route verification (rp_filter). Do so by running the following command on the Administration Server:

```
echo 0 > /proc/sys/net/ipv4/conf/all/rp_filter
```

If this setting solves the problem, make it permanent by editing /etc/sysctl.conf and setting the value for net.ipv4.conf.all.rp_filter to 0.

Q: Can I change the host name of the Administration Server?

A: No, after you have run **install-suse-cloud** you cannot change the host name anymore. Services like Crowbar, Chef, and the RabbitMQ will fail when having changed the host name.

Q: What to do when browsing the Chef Web UI gives a Tampered with cookie error?

A: You probably have an old cookie in your browser from a previous Chef installation on the same IP. Remove the cookie named _chef_server_session_id and try again.

Q: How to make custom software repositories from an external server (for example a remote SMT or SUSE Manager server) available for the nodes?

A: Custom repositories need to be added using the YaST Crowbar module:

1. Start the YaST Crowbar module and switch to the *Repositories* tab: *YaST* › *Miscellaneous* › *Crowbar* › *Repositories*.

2. Choose *Add Repositories*

3. Enter the following data:

   Name
       A unique name to identify the repository.

   URL
       Link or path to the repository.

Ask On Error

> Access errors to a repository are silently ignored by default. To ensure that you get notified of these errors, set the `Ask On Error` flag.

Target Platform/Architecture

> Currently only repositories for *SLE 12 SP1* on the *x86_64* architecture are supported. Make sure to select both options.

4. Save your settings selecting *OK*.

12.1.2   OpenStack Node Deployment

Q: How can I log in to a node as `root`?

A: By default you cannot directly log in to a node as `root`, because the nodes were set up without a `root` password. You can only log in via SSH from the Administration Server. You should be able to log in to a node with **ssh root@***NAME* where *NAME* is the name (alias) of the node.

If name resolution does not work, go to the Crowbar Web interface and open the *Node Dashboard*. Click the name of the node and look for its *admin (eth0) IP Address*. Log in to that IP address via SSH as user `root`.

Q: What to do if a node refuses to boot or boots into a previous installation?

A: Make sure to change the boot order in the BIOS of the node, so that the first boot option is to boot from the network/boot using PXE.

Q: What to do if a node hangs during hardware discovery after the very first boot using PXE into the "SLEShammer" image?

A: The `root` login is enabled at a very early state in discovery mode, so chances are high that you can log in for debugging purposes as described in *Q:*. If logging in as `root` does not work, you need to set the `root` password manually. This can either be done by setting the password via the Kernel command line as explained in *Q:*, or by creating a hook as explained below:

1. Create a directory on the Administration Server named `/updates/discovering-pre`

```
mkdir /updates/discovering-pre
```

2. Create a hook script `setpw.hook` in the directory created in the previous step:

```
cat > /updates/discovering-pre/setpw.hook <<EOF
#!/bin/sh
echo "root:linux" | chpasswd
EOF
```

3. Make the script executable:

```
chmod a+x  /updates/discovering-pre/setpw.hook
```

If you are still cannot log in, you very likely hit a bug in the discovery image. Report it at http://bugzilla.suse.com/.

Q: How to provide Kernel Parameters for the SLEShammer Discovery Image?

A: Kernel Parameters for the SLEShammer Discovery Image can be provided via the Provisioner barclamp. The following example shows how to set a `root` password:

1. Open a browser and point it to the Crowbar Web interface available on the Administration Server, for example `http://192.168.124.10/`. Log in as user `crowbar`. The password is `crowbar` by default, if you have not changed it.

2. Open *Barclamps* › *Crowbar* and click *Edit* in the *Provisioner* row.

3. Click *Raw* in the *Attributes* section and add the Kernel parameter(s) to the `"discovery": { "append": "" }` line, for example;

```
"discovery": {
  "append": "DISCOVERY_ROOT_PASSWORD=PASSWORD"
},
```

4. *Apply* the proposal without changing the assignments in the *Deployment* section.

Q: What to do when a deployed node fails to boot using PXE with the following error message:

```
Could not find kernel image:
        ../suse-12.1/install/boot/x86_64/loader/linux
```

?

A: The installation repository on the Administration Server at `/srv/tftpboot/suse-12.1/install` has not been set up correctly to contain the SUSE Linux Enterprise Server 12 SP1 installation media. Review the instructions at *Section 5.1, "Copying the Product Media Repositories"*.

Q: Why does my deployed node hang at `Unpacking initramfs` during boot when using PXE?

A: The node probably does not have enough RAM. You need at least 2 GB RAM.

Q: What to do if a node is reported to be in the state `Problem`? What to do if a node hangs at

```
Executing AutoYast script: /var/adm/autoinstall/init.d/crowbar_join
```

after the installation has been finished?

A: Be patient—the AutoYaST script may take a while to finish. If it really hangs, log in to the node as `root` (see *Q:* for details). Check for error messages at the end of `/var/log/crowbar/crowbar_join/chef.log`. Fix the errors and restart the AutoYaST script by running the following command:

```
rccrowbar_join start
```

If successful, the node will be listed in state `Ready`, when the script has finished.

If that does not help or if the log does not provide useful information, proceed as follows:

1. Log in to the Administration Server and run the following command:

   ```
   crowbar crowbar transition $NODE
   ```

   NODE needs to be replaced by the alias name you have given to the node when having installed it. Note that this name needs to be prefixed with `$`.

2. Log in to the node and run `chef-client`.

3. Check the output of the command for failures and error messages and try to fix the cause of these messages.

4. Reboot the node.

If the node is in a state where login in from the Administration Server is not possible, you need to create a `root` password for it as described in *Direct `root` Login*. Now re-install the node by going to the node on the Crowbar Web interface and clicking *Reinstall.* After having been re-installed, the node will hang again, but now you can log in and check the log files to find the cause.

Q: Where to find more information when applying a barclamp proposal fails?

A: Check the Chef client log files on the Administration Server located at `/var/log/crow-bar/chef-client/d*.log`. Further information is available from the Chef client log files located on the node(s) affected by the proposal (`/var/log/chef/client.log`), and from the log files of the service that failed to be deployed. Additional information may be gained from the Crowbar Web UI log files on the Administration Server. For a list of log file locations refer to *Appendix A, Log Files*.

Q: How to Prevent the Administration Server from Installing the OpenStack Nodes (Disable PXE and DNS Services)?

A: By default, the OpenStack nodes are installed by booting a discovery image from the Administration Server using PXE. They get allocated and then boot via PXE into an automatic installation (see *Section 9.2, "Node Installation"* for details). If you want to install the OpenStack nodes manually or with a custom provisioning tool, you need to disable the PXE boot service and the DNS service on the Administration Server.

As a consequence you also need to provide an external DNS server. Such a server needs to comply with the following requirements:

- It needs to handle all domain to IP requests for SUSE OpenStack Cloud.

- It needs to handle all IP to domain requests for SUSE OpenStack Cloud.

- It needs to forward unknown requests to other DNS servers.

To disable the PXE and DNS services when setting up the Administration Server, proceed as follows:

The following steps need to be performed *before* starting the SUSE OpenStack Cloud Crowbar installation.

1. Create the file /etc/crowbar/dns.json with the following content:

```
{
  "attributes": {
    "dns": {
      "nameservers": [ "DNS_SERVER", "DNS_SERVER2" ],
      "auto_assign_server": false
    }
  }
}
```

Replace *DNS_SERVER* and *DNS_SERVER2* with the IP address(es) of the external DNS server(s). Specifying more than one server is optional.

2. Create the file /etc/crowbar/provisioner.json with the following content:

```
{
  "attributes": {
    "provisioner": {
      "enable_pxe": false
    }
  }
}
```

3. If these files are present when the SUSE OpenStack Cloud Crowbar installation is started, the Administration Server will be set up using external DNS services and no PXE boot server.

In case you already have deployed SUSE OpenStack Cloud, proceed as follows to disable the DNS and PXE services on the Administration Server:

PROCEDURE 12.2: DISABLING PXE/DNS ON AN ADMINISTRATION SERVER RUNNING CROWBAR

1. Open a browser and point it to the Crowbar Web interface available on the Administration Server, for example `http://192.168.124.10/`. Log in as user `crowbar`. The password is `crowbar` by default, if you have not changed it.

2. Open *Barclamps* › *Crowbar* and click *Edit* in the *Provisioner* row.

3. Click *Raw* in the *Attributes* section and change the value for *enable_pxe* to `false`:

```
"enable_pxe": false,
```

4. *Apply* the proposal without changing the assignments in the *Deployment* section.

5. Change to the *DNS* barclamp via *Barclamps* › *Crowbar* and click *Edit* in the *DNS* row.

6. Click *Raw* in the *Attributes* section. Change the value for *auto_assign_server* to `false` and add the address(es) for the external name server(s):

```
"auto_assign_server": false,
"nameservers": [
  "DNS_SERVER",
  "DNS_SERVER2"
],
```

Replace *DNS_SERVER* and *DNS_SERVER2* with the IP address(es) of the external DNS server(s). Specifying more than one server is optional.

7. *Save* your changes, but do not apply them, yet!

8. In the *Deployment* section of the barclamp remove all nodes from the *dns-server* role, but do not change the assignments for the *dns-client* role.

9. *Apply* the barclamp.

10. When the DNS barclamp has been successfully applied, log in to the Administration Server and stop the DNS service:

```
systemctl stop named
```

Now that the PXE and DNS services are disabled you can install SUSE Linux Enterprise Server 12 SP1 on the OpenStack nodes. When a node is ready, add it to the pool of nodes as described in *Section 9.3, "Converting Existing SUSE Linux Enterprise Server 12 SP1 Machines Into SUSE OpenStack Cloud Nodes"*.

Q: I have installed a new hard disk on a node that was already deployed. Why is it ignored by Crowbar?

A: When adding a new hard disk to a node that has already been deployed, it can take up to 15 minutes before the new disk is detected.

Q: How to install additional packages (for example a driver) when nodes are deployed?

A: SUSE OpenStack Cloud offers the possibility to install additional packages that are not part of the default scope of packages installed on the OpenStack nodes. This is for example required if your hardware is only supported by a third party driver. It is also useful if your setup requires to install additional tools that would otherwise need to be installed manually.

Prerequisite for using this feature is that the packages are available in a repository known on the Administration Server. Refer to *Q:* for details, if the packages you want to install are not part of the repositories already configured.

To add packages for installation on node deployment, proceed as follows:

1. Open a browser and point it to the Crowbar Web interface on the Administration Server, for example `http://192.168.124.10/`. Log in as user `crowbar`. The password is `crowbar` by default, if you have not changed it during the installation.

2. Go to *Barclamps* › *Crowbar* and click the *Edit* button for *Provisioner*.

3. Next click *Raw* in the *Attributes* page to open an editable view of the provisioner configuration.

4. Add the following JSON code *before* the last closing curly bracket (replace the *PACK-AGE* placeholders with real package names):

```
        "packages": {
    "suse-12.1": ["PACKAGE_1", "PACKAGE_2"],
  }
```

Note that these packages will get installed on all OpenStack nodes. If the change to the Provisioner barclamp is made after nodes have already been deployed, the packages will be installed on the affected nodes with the next run of Chef or **crowbar-register**. Package names will be validated against the package naming guidelines to prevent script-injection.

12.1.3 Miscellaneous

Q: How to change the nova default configuration?

A: To change the nova default configuration, the respective Chef cookbook file needs to be adjusted. This files is stored on the Administration Server at /opt/dell/chef/cookbooks/nova/templates/default/nova.conf.erb. To activate changes to these files, the following command needs to be executed:

```
barclamp_install.rb --rpm /opt/dell/barclamps/openstack/
```

12.2 Support

Before contacting support to help you with a problem on SUSE OpenStack Cloud, it is strongly recommended that you gather as much information about your system and the problem as possible. For this purpose, SUSE OpenStack Cloud ships with a tool called **supportconfig**. It gathers system information such as the current kernel version being used, the hardware, RPM database, partitions, and other items. **supportconfig** also collects the most important log files, making it easier for the supporters to identify and solve your problem.

It is recommended to always run **supportconfig** on the Administration Server and on the Control Node(s). If a Compute Node or a Storage Node is part of the problem, run **supportconfig** on the affected node as well. For details on how to run **supportconfig**, see http://www.suse.com/documentation/sles-12/book_sle_admin/data/cha_adm_support.html.

12.2.1 Applying PTFs (Program Temporary Fixes) Provided by the SUSE L3 Support

Under certain circumstances, the SUSE support may provide temporary fixes, the so-called PTFs, to customers with an L3 support contract. These PTFs are provided as RPM packages. To make them available on all nodes in SUSE OpenStack Cloud, proceed as follows.

1. Download the packages from the location provided by the SUSE L3 Support to a temporary location on the Administration Server.

2. Move the packages from the temporary download location to the following directories on the Administration Server:

   "noarch" packages (`*.noarch.rpm`):

   ```
   /srv/tftpboot/suse-12.1/x86_64/repos/PTF/rpm/noarch/
   /srv/tftpboot/suse-12.1/s390x/repos/PTF/rpm/noarch/
   ```

   "x86_64" packages (`*.x86_64.rpm`)

   ```
   /srv/tftpboot/suse-12.1/x86_64/repos/PTF/rpm/x86_64/
   ```

   "s390x" packages (`*.s390x.rpm`)

   ```
   /srv/tftpboot/suse-12.1/s390x/repos/PTF/rpm/s390x/
   ```

3. Create or update the repository metadata:

   ```
   createrepo-cloud-ptf
   ```

4. The repositories are now set up and are available for all nodes in SUSE OpenStack Cloud except for the Administration Server. In case the PTF also contains packages to be installed on the Administration Server, make the repository available on the Administration Server as well:

```
zypper ar -f /srv/tftpboot/suse-12.1/x86_64/repos/PTF PTF
```

5. To deploy the updates, proceed as described in *Section 9.4.1, "Deploying Node Updates with the Updater Barclamp"*. Alternatively, run **zypper up** manually on each node.

A Log Files

Find a list of log files below, sorted according to the nodes where they can be found.

A.1 On the Administration Server

- Crowbar Web Interface: `/var/log/crowbar/production.log`

- Chef server: `/var/log/chef/server.log`

- Chef expander: `/var/log/chef/expander.log`

- Chef client (for the Administration Server only): `/var/log/chef/client.log`

- Upgrade log files (only available if the Administration Server has been upgraded from a previous version using **suse-cloud-upgrade**): `/var/log/crowbar/upgrade/*`

- Apache SOLR (Chef's search server): `/var/log/chef/solr.log`

- HTTP (AutoYaST) installation server for provisioner barclamp: `/var/log/apache2/provisioner-{access,error}_log`

- Log file from mirroring SMT repositories (optional): `/var/log/smt/smt-mirror.log`

- Default SUSE log files: `/var/log/messages`, `/var/log/zypper.log` etc.

- Syslogs for all nodes: `/var/log/nodes/*.log` (these are collected via remote syslogging)

- Other client node log files saved on the Administration Server:

  - `/var/log/crowbar/sledgehammer/d*.log`: Initial Chef client run on nodes booted using PXE prior to discovery by Crowbar.

  - `/var/log/crowbar/chef-client/d*.log`: Output from Chef client when proposals are applied to nodes. This is the first place to look if a barclamp proposal fails to apply.

A.2 On All Other Crowbar Nodes

Logs for when the node registers with the Administration Server:

- `/var/log/crowbar/crowbar_join/errlog`

- `/var/log/crowbar/crowbar_join/$TOPIC.{log,err}`: STDOUT/STDERR from running commands associated with $TOPIC when the node joins the Crowbar cluster. $TOPIC can be:

  - `zypper`: package management activity

  - `ifup`: network configuration activity

  - `Chef`: Chef client activity

  - `time`: starting of ntp client

- Chef client log: `/var/log/chef/client.log`

- Default SUSE log files: `/var/log/messages`, `/var/log/zypper.log` etc.

A.3 On the Control Node(s)

On setups with multiple Control Nodes log files for certain services (such as `keystone.log`) are only available on the node where the respective service is deployed.

- `/var/log/apache2/openstack-dashboard-*`: Logs for the OpenStack Dashboard

- `/var/log/ceilometer/*`: Ceilometer log files.

- `/var/log/cinder/*`: Cinder log files.

- `/var/log/glance/*`: Glance; log files.

- `/var/log/heat/*`: Heat log files.

- `/var/log/keystone/*`: Keystone log files.

- `/var/log/neutron/*`: Neutron log files.

- `/var/log/nova/*`: various log files relating to Nova services.

- `/var/log/rabbitmq/*`: RabbitMQ log files.

- `/var/log/swift/*`: Swift log files.

A.4 On Compute Nodes

`/var/log/nova/nova-compute.log`

A.5 On Nodes with Ceph Barclamp

`/var/log/ceph/*.log`

B Repository Locations

The following tables show the locations of all repositories that can be used for SUSE OpenStack Cloud.

TABLE B.1: SMT REPOSITORIES HOSTED ON THE ADMINISTRATION SERVER

Repository	Directory
Mandatory Repositories	
SLES12-SP1-Pool	`/srv/www/htdocs/repo/SUSE/Products/SLE-SERVER/12-SP1/x86_64/product/`
SLES12-SP1-Updates	`/srv/www/htdocs/repo/SUSE/Updates/SLE-SERVER/12-SP1/x86_64/update/`
SUSE-OpenStack-Cloud-6-Pool	`/srv/www/htdocs/repo/SUSE/Products/OpenStack-Cloud/6/x86_64/product/`
SUSE-OpenStack-Cloud-6-Updates	`/srv/www/htdocs/repo/SUSE/Updates/OpenStack-Cloud/6/x86_64/update/`
Optional Repositories	
SLE-HA12-SP1-Pool	`/srv/www/htdocs/repo/SUSE/Products/SLE-HA/12-SP1/x86_64/product/`
SLE-HA12-SP1-Updates	`/srv/www/htdocs/repo/SUSE/Updates/SLE-HA/12-SP1/x86_64/update/`
SUSE-Enterprise-Storage-2.1-Pool	`/srv/www/htdocs/repo/SUSE/Products/Storage/2.1/x86_64/product/`
SUSE-Enterprise-Storage-2.1-Updates	`/srv/www/htdocs/repo/SUSE/Updates/Storage/2.1/x86_64/update/`

TABLE B.2: SMT REPOSITORIES HOSTED ON A REMOTE SERVER

Repository	URl
Mandatory Repositories	
SLES12-SP1-Pool	http://*smt.example.com*/repo/SUSE/Products/SLE-SERVER/12-SP1/x86_64/product/
SLES12-SP1-Updates	http://*smt.example.com*/repo/SUSE/Updates/SLE-SERVER/12-SP1/x86_64/update/
SUSE-OpenStack-Cloud-6-Pool	http://*smt.example.com*/repo/SUSE/Products/OpenStack-Cloud/6/x86_64/product/
SUSE-OpenStack-Cloud-6-Updates	http://*smt.example.com*/repo/SUSE/Updates/OpenStack-Cloud/6/x86_64/update/
Optional Repositories	
SLE-HA12-SP1-Pool	http://*smt.example.com*/repo/SUSE/Products/SLE-HA/12-SP1/x86_64/product/
SLE-HA12-SP1-Updates	http://*smt.example.com*/repo/SUSE/Updates/SLE-HA/12-SP1/x86_64/update/
SUSE-Enterprise-Storage-2.1-Pool	http://*smt.example.com*/repo/SUSE/Products/Storage/2.1/x86_64/product/
SUSE-Enterprise-Storage-2.1-Updates	http://*smt.example.com*/repo/SUSE/Updates/Storage/2.1/x86_64/update/

TABLE B.3: SUSE MANAGER REPOSITORIES (CHANNELS)

Repository	URL
Mandatory Repositories	
SLES12-SP1-Updates	http://manager.example.com/ks/dist/child/sles12-sp1-updates-x86_64/sles12-sp1-x86_64/

Repository	URL
SUSE-OpenStack-Cloud-6-Pool	http://manager.example.com/ks/dist/child/suse-openstack-cloud-6-pool-x86_64/sles12-sp1-x86_64/
SUSE-OpenStack-Cloud-6--Updates	http://manager.example.com/ks/dist/child/suse-openstack-cloud-6-updates-x86_64/sles12-sp1-x86_64/
Optional Repositories	
SLE-HA12-SP1-Pool	http://manager.example.com/ks/dist/child/sle-ha12-sp1-pool-x86_64/sles12-sp1-x86_64/
SLE-HA12-SP1-Updates	http://manager.example.com/ks/dist/child/sle-ha12-sp1-updates-x86_64/sles12-sp1-x86_64/
SUSE-Enterprise-Storage-2.1-Pool	http://manager.example.com/ks/dist/child/suse-enterprise-storage-2.1-pool-x86_64/sles12-sp1-x86_64/
SUSE-Enterprise-Storage-2.1-Updates	http://manager.example.com/ks/dist/child/suse-enterprise-storage-2.1-updates-x86_64/sles12-sp1-x86_64/

The following table shows the default repository locations that are recommended to use when manually copying, synchronizing our mounting the repositories. When choosing these locations, it is sufficient to set the repository location in YaST Crowbar to *Custom*. You do not need to specify a detailed location for each repository. Refer to *Section 5.2.4, "Alternative Ways to Make the Repositories Available"* and *Section 7.4, "Repositories"* for details.

TABLE B.4: DEFAULT REPOSITORY LOCATIONS ON THE ADMINISTRATION SERVER

Channel	Directory on the Administration Server
Mandatory Repositories	
SLES12-SP1-Pool	`/srv/tftpboot/suse-12.1/x86_64/repos/SLES12-SP1-Pool/`
SLES12-SP1-Updates	`/srv/tftpboot/suse-12.1/x86_64/repos/SLES12-SP1-Updates/`
SUSE-OpenStack-Cloud-6-Pool	`/srv/tftpboot/suse-12.1/x86_64/repos/SUSE-OpenStack-Cloud-6-Pool/`

Channel	Directory on the Administration Server
SUSE-OpenS-tack-Cloud-6-Updates	`/srv/tftpboot/suse-12.1/x86_64/repos/SUSE-OpenS-tack-Cloud-6-Updates`
Optional Repositories	
SLE-HA12-SP1-Pool	`/srv/tftpboot/suse-12.1/x86_64/repos/SLE-HA12-SP1`
SLE-HA12-SP1-Up-dates	`/srv/tftpboot/suse-12.1/x86_64/repos/SLE-HA12-SP1-Up-dates`
SUSE-Enterprise-Stor-age-2.1-Pool	`/srv/tftpboot/suse-12.1/x86_64/repos/SUSE-Enter-prise-Storage-2.1-Pool`
SUSE-Enterprise-Stor-age-2.1-Updates	`/srv/tftpboot/suse-12.1/x86_64/repos/SUSE-Enter-prise-Storage-2.1-Updates`

C Roles and Services in SUSE OpenStack Cloud

The following table lists all roles (as defined in the barclamps), and their associated services. As of SUSE OpenStack Cloud 6 this list is work in progress. Services can be manually started and stopped with the commands **systemctl start** *SERVICE* and **systemctl stop** *SERVICE*.

Role	Service
calamari	`cthulhu`
ceilometer-agent	`openstack-ceilometer-agent-compute`
ceilometer-polling ceilometer-server ceilometer-swift-proxy-middle-ware	`openstack-ceilometer-agent-notification`
	`openstack-ceilometer-alarm-evaluator`
	`openstack-ceilometer-alarm-notifier`
	`openstack-ceilometer-api`
	`openstack-ceilometer-collector`
	`openstack-ceilometer-polling`
ceph-mon	`ceph-mon@*`
ceph-osd	`ceph-osd@*`
ceph-radosgw	`ceph-radosgw@*`
cinder-controller	`openstack-cinder-api`
	`openstack-cinder-scheduler`
cinder-volume	`openstack-cinder-volume`
database-server	`postgresql`
glance-server	`openstack-glance-api`
	`openstack-glance-registry`

Role	Service
heat-server	`openstack-heat-api-cfn`
	`openstack-heat-api-cloudwatch`
	`openstack-heat-api`
	`openstack-heat-engine`
horizon	`apache2`
keystone-server	`openstack-keystone`
manila-server	`openstack-manila-api`
	`openstack-manila-scheduler`
manila-share	`openstack-manila-share`
neutron-server	`openstack-neutron`
nova-compute-*	`openstack-nova-compute`
	`openstack-neutron-openvswitch-agent` (when neutron is deployed with openvswitch)
nova-controller	`openstack-nova-api`
	`openstack-nova-cert`
	`openstack-nova-conductor`
	`openstack-nova-consoleauth`
	`openstack-nova-novncproxy`
	`openstack-nova-objectstore`
	`openstack-nova-scheduler`
rabbitmq-server	`rabbitmq-server`

Role	Service
swift-dispersion	none
swift-proxy	`openstack-swift-proxy`
swift-ring-compute	none
swift-storage	`openstack-swift-account-auditor`
	`openstack-swift-account-reaper`
	`openstack-swift-account-replicator`
	`openstack-swift-account`
	`openstack-swift-container-auditor`
	`openstack-swift-container-replicator`
	`openstack-swift-container-sync`
	`openstack-swift-container-updater`
	`openstack-swift-container`
	`openstack-swift-object-auditor`
	`openstack-swift-object-expirer`
	`openstack-swift-object-replicator`
	`openstack-swift-object-updater`
	`openstack-swift-object`
trove-server	`openstack-trove-api`
	`openstack-trove-conductor`
	`openstack-trove-taskmanager`

D The Network Barclamp Template File

The Crowbar network barclamp provides two functions for the system. The first is a common role to instantiate network interfaces on the Crowbar managed systems. The other function is address pool management. While the addresses can be managed with the YaST Crowbar module, complex network setups require to manually edit the network barclamp template file `/etc/crowbar/network.json`. This section explains the file in detail. Settings in this file are applied to all nodes in SUSE OpenStack Cloud.

 Warning: No Network Changes After Completed the SUSE OpenStack Cloud Crowbar installation

After you have completed the SUSE OpenStack Cloud Crowbar installation, you cannot change the network setup anymore. If doing so, you would need to completely set up the Administration Server again.

The only exception from this rule is the interface map. This section can be changed at a later stage as well. See *Section D.3, "Interface Map"* for details.

D.1 Editing `network.json`

The `network.json` is located in `/etc/crowbar/`. To edit it, open it in an editor of your choice. The template has the following general structure:

```
{
    "attributes" : {
        "mode" : "value",
        "start_up_delay" : value,
        "teaming" : { "mode": value }, ❶
        "network" : {
            "interface_map" ❷ : [
                ...
            ],
            "conduit_map" ❸ : [
                ...
            ],
```

```
        "networks"❹ : {
            ...
        },
    }
  }
}
```

① General attributes. Refer to *Section D.2, "Global Attributes"* for details.

② Interface map section. Defines the order in which the physical network interfaces are to be used. Refer to *Section D.3, "Interface Map"* for details.

③ Network conduit section defining the network modes and the network interface usage. Refer to *Section D.4, "Network Conduits"* for details.

④ Network definition section. Refer to *Section D.5, "Network Definitions"* for details.

 Note: Order of Elements

The order in which the entries in the `network.json` file appear may differ from the one listed above. Use your editor's search function to find certain entries.

D.2 Global Attributes

The most important options to define in the global attributes section are the default values for the network and bonding modes. The following global attributes exist:

```
{
  "attributes" : {
    "mode" : "single",①
    "start_up_delay" : 30,②
    "teaming" : { "mode": 5 },③
    "network" : {
      "interface_map" : [
        ...
      ],
      "conduit_map" : [
        ...
```

```
        ],
        "networks" : {
            ...
        },
    }
  }
}
```

❶ Network mode. Defines the configuration name (or name space) to be used from the conduit_map (see *Section D.4, "Network Conduits"*). This allows to define multiple configurations (single, dual, and team are preconfigured) and switch them by changing this parameter.

❷ Time (in seconds) the Chef-client waits for the network interfaces to become online before running into a time-out.

❸ Default bonding mode. See https://www.kernel.org/doc/Documentation/networking/bonding.txt for a list of available modes.

D.3 Interface Map

By default physical network interfaces are used in the order they appear under `/sys/class/net/`. In case you want to apply a different order, you need to create an interface map where you can specify a custom order of the bus IDs. Interface maps are created for specific hardware configurations and are applied to all machines matching this configuration.

```
{
  "attributes" : {
    "mode" : "single",
    "start_up_delay" : 30,
    "teaming" : { "mode": 5 },
    "network" : {
      "interface_map" : [
        {
          "pattern" : "PowerEdge R610"❶ ,
          "serial_number" : "0x02159F8E"❷ ,
          "bus_order" : [❸
```

```
            "0000:00/0000:00:01",
            "0000:00/0000:00:03"
        ]
    }
    ...
],
"conduit_map" : [
    ...
],
"networks" : {
    ...
},
```

1 Hardware specific identifier. This identifier can be obtained by running the command **dmidecode** -s system-product-name on the machine you want to identify. You can log in to a node during the hardware discovery phase (when booting the SLEShammer image) via the Administration Server.

2 Additional hardware specific identifier. This identifier can be used in case two machines have the same value for *pattern*, but different interface maps are needed. Specifying this parameter is optional (it is not included in the default network.json file). The serial number of a machine can be obtained by running the command **dmidecode** -s system-serial-number on the machine you want to identify.

3 Bus IDs of the interfaces. The order in which they are listed here defines the order in which Chef addresses the interfaces. The IDs can be obtained by listing the contents of /sys/class/net/.

> **❗ Important: PXE Boot Interface Must be Listed First**
>
> The physical interface used to boot the node via PXE must always be listed first.

Note: Interface Map Changes Allowed After Having Completed the "SUSE OpenStack Cloud Crowbar Installation

Contrary to all other sections in `network.json`, you can change interface maps after having completed the SUSE OpenStack Cloud Crowbar installation. However, nodes that are already deployed and affected by these changes need to be deployed again. Therefore it is not recommended to make changes to the interface map that affect active nodes.

If you change the interface mappings after having completed the SUSE OpenStack Cloud Crowbar installation you *must not* make your changes by editing `network.json`. You must rather use the Crowbar Web interface and open *Barclamps › Crowbar › Network › Edit*. Activate your changes by clicking *Apply*.

D.3.1   Interface Map Example

EXAMPLE D.1: CHANGING THE NETWORK INTERFACE ORDER ON A MACHINE WITH FOUR NICS

1. Get the machine identifier by running the following command on the machine to which the map should be applied:

```
~ # dmidecode -s system-product-name
AS 2003R
```

The resulting string needs to be entered on the *pattern* line of the map. It is interpreted as a Ruby regular expression (see http://www.ruby-doc.org/core-2.0/Regexp.html for a reference). Unless the pattern starts with `^` and ends with `$` a substring match is performed against the name return from the above commands.

2. List the interface devices in `/sys/class/net` to get the current order and the bus ID of each interface:

```
~ # ls -lgG /sys/class/net/ | grep eth

lrwxrwxrwx 1 0 Jun 19 08:43 eth0 -> ../../devices/pci0000:00/0000:00:1c.0/0000:09:00.0/net/eth0

lrwxrwxrwx 1 0 Jun 19 08:43 eth1 -> ../../devices/pci0000:00/0000:00:1c.0/0000:09:00.1/net/eth1

lrwxrwxrwx 1 0 Jun 19 08:43 eth2 -> ../../devices/pci0000:00/0000:00:1c.0/0000:09:00.2/net/eth2

lrwxrwxrwx 1 0 Jun 19 08:43 eth3 -> ../../devices/pci0000:00/0000:00:1c.0/0000:09:00.3/net/eth3
```

The bus ID is included in the path of the link target—it is the following string: `../../`
`devices/pciBUS ID/net/eth0`

3. Create an interface map with the bus ID listed in the order the interfaces should be
   used. Keep in mind that the interface from which the node is booted using PXE must
   be listed first. In the following example the default interface order has been changed
   to `eth0`, `eth2`, `eth1` and `eth3`.

```
{
    "attributes" : {
        "mode" : "single",
        "start_up_delay" : 30,
        "teaming" : { "mode": 5 },
        "network" : {
            "interface_map" : [
                {
                    "pattern" : "AS 2003R",
                    "bus_order" : [
                        "0000:00/0000:00:1c.0/0000:09:00.0",
                        "0000:00/0000:00:1c.0/0000:09:00.2",
                        "0000:00/0000:00:1c.0/0000:09:00.1",
                        "0000:00/0000:00:1c.0/0000:09:00.3"
                    ]
                }
                ...
            ],
            "conduit_map" : [
                ...
            ],
            "networks" : {
                ...
            },
        }
    }
}
```

D.4 Network Conduits

Network conduits define mappings for logical interfaces—one or more physical interfaces bonded together. Each conduit can be identified by a unique name, the *pattern*. This pattern is also called "Network Mode" in this document.

Several network modes are already pre-defined. The most important ones are:

single: Only use the first interface for all networks. VLANs will be added on top of this single interface.

dual: Use the first interface as the admin interface and the second one for all other networks. VLANs will be added on top of the second interface.

team: Bond first two interfaces. VLANs will be added on top of the bond.

See *Section 2.1.2, "Network Modes"* for detailed descriptions. Apart from these modes a fallback mode `".*/.*/.*"` is also pre-defined—it is applied in case no other mode matches the one specified in the global attributes section. These modes can be adjusted according to your needs. It is also possible to define a custom mode.

The mode name that is specified with `mode` in the global attributes section is deployed on all nodes in SUSE OpenStack Cloud. It is not possible to use a different mode for a certain node. However, you can define "sub" modes with the same name that only match machines with a certain number of physical network interfaces or machines with certain roles (all Compute Nodes for example).

```
{
    "attributes" : {
        "mode" : "single",
        "start_up_delay" : 30,
        "teaming" : { "mode": 5 },
        "network" : {
            "interface_map" : [
                ...
            ],
            "conduit_map" : [
                {
                    "pattern" : "team/.*/.*"❶,
                    "conduit_list" : {
                        "intf2"❷ : {
```

```
            "if_list" : ["1g1","1g2"] ❸ ,
            "team_mode" : 5 ❹
          },
          "intf1" : {
            "if_list" : ["1g1","1g2"],
            "team_mode" : 5
          },
          "intf0" : {
            "if_list" : ["1g1","1g2"],
            "team_mode" : 5
          }
        }
      },
      ...
    ],
    "networks" : {
      ...
    },
  }
}
```

❶ This line contains the pattern definition for a mode. The value for pattern must have the following form:

```
mode_name/number_of_nics/node_role
```

It is interpreted as a Ruby regular expression (see http://www.ruby-doc.org/core-2.0/Regexp.html for a reference).

mode_name
Name of the network mode. This string is used to reference the mode from the general attributes section.

number_of_nics

> Normally it is not possible to apply different network modes to different roles—you can only specify one mode in the global attributes section. However, it does not make sense to apply a network mode that bonds three interfaces on a machine with only two physical network interfaces. This option enables you to create modes for nodes with a given number of interfaces.

node_role

> This part of the pattern lets you create matches for a certain node role. This enables you to create network modes for certain roles, for example the Compute Nodes (role: *nova-compute*) or the Swift nodes (role: *swift-storage*). See *Example D.3, "Network Modes for Certain Roles"* for the full list of roles.

2 The logical network interface definition. Each conduit list must contain at least one such definition. This line defines the name of the logical interface. This identifier must be unique and will also be referenced in the network definition section. It is recommended to stick with the pre-defined naming scheme with `intf0` for "Interface 0", `intf1` for "Interface 1", etc. If you change the name (not recommended), you also need to change all references in the network definition section.

3 This line maps one or more *physical* interfaces to the logical interface. Each entry represents a physical interface. If more than one entry exists, the interfaces are bonded—either with the mode defined in the *team_mode* attribute of this conduit section or, if that is not present, by the globally defined *teaming* attribute.

The physical interfaces definition needs to fit the following pattern:

```
[Quantifier][Speed][Interface Number]
```

Valid examples are `+1g2`, `10g1` or `?1g2`.

Quantifier

> Specifying the quantifier is optional. The following values may be entered:

> `+` : at least the speed specified afterwards (specified value or higher)
> `-` : at most the speed specified afterwards (specified value or lower)
> `?` : any speed (speed specified afterwards is ignored)
> If no quantifier is specified, the exact speed specified is used.

Speed

Specifying the interface speed is mandatory (even if using the `?` quantifier). The following values may be entered:

`10m`: 10 Mbit

`100m`: 100 Mbit

`1g`: 1 Gbit

`10g`: 10 Gbit

Order

Position in the interface order. Specifying this value is mandatory. The interface order is defined by the order in which the interfaces appear in `/sys/class/net` (default) or, if existing, by an interface map. The order is also linked to the speed in this context, so `1g1` means "The first 1Gbit interface", `+1g1` means "The first 1Gbit or 10Gbit interface". `?1g1` would match the very first interface, regardless of its speed.

 Note: Ordering Numbers

Ordering numbers start with `1` rather than with `0`.

④ The bonding mode to be used for this logical interface. Overwrites the default set in the global attributes section *for this interface*. See https://www.kernel.org/doc/Documentation/networking/bonding.txt for a list of available modes. Specifying this option is optional—if not specified here, the global setting applies.

D.4.1 Network Conduit Examples

EXAMPLE D.2: NETWORK MODES FOR DIFFERENT NIC NUMBERS

The following example defines a network mode named `my_mode` for nodes with 6, 3 and an arbitrary number of network interfaces. Since the first mode that matches is applied, it is important that the specific modes (for 6 and 3 NICs) are listed before the general one:

```
{
    "attributes" : {
        "mode" : "single",
        "start_up_delay" : 30,
        "teaming" : { "mode": 5 },
```

```
        "network" : {
          "interface_map" : [
            ...
          ],
          "conduit_map" : [
            {
              "pattern" : "my_mode/6/.*",
              "conduit_list" : {
                ...
              }
            },
            {
              "pattern" : "my_mode/3/.*",
              "conduit_list" : {
                ...
              }
            },
            {
              "pattern" : "my_mode/.*/.*",
              "conduit_list" : {
                ...
              }
            },
            ...
          ],
          "networks" : {
            ...
          },
        }
      }
}
```

EXAMPLE D.3: NETWORK MODES FOR CERTAIN ROLES

The following example defines network modes for Compute Nodes with four physical interfaces, the Administration Server (role `crowbar`), the Control Node, and a general mode applying to all other nodes.

```
{
    "attributes" : {
        "mode" : "single",
        "start_up_delay" : 30,
        "teaming" : { "mode": 5 },
        "network" : {
            "interface_map" : [
                ...
            ],
            "conduit_map" : [
             {
                "pattern" : "my_mode/4/nova-compute",
                "conduit_list" : {
                  ...
                }
             },
             {
                "pattern" : "my_mode/.*/crowbar",
                "conduit_list" : {
                   ...
                }
             },
             {
                "pattern" : "my_mode/.*/nova-controller",
                "conduit_list" : {
                   ...
                }
             },
             {
                "pattern" : "my_mode/.*/.*",
                "conduit_list" : {
                   ...
                 }
             },
             ...
```

```
            ],
            "networks" : {
                ...
            },
        }
    }
}
```

The following values for `node_role` can be used:

`ceilometer-polling`

`ceilometer-server`

`ceph-calamari`

`ceph-mon`

`ceph-osd`

`ceph-radosgw`

`cinder-controller`

`cinder-volume`

`crowbar`

`database-server`

`glance-server`

`heat-server`

`horizon-server`

`keystone-server`

`manila-server`

`manila-share`

`neutron-network`

`neutron-server`

`nova-controller`

`nova-compute-*`

`rabbitmq-server`

`trove-server`

`swift-dispersion`

`swift-proxy`

`swift-ring-compute`

`swift-storage`

The role `crowbar` refers to the Administration Server.

Apart from the roles listed under *Example D.3, "Network Modes for Certain Roles"* each node in SUSE OpenStack Cloud has a unique role, which lets you create modes matching exactly one node. The role is named after the scheme `crowbar-d` *FULLY QUALIFIED HOSTNAME*. The *FULLY QUALIFIED HOSTNAME* in turn is composed of the MAC address of the network interface used to boot the node via PXE and the domain name configured on the Administration Server. Colons and periods are replaced with underscores. An example role name would be: `crowbar-d1a-12-05-1e-35-49_my_cloud`.

Network mode definitions for certain machines must be listed first in the conduit map. This prevents other, general rules which would also map from being applied.

```
{
    "attributes" : {
        "mode" : "single",
        "start_up_delay" : 30,
        "teaming" : { "mode": 5 },
        "network" : {
            "interface_map" : [
                ...
            ],
            "conduit_map" : [
              {
                "pattern" : "my_mode/.*/crowbar-d1a-12-05-1e-35-49_my_cloud",
                "conduit_list" : {
                    ...
                }
              },
                ...
            ],
            "networks" : {
                ...
            },
        }
    }
}
```

```
        }
```

D.5 Network Definitions

The network definitions contain IP address assignments, the bridge and VLAN setup and settings for the router preference. Each network is also assigned to a logical interface defined in the network conduit section. In the following the network definition is explained using the example of the admin network definition:

```
{
    "attributes" : {
        "mode" : "single",
        "start_up_delay" : 30,
        "teaming" : { "mode": 5 },
        "network" : {
            "interface_map" : [
                ...
            ],
            "conduit_map" : [
                ...
            ],
            "networks" : {
                "admin" : {
                    "conduit" : "intf0"❶,
                    "add_bridge" : false❷,
                    "use_vlan" : false❸,
                    "vlan" : 100❹,
                    "router_pref" : 10❺,
                    "subnet" : "192.168.124.0"❻,
                    "netmask" : "255.255.255.0",
                    "router" : "192.168.124.1",
                    "broadcast" : "192.168.124.255",
                    "ranges" : {
                        "admin" : {
                            "start" : "192.168.124.10",
```

```
        "end" : "192.168.124.11"
      },
      "switch" : {
        "start" : "192.168.124.241",
        "end" : "192.168.124.250"
      },
      "dhcp" : {
        "start" : "192.168.124.21",
        "end" : "192.168.124.80"
      },
      "host" : {
        "start" : "192.168.124.81",
        "end" : "192.168.124.160"
      }
    }
  },
  "nova_floating": {
    "add_ovs_bridge": false❼,
    "bridge_name": "br-public"❽,
    ....
  }
  ...
  },
}
}
```

❶ Logical interface assignment. The interface must be defined in the network conduit section and must be part of the active network mode.

❷ Bridge setup. Do not touch. Should be `false` for all networks.

❸ Create a VLAN for this network. Changing this setting is not recommended.

❹ ID of the VLAN. Change this to the VLAN ID you intend to use for the specific network if required. This setting can also be changed using the YaST Crowbar interface. The VLAN ID for the `nova-floating` network must always match the one for the `public network`.

⑤ Router preference, used to set the default route. On nodes hosting multiple networks the router with the lowest `router_pref` becomes the default gateway. Changing this setting is not recommended.

⑥ Network address assignments. These values can also be changed by using the YaST Crowbar interface.

⑦ Openvswitch virtual switch setup. This attribute is maintained by Crowbar on a per-node level and should not be changed manually.

⑧ Name of the openvswitch virtual switch. This attribute is maintained by Crowbar on a per-node level and should not be changed manually.

ⓘ Important: VLAN Settings

As of SUSE OpenStack Cloud 6, using a VLAN for the admin network is only supported on a native/untagged VLAN. If you need VLAN support for the admin network, it must be handled at switch level.

When deploying Compute Nodes with Microsoft Hyper-V or Windows Server, you must *not* use openvswitch with gre. Instead, use openvswitch with VLAN (recommended) or linuxbridge as a plugin for Neutron.

When changing the network configuration with YaST or by editing `/etc/crowbar/network.json` you can define VLAN settings for each network. For the networks `nova-fixed` and `nova-floating`, however, special rules apply:

nova-fixed: The *USE VLAN* setting will be ignored. However, VLANs will automatically be used if deploying Neutron with VLAN support (using the plugins linuxbridge, openvswitch plus VLAN or cisco plus VLAN). In this case, you need to specify a correct *VLAN ID* for this network.

nova-floating: When using a VLAN for `nova-floating` (which is the default), the *USE VLAN* and *VLAN ID* settings for *nova-floating* and *public* need to be the same. When not using a VLAN for `nova-floating`, it needs to use a different physical network interface than the `nova_fixed` network.

E Configuring Role Based Access Control (RBAC)

To limit users' access rights (or to define more fine-grained access rights), you can use Role Based Access Control (RBAC, only available with Keystone v3). In the example below, we will create a new role (`ProjectAdmin`) that allows users with this role to add and remove other users to the `Member` role on the same project.

To create a new role that can be assigned to a user-project pair, the following basic steps are needed:

1. Create a custom `policy.json` file for the Keystone service. On the node where the `keystone-server` role is deployed, copy the file to `/etc/keystone/CUSTOM_policy.json`. For details, see *Section E.1, "Editing `policy.json`"*.

2. Create a custom `keystone_policy.json` file for the Horizon service. On the node where the `nova_dashboard-server` role is deployed, copy the custom `keystone_policy.json` file to `/srv/www/openstack-dashboard/openstack_dashboard/conf/` (default directory for policy files in Horizon). For details, see *Section E.2, "Editing `keystone_policy.json`"*.

3. Make the Keystone service aware of the `CUSTOM_policy.json` file by editing and reapplying the *Keystone* barclamp. For details, see *Section E.3, "Adjusting the Keystone Barclamp Proposal"*.

4. Make the Horizon service aware of the `keystone_policy.json` file by editing and reapplying the *Horizon* barclamp. For details, see *Section E.4, "Adjusting the Horizon Barclamp Proposal"*.

E.1 Editing `policy.json`

The `policy.json` file is located in `/etc/keystone/` on the node where the `keystone-server` role is deployed.

1. Copy `/etc/keystone/policy.json` and save it under a different name, for example `CUSTOM_policy.json`.

Important: Use Different File Name

If you use the same name as the original file, your custom file will be overwritten by the next package update.

2. To edit the file, open it in an editor of your choice.

3. To add the new role, enter the following two lines at the beginning of the file:

```
{
  "subadmin": "role:ProjectAdmin",
  "projectadmin": "rule:subadmin and project_id:%(target.project.id)s",
  [...]
```

4. Adjust the other rules in the file accordingly:

```
  "identity:get_domain": "rule:admin_required or rule:subadmin",
  [...]
  "identity:get_project": "rule:admin_required or rule:projectadmin",
  [...]
  "identity:list_user_projects": "rule:admin_or_owner or rule:projectadmin",
  [...]
  "identity:update_project": "rule:admin_required or rule:projectadmin",
  [...]
  "identity:get_user": "rule:admin_required or rule:projectadmin",
  "identity:list_users": "rule:admin_required or rule:subadmin",
  [...]
  "identity:list_groups": "rule:admin_required or rule:subadmin",
  [...]
  "identity:list_roles": "rule:admin_required or rule:subadmin",
  [...]
  "identity:list_grants": "rule:admin_required or (rule:subadmin and
project_id:%(target.project.id)s)",
  "identity:create_grant": "rule:admin_required or (rule:subadmin and
project_id:%(target.project.id)s and 'Member':%(target.role.name)s)",
  "identity:revoke_grant": "rule:admin_required or (rule:subadmin and
project_id:%(target.project.id)s and 'Member':%(target.role.name)s)",
```

```
[...]
    "identity:list_role_assignments": "rule:admin_required or rule:subadmin",
```

5. Save the changes and copy the file to /etc/keystone/*CUSTOM*_policy.json on the node where the `keystone-server` role is deployed (usually a Control Node or a cluster if you use a High Availability setup).

E.2 Editing `keystone_policy.json`

By default, the `keystone_policy.json` file is located in /srv/www/openstack-dashboard/openstack_dashboard/conf/ on the node where the `nova_dashboard-server` role is deployed. It is similar (but not identical) to `policy.json` and defines which actions the user with a certain role is allowed to execute in Horizon. If the user is not allowed to execute a certain action, the OpenStack Dashboard will show an error message.

1. Copy /srv/www/openstack-dashboard/openstack_dashboard/conf/ `keystone_policy.json` and save it under a different name, for example *CUSTOM*_keystone_policy.json.

   ❗ Important: Use Different File Name

   If you use the same name as the original file, your custom file will be overwritten by the next package update.

2. To edit the file, open it in an editor of your choice.

3. To add the new role, enter the following two lines at the beginning of the file:

```
{
  "subadmin": "role:ProjectAdmin",
  "projectadmin": "rule:subadmin and project_id:%(target.project.id)s",
  [...]
```

4. Adjust the other rules in the file accordingly:

```
  "identity:get_project": "rule:admin_required or rule:projectadmin",
  [...]
```

```
"identity:list_user_projects": "rule:admin_or_owner or rule:projectadmin",
[...]
"identity:get_user": "rule:admin_required or rule:projectadmin",
"identity:list_users": "rule:admin_required or rule:subadmin",
[...]
"identity:list_roles": "rule:admin_required or rule:subadmin",
[...]
"identity:list_role_assignments": "rule:admin_required or rule:subadmin",
```

5. Save the changes and copy the file to `/srv/www/openstack-dash-board/openstack_dashboard/conf/CUSTOM_keystone_policy.json` on the node where the `nova_dashboard-server` role is deployed.

E.3 Adjusting the *Keystone* Barclamp Proposal

1. Log in to the Crowbar Web interface.

2. Select *Barclamps* › *All barclamps*.

3. Go to the *Keystone* barclamp and click *Edit*.

4. In the *Attributes* section, click *Raw*. This shows the complete configuration file and allows you to edit it directly.

5. Adjust the `policy_file` parameter to point to the `CUSTOM_policy.json` file. For example:

```
{
  [...]
  "policy_file": "mypolicy.json",
}
```

6. *Save* and *Apply* the changes to the Keystone barclamp.

E.4 Adjusting the *Horizon* Barclamp Proposal

1. Log in to the Crowbar Web interface.

2. Select *Barclamps* > *All barclamps*.

3. Go to the *Horizon* barclamp and click *Edit*.

4. In the *Attributes* section, click *Raw*. This shows the complete configuration file and allows you to edit it directly.

5. If needed, adjust the `policy_file_path` parameter to point to the directory where you copied the newly added *CUSTOM*_keystone_policy.json file. By default, its value is an empty string—this means that the default directory will be used.

6. Enter the new file's name as value of the `identity` parameter within the `policy_file` section (❶):

```
{
   "policy_file_path": "",
   "policy_file": {
      "identity": "mykeystone_policy.json",  ❶
      "compute": "nova_policy.json",
      "volume": "cinder_policy.json",
      "image": "glance_policy.json",
      "orchestration": "heat_policy.json",
      "network": "neutron_policy.json",
      "telemetry": "ceilometer_policy.json"
```

7. *Save* and *Apply* the changes to the Horizon barclamp.

F Setting up a Netboot Environment for Microsoft* Windows

Setting up Compute Nodes running Microsoft Windows Server 2012 R2, Microsoft Windows Server 2012, Microsoft Hyper-V Server 2012 R2 or Microsoft Hyper-V Server 2012 requires to configure the Administration Server to be able to provide the netboot environment for node installation. The environment is generated from a machine running Microsoft Windows Server or Microsoft Hyper-V Server.

F.1 Requirements

The following requirements must be met to successfully deploy Hyper-V:

* Provide a separate machine running Microsoft Windows Server 2012 R2, Microsoft Windows Server 2012, Microsoft Hyper-V Server 2012 R2 or Microsoft Hyper-V Server 2012. The machine must be able to access the Administration Server and the Internet.

* Install Samba (package `samba`) and the Microsoft Hyper-V tools (package `hyper-v`) on the Administration Server.

F.2 Providing a Hyper-V Netboot Environment

To provide a Hyper-V netboot environment on the Administration Server, a samba share, that can be mounted on the Windows machine, is created on the Administration Server. Among others, this share contains the Hyper-V tools which provide Windows scripts to generate the environment.

PROCEDURE F.1: PREPARING THE ADMINISTRATION SERVER

1. Ensure that the requirements listed at *Section F.1, "Requirements"* are met.

2. If you have more than one hard disk, edit `/srv/tftpboot/adk-tools/build_winpe.ps1` and adjust the value for `$install_media` accordingly.

3. Make sure the Samba daemons `smb` and `nmb` are automatically started during boot and are currently running by executing the following commands:

```
systemctl enable smb nmb
systemctl start smb nmb
```

4. Edit the Samba configuration file `/etc/samba/smb.conf` and add the following share:

```
[reminst]
        comment = MS Windows remote install
        guest ok = Yes
        inherit acls = Yes
        path = /srv/tftpboot
        read only = No
        force user = root
```

By default, the workgroup name is set to `WORKGROUP` in the `[global]` section of `/etc/samba/smb.conf`. Adjust it, if needed.

5. Reload the smb service:

```
rcsmb reload
```

When Samba is properly configured on the Administration Server, log in to the machine running Microsoft Windows Server or Microsoft Hyper-V Server and generate the environment:

PROCEDURE F.2: NETBOOT ENVIRONMENT GENERATION

1. Log in to the Microsoft Windows Server or Microsoft Hyper-V Server machine. Connect the device name `X:` to the Samba share `\\crowbar\reminst` configured on the Administration Server (which is named `crowbar` by default) in the previous step. This can either be done from the Explorer or on the command line with the **net use x: \\crowbar\reminst** command.

2. Device `X:` contains a directory `X:\adk-tools` with image creation scripts for either Windows Server 2012 R2 `build_winpe_windows-6.3.ps1`), Windows Server 2012 (`build_winpe_windows-6.2.ps1`), Hyper-V Serv-

er 2012 R2 (`build_winpe_hyperv-6.3.ps1`) or Hyper-V Server 2012 (`build_winpe_hyperv-6.2.ps1`). Build the image by running the following commands on the command line:

Windows Server 2012 R2

```
powershell -ExecutionPolicy Bypass x:\adk-tools
\build_winpe_windows-6.3.ps1
```

Windows Server 2012

```
powershell -ExecutionPolicy Bypass x:\adk-tools
\build_winpe_windows-6.2.ps1
```

Hyper-V Server 2012 R2

```
powershell -ExecutionPolicy Bypass x:\adk-tools\build_winpe_hyperv-6.3.ps1
```

Hyper-V Server 2012

```
powershell -ExecutionPolicy Bypass x:\adk-tools\build_winpe_hyperv-6.2.ps1
```

Executing the script requires Internet access, because additional software needs to be downloaded.

After the netboot environment is set up, you can choose either *Windows Server 2012 R2*, *Windows Server 2012*, *Hyper-V Server 2012 R2* or *Hyper-V Server 2012* as the *Target Platform* for newly discovered nodes from the *Node Dashboard*.

G VMware vSphere Installation Instructions

SUSE OpenStack Cloud supports the Nova Compute VMware vCenter driver which enables access to advanced features such as vMotion, High Availability, and Dynamic Resource Scheduling (DRS). However, VMware vSphere is not supported "natively" by SUSE OpenStack Cloud—it rather delegates requests to an existing vCenter. It requires preparations at the vCenter and post install adjustments of the Compute Node.

G.1 Requirements

The following requirements must be met to successfully deploy a Nova Compute VMware node:

- VMware vSphere vCenter 5.1 or higher

- VMware vSphere ESXi nodes 5.1 or higher

- A separate Compute Node that acts as a proxy to vCenter is required. Minimum system requirements for this node are:

  CPU: x86_64 with 2 cores (4 recommended)
  RAM: 2 GB (8 GB recommended)
  Disk space: 4 GB (30 GB recommended)
  See *Section G.3, "Finishing the Nova Compute VMware Node Installation"* for setup instructions.

- Neutron must not be deployed with the `openvswitch with gre` plug-in. See *Section 10.11, "Deploying Neutron"* for details.

- Security groups are only supported when running VMWare NSX. You need to deploy Neutron with the *vmware* plug-in to have security group support. This is also a prerequisite for `gre` tunnel support.

G.2 Preparing the VMware vCenter Server

SUSE OpenStack Cloud requires the VMware vCenter server to run version 5.1 or better. You need to create a single data center for SUSE OpenStack Cloud (multiple data centers are currently not supported):

1. Log in to the vCenter Server using the vSphere Web Client

2. Choose *Hosts and Clusters* and create a single *Datacenter*

3. Set up a *New Cluster* which has *DRS* enabled.

4. Set *Automation Level* to `Fully Automated` and *Migration Threshold* to `Aggressive`.

5. Create shared storage. Only shared storage is supported and data stores must be shared among all hosts in a cluster. It is recommended to remove data stores not intended for OpenStack from clusters being configured for OpenStack. Multiple data stores can be used per cluster.

6. Create a port group with the same name as the `vmware.integration_bridge` value in `nova.conf` (default is br-int). All VM NICs are attached to this port group for management by the OpenStack networking plug-in. Assign the same VLAN ID as for the neutron network. On the default network setup this is the same VLAN ID as for the `nova_fixed` network. Use *YaST › Miscellaneous › Crowbar › Networks* to look up the VLAN ID.

G.3 Finishing the Nova Compute VMware Node Installation

Deploy Nova as described in *Section 10.12, "Deploying Nova"* on a single Compute Node and fill in the *VMWare vCenter Settings* attributes:

vCenter IP Address

IP address of the vCenter server.

vCenter Username / vCenter Password

vCenter login credentials.

Cluster Names

A comma-separated list of cluster names you have added on the vCenter server.

Regex to match the name of a datastore

Regular expression to match the name of a data store. If you have several data stores, this option allows you to specify the data stores to use with Nova Compute. For example, the value `nas.*` selects all data stores that have a name starting with `nas`. If this option is omitted, Nova Compute uses the first data store returned by the vSphere API. However, it is recommended not to use this option and to remove data stores that are not intended for OpenStack instead.

VLAN Interface

The physical interface that is to be used for VLAN networking. The default value of `vmnic0` references the first available interface ("eth0"). `vmnic1` would be the second interface ("eth1").

CA file for verifying the vCenter certificate

Absolute path to the vCenter CA certificate.

vCenter SSL Certificate is insecure (for instance, self-signed)

Default value: `false` (the CA truststore is used for verification). Set this option to `true` when using self-signed certificates to disable certificate checks. This setting is for testing purposes only and must not be used in production environments!

FIGURE G.1: THE NOVA BARCLAMP: VMWARE CONFIGURATION

G.4 Making the Nova Compute VMware Node Highly Available

OpenStack does not support deploying multiple VMware Compute Nodes. As a workaround, set up an instance on the vSphere Cluster, register it with Crowbar and deploy the `nova-compute-vmware` role on this node:

1. Create an instance on the vSphere Cluster and install SLES 11 SP3.

2. Configure a network interface in a way that it can access the SUSE OpenStack Cloud admin network.

3. Enable the High-Availability flag in vCenter for this instance.

4. Follow the instructions at *Section 9.3, "Converting Existing SUSE Linux Enterprise Server 12 SP1 Machines Into SUSE OpenStack Cloud Nodes"* to register the instance with the Administration Server and add it to the pool of nodes available for deployment.

5. Deploy the `nova-compute-vmware` role on the new node as described in *Section 10.12, "Deploying Nova"* **and** *Section G.3, "Finishing the Nova Compute VMware Node Installation"*.

H Using Cisco Nexus Switches with Neutron

H.1 Requirements

The following requirements must be met to use Cisco Nexus switches with Neutron:

- Cisco Nexus series 3000, 5000 or 7000

- All Compute Nodes must be equipped with at least two network cards.

- The switch needs to have the XML management interface enabled. SSH access to the management interface must be enabled (refer to the switch's documentation for details).

- Enable VLAN trunking for all Neutron managed VLANs on the switch port to which the controller node running Neutron is connected to.

- If VLAN configurations for Neutron managed VLANs already exist on the switch (for example from a previous SUSE OpenStack Cloud deployment), you need to delete them via the switch's management interface prior to deploying Neutron.

- When using the Cisco plugin, Neutron reconfigures the VLAN trunk configuration on all ports used for the `nova-fixed` traffic (the traffic between the instances). This requires to configure separate network interfaces exclusively used by `nova-fixed`. This can be achieved by adjusting `/etc/crowbar/network.json` (refer to *Appendix D, The Network Barclamp Template File*). The following example shows an appropriate configuration for dual mode, where *nova-fixed* has bee mapped to conduit *intf1* and all other networks to other conduits. Configuration attributes not relevant in this context have been replaced with
....

EXAMPLE H.1: EXCLUSIVELY MAPPING *NOVA-FIXED* TO CONDUIT *INTF1* IN DUAL MODE

```
{
    "attributes" : {
      "network" : {
        "conduit_map" : [
          ...
        ],
        "mode" : "single",
```

```
    "networks" : {
        "nova_fixed" : {
            ...,
            "conduit" : "intf1"
        },
        "nova_floating" : {
            ...,
            "conduit" : "intf0"
        },
        "public" : {
            ...,
            "conduit" : "intf0"
        },
        "storage" : {
            ...,
            "conduit" : "intf0"
        },
        "os_sdn" : {
            ...,
            "conduit" : "intf0"
        },
        "admin" : {
            ...,
            "conduit" : "intf0"
        },
        "bmc" : {
            ...,
            "conduit" : "bmc"
        },
        "bmc_vlan" : {
            ...,
            "conduit" : "intf2"
        },
    },
    ...,
},
```

```
        }
}
```

- Make a note of all switch ports to which the interfaces using the `nova-fixed` network on the Compute Nodes are connected. This information will be needed when deploying Neutron.

H.2   Deploying Neutron with the Cisco Plugin

1. Create a Neutron barclamp proposal in the Crowbar Web interface.

2. Select *cisco* as the *Plugin* and *vlan* for *Mode*.

3. The *Cisco Switch Credentials* table will be faded out. Enter the *IP Address*, the SSH *Port* number and the login credentials for the switch's management interface. If you have multiple switches, open a new row in the table by clicking *Add* and enter the data for another switch.

FIGURE H.1: THE NEUTRON BARCLAMP: CISCO PLUGIN

4. Choose whether to encrypt public communication (*HTTPS*) or not (*HTTP*). If choosing *HTTPS*, refer to *SSL Support: Protocol* for configuration details.

5. Choose a node for deployment and *Apply* the proposal.

6. **Deploy Nova** (see *Section 10.12, "Deploying Nova"*), **Horizon** (see *Section 10.13, "Deploying Horizon (OpenStack Dashboard)"* and all other remaining barclamps.

7. When all barclamps have been deployed, return to the Neutron barclamp by choosing *Barclamps › OpenStack › Neutron › Edit*. The proposal now contains an additional table named *Assign Switch Ports*, listing all Compute Nodes.

   For each Compute Node enter the switch it is connected to and the port number from the notes you took earlier. The values need to be entered like the following: `1/13` or `Eth1/20`.

8. When you have entered the data for all Compute Nodes, re-apply the proposal.

 Important: Deploying Additional Compute Nodes

Whenever you deploy additional Compute Nodes to an active SUSE OpenStack Cloud deployment using the Cisco plugin with Neutron, you need to update the Neutron barclamp proposal by entering their port data as described in the previous step.

 Note: Verifying the Setup

To verify if Neutron was correctly deployed, do the following:

1. Launch an instance (refer to the *End User Guide*, chapter *Launch instances* for instructions).

2. Find out which VLAN was assigned to the network by running the command **neutron net-show fixed**. The result lists a *segmentation_id* matching the VLAN.

3. Log in to the switch's management interface and list the VLAN configuration. If the setup was deployed correctly, the port of the Compute Node the instance is running on, is in trunk mode for the matching VLAN.

I Crowbar Batch

This is the documentation for the `crowbar batch` subcommand.

I.1 Description

`crowbar batch` provides a quick way of creating, updating, and applying Crowbar proposals. It can be used to:

- accurately capture the configuration of an existing Crowbar environment.

- drive Crowbar to build a complete new environment from scratch.

- capture one SUSE OpenStack Cloud environment and then reproduce it on another set of hardware (provided hardware and network configuration match to an appropriate extent).

- automatically update existing proposals.

As the name suggests, `crowbar batch` is intended to be run in "batch mode", that is mostly unattended. It has two modes of operation:

crowbar batch export

Exports a YAML file which describes existing proposals and how their parameters deviate from the default proposal values for that barclamp.

crowbar batch build

Imports a YAML file in the same format as above, and uses it to build new proposals if they don't yet exist, and then update the existing proposals so that their parameters match those given in the YAML file.

I.2 YAML file format

Here is an example YAML file. At the top-level, there is a proposals array, each entry of which is a hash representing a proposal:

```
proposals:
- barclamp: provisioner
```

```
  # Proposal name defaults to 'default'.
  attributes:
    shell_prompt: USER@ALIAS:CWD SUFFIX
- barclamp: database
  # Default attributes are good enough, so we just need to assign
  # nodes to roles:
  deployment:
    elements:
      database-server:
        - "@@controller1@@"
- barclamp: rabbitmq
  deployment:
    elements:
      rabbitmq-server:
        - "@@controller1@@"
```

 Note: Reserved Indicators in YAML

Note that the characters @ and ` are reserved indicators in YAML. They can appear anywhere in a string *except at the beginning*. Therefore a string such as @@controller1@@ needs to be quoted using double quotes.

I.2.1 Top-level proposal attributes

barclamp

Name of the barclamp for this proposal (required).

name

Name of this proposal (optional; default is default). In **build** mode, if the proposal does not already exist, it will be created.

attributes

An optional nested hash containing any attributes for this proposal which deviate from the defaults for the barclamp.

In **export** mode, any attributes set to the default values are excluded to keep the YAML as short and readable as possible.

In **build** mode, these attributes are deep-merged with the current values for the proposal. If the proposal didn't already exist, batch build will create it first, so the attributes are effectively merged with the default values for the barclamp's proposal.

wipe_attributes

An optional array of paths to nested attributes which should be removed from the proposal. Each path is a period-delimited sequence of attributes; for example `pacemaker.stonith.sbd.nodes` would remove all SBD nodes from the proposal if it already exists. If a path segment contains a period, it should be escaped with a backslash, for example `segment-one.segment\.two.segment_three`.

This removal occurs before the deep merge described above. For example a batch build with a YAML file which included `pacemaker.stonith.sbd.nodes` in `wipe_attributes` of a pacemaker barclamp proposal would ensure that at the end of the run, only SBD nodes listed in the attributes sibling hash would be used. In contrast, without the `wipe_attributes` entry, the SBD nodes given would be appended to any SBD nodes already defined in the proposal.

deployment

A nested hash defining how and where this proposal should be deployed.

In **build** mode, this hash is deep-merged in the same way as the attributes hash, except that the array of elements for each Chef role is reset to the empty list before the deep merge. This special exception may change in the future.

I.2.2   Node Alias Substitutions

Any string anywhere in the YAML which is of the form `@@node@@`, and where *node* is a node alias will be substituted for the name of that node. For example if `controller1` is a Crowbar alias for node `d52-54-02-77-77-02.mycloud.com`, then `@@controller1@@` will be substituted for that host name. This allows YAML files to be reused across environments.

I.3 Options

In addition to the standard options available to every **crowbar** subcommand (run **crowbar batch --help** for a full list), there are some extra options specifically for **crowbar batch**:

--include <barclamp[.proposal]>
> Only include the barclamp / proposals given.
>
> This option can be repeated multiple times. The inclusion value can either be the name of a barclamp (for example, `pacemaker`) or a specifically named proposal within the barclamp (for example, `pacemaker.network_cluster`).
>
> If it is specified, then only the barclamp / proposals specified are included in the build or export operation, and all others are ignored.

--exclude <barclamp[.proposal]>
> This option can be repeated multiple times. The exclusion value is the same format as for `--include`. The barclamps / proposals specified are excluded from the build or export operation.

--timeout <seconds>
> Change the timeout for Crowbar API calls.
>
> As Chef's run lists grow, some of the later OpenStack barclamp proposals (for example Nova, Horizon, or Heat) can take over 5 or even 10 minutes to apply. Therefore you may need to increase this timeout to 900 seconds in some circumstances.

J Recovering Clusters to a Healthy State

If one node in your cluster refuses to rejoin the cluster, it is most likely that the node has not been shut down cleanly. This can either be due to manual intervention or because the node has been fenced (shut down) by the STONITH mechanism of the cluster, to protect the integrity of data in case of a split-brain scenario.

The following sections refer to problems with the Control Nodes cluster and show how to recover your degraded cluster to full strength. This takes the following basic steps:

1. *Re-adding the Node to the Cluster*

2. *Recovering Crowbar and Chef*

3. In addition, you may need to reset resource failcounts in order to allow resources to start on the node you have re-added to the cluster. See *Section J.4, "Cleaning Up Resources"*.

4. In addition, you may need to manually remove the maintenance mode flag from a node. See *Section J.5, "Removing the Maintenance Mode Flag from a Node"*.

For a list of possible symptoms that help you to diagnose a degraded cluster, see *Section J.1, "Symptoms of a Degraded Control Node Cluster"*.

J.1 Symptoms of a Degraded Control Node Cluster

The following incidents may occur if a Control Node in your cluster has been shut down in an unclean state:

- A VM reboots although the SUSE OpenStack Cloud administrator did not trigger this action.

- One of the Control Node in the Crowbar Web interface is in status `Problematic`, signified by a red dot next to the node.

- The Hawk Web interface stops responding on one of the Control Nodes, while it is still responding on the others.

- The SSH connection to one of the Control Nodes freezes.

- The OpenStack services stop responding for a short while.

J.2   Re-adding the Node to the Cluster

1. Reboot the node.

2. Connect to the node via SSH from the Administration Server.

3. If you have a 2-node cluster, remove the block file that is created on a node during start of the cluster service:

```
root # rm /var/spool/corosync/block_automatic_start
```

The block file avoids STONITH deathmatches for 2-node clusters (where each node kills the other one, resulting in both nodes rebooting all the time). When Corosync shuts down cleanly, the block file is automatically removed. Otherwise the block file is still present and prevents the cluster service from (re-)starting on that node.

4. Start the cluster service on the cluster node:

```
root # systemctl start pacemaker
```

J.3   Recovering Crowbar and Chef

Making the Pacemaker node rejoin the cluster is not enough. All nodes in the cloud (including the Administration Server) need to be aware that this node is back online. This requires the following steps for Crowbar and Chef:

1. Log in to the node you have re-added to the cluster.

2. Re-register the node with Crowbar by executing:

```
root # service crowbar_join start
```

3. Log in to one of the *other* Control Nodes.

4. Trigger a Chef run:

```
root # chef-client
```

J.4 Cleaning Up Resources

A resource will be automatically restarted if it fails, but each failure increases the resource's failcount. If a `migration-threshold` has been set for the resource, the node will no longer run the resource when the number of failures reaches the migration threshold. To allow the resource to start again on the node, reset the resources failcount by cleaning up the resource manually. You can clean up individual resources by using the Hawk Web interface or all in one go as described below:

1. Log in to one of the cluster nodes.

2. Clean-up all stopped resources with the following command:

```
root # crm_resource -o | \
  awk '/\tStopped |Timed Out/ { print $1 }' | \
  xargs -n1 crm resource cleanup
```

J.5 Removing the Maintenance Mode Flag from a Node

During normal operation, chef-client sometimes needs to place a node into maintenance mode. The node is kept in maintenance mode until the chef-client run finishes. However, if the chef-client run fails, the node may be left in maintenance mode. In that case, the cluster management tools like crmsh or Hawk will show all resources on that node as unmanaged. To remove the maintenance flag:

1. Log in the cluster node.

2. Disable the maintenance mode with:

```
root # crm node ready
```

K Documentation Updates

This chapter lists content changes for this document since the release of SUSE® OpenStack Cloud 2.0.

This manual was updated on the following dates:

K.1 March, 2016 (Initial Release SUSE OpenStack Cloud 6)

General

- Renamed SUSE Cloud to SUSE OpenStack Cloud.

- Reorganized the manual by introducing parts and splitting long chapters to improve readability.

- All nodes including the Administration Server are now based on SUSE Linux Enterprise Server 12 SP1. The documentation has been updated accordingly.

- Rewrote large parts of *Chapter 5, Software Repository Setup* because repository handling in SUSE OpenStack Cloud has been made easier. Furthermore, repositories are no longer provided by the Novell Customer Center, but rather by the SUSE Customer Center.

- **Added** *Chapter 8, The Crowbar Web Interface.*

- Added documentation for the new Web interface-based installation of the Administration Server (*Section 7.6.1, "Starting the SUSE OpenStack Cloud Crowbar Installation from the Web Interface"*).

- A new backup procedure has been added to SUSE OpenStack Cloud (*Section 11.5, "Backing Up and Restoring the Administration Server"*).

- *Section 11.3, "Upgrading from SUSE OpenStack Cloud 5 to SUSE OpenStack Cloud 6"* is now done via a Web interface.

- Added *Section 11.2, "Service Order on SUSE OpenStack Cloud Start-up or Shutdown"*.

- Added *Appendix J, Recovering Clusters to a Healthy State*.

- SUSE OpenStack Cloud 6 supports Manila a Shared File System Service (*Section 10.10, "Deploying Manila"*).

- Added *Appendix E, Configuring Role Based Access Control (RBAC)*.

Bugfixes

- Updated repository links and paths in *Chapter 5, Software Repository Setup* (http://bugzilla.suse.com/show_bug.cgi?id=862056, http://bugzilla.suse.com/show_bug.cgi?id=956681, and https://bugzilla.suse.com/show_bug.cgi?id=956686).

- Provided a full list of OpenStack roles and services in *Appendix C, Roles and Services in SUSE OpenStack Cloud* (http://bugzilla.suse.com/show_bug.cgi?id=875149).

- SUSE OpenStack Cloud does not support High Availability for the LBaaS service plugin (http://bugzilla.suse.com/show_bug.cgi?id=881510).

- Provided instructions on how to change keymap on Compute Nodes (http://bugzilla.suse.com/show_bug.cgi?id=906846).

- Added a link to the SUSE Enterprise Storage documentation to *Section 2.6.4.2, "Ceph —Avoiding Points of Failure"* (http://bugzilla.suse.com/show_bug.cgi?id=917344).

- An HA setup for Trove is not supported (http://bugzilla.suse.com/show_bug.cgi?id=919471).

- Added the new section *Section 11.2, "Service Order on SUSE OpenStack Cloud Start-up or Shutdown"*. (http://bugzilla.suse.com/show_bug.cgi?id=919476).

- Repositories are distributed by the SUSE Customer Center (http://bugzilla.suse.com/show_bug.cgi?id=919844).

- Updates on adding an external Ceph cluster at *Section 9.4.4.2, "Making Ceph Available on the SUSE OpenStack Cloud Nodes"* (http://bugzilla.suse.com/show_bug.cgi?id=923117 and http://bugzilla.suse.com/show_bug.cgi?id=924001).

- Added documentation for VXLAN support at *Section 10.11, "Deploying Neutron"* (http://bugzilla.suse.com/show_bug.cgi?id=923218).

- HA cluster nodes need to be put into maintenance mode prior to updating packages (http://bugzilla.suse.com/show_bug.cgi?id=923962).

- Added an explanation on Distributed Virtual Routers (DVR) to *Section 10.11, "Deploying Neutron"* (http://bugzilla.suse.com/show_bug.cgi?id=925438).

- New technology preview feature: Docker support (http://bugzilla.suse.com/show_bug.cgi?id=926224).

- Added instructions on how to disable PXE and DNS services on the Administration Server to allow custom provisioning at *Q & A 12.1.2, "OpenStack Node Deployment"* (http://bugzilla.suse.com/show_bug.cgi?id=929081 and https://bugzilla.suse.com/show_bug.cgi?id=920826).

- Added instructions on how to enable jumbo frames at *Section 7.5, "Custom Network Configuration"* (http://bugzilla.suse.com/show_bug.cgi?id=930744).

- Added the new appendix *Appendix E, Configuring Role Based Access Control (RBAC)* (http://bugzilla.suse.com/show_bug.cgi?id=931856).

- Ceilometer is also supported on HyperV Compute Nodes (http://bugzilla.suse.com/show_bug.cgi?id=932314).

- Added instructions on how to install additional packages to *Q & A 12.1.1, "Admin Node Deployment"* (http://bugzilla.suse.com/show_bug.cgi?id=936244).

- Public and floating networks can be split using different VLANs (http://bugzilla.suse.com/show_bug.cgi?id=936984).

- Calamari needs to be deployed on a dedicated node (http://bugzilla.suse.com/show_bug.cgi?id=940189).

- Setting `REPOS_SKIP_CHECKS` is no longer needed on SUSE OpenStack Cloud 6 (http://bugzilla.suse.com/show_bug.cgi?id=940941).

- Provided better examples for `/etc/crowbar/network.json` in *Appendix D, The Network Barclamp Template File* (http://bugzilla.suse.com/show_bug.cgi?id=944074).

- Added a solution for fixing nodes in state `Problem` at *Q & A 12.1.2, "OpenStack Node Deployment"* (http://bugzilla.suse.com/show_bug.cgi?id=945436).

- The openvswitch with VLAN configuration for neutron-l3 no longer requires a 4 NIC configuration (http://bugzilla.suse.com/show_bug.cgi?id=946874).

- The Web interface now contains a *Repositories* screen showing an overview of the repositories of SUSE OpenStack Cloud (http://bugzilla.suse.com/show_bug.cgi?id=952643).

- Added documentation for the Cisco USC support at *Section 8.2.3, "Utilities"* (http://bugzilla.suse.com/show_bug.cgi?id=953982).

- Added the FAQ *Q:* (http://bugzilla.suse.com/show_bug.cgi?id=954413).

- SUSE OpenStack Cloud 6 supports Manila a Shared File System Service (http://bugzilla.suse.com/show_bug.cgi?id=956234).

- Errors in *Section 10.1.1, "Delete a Proposal That Already Has Been Deployed"* have been fixed (http://bugzilla.suse.com/show_bug.cgi?id=956244).

- Renamed SUSE Cloud to SUSE OpenStack Cloud (http://bugzilla.suse.com/show_bug.cgi?id=956431).

- Updates for the Swift barclamp (http://bugzilla.suse.com/show_bug.cgi?id=956659).

- Updates for the Glance barclamp (http://bugzilla.suse.com/show_bug.cgi?id=956664).

- Updates for the Cinder barclamp (http://bugzilla.suse.com/show_bug.cgi?id=956666).

- Updates for the Neutron barclamp (http://bugzilla.suse.com/show_bug.cgi?id=956669).

- Updates for the Nova barclamp (http://bugzilla.suse.com/show_bug.cgi?id=956900).

- OpenAIS has been replaced by Corosync (http://bugzilla.suse.com/show_bug.cgi?id=956670).

- Updates for the list of services at *Section 2.3, "SSL Encryption"* (http://bugzilla.suse.com/show_bug.cgi?id=956675).

- Updates for the Ceilometer barclamp (http://bugzilla.suse.com/show_bug.cgi?id=956676).

- Updates for *Section 2.5, "Software Requirements"* (http://bugzilla.suse.com/show_bug.cgi?id=956679).

- Updated *Chapter 4, Installing and Setting Up an SMT Server on the Administration Server (Optional)* (http://bugzilla.suse.com/show_bug.cgi?id=956680).

- Minor changes in *Section 12.1, "FAQ"* (http://bugzilla.suse.com/show_bug.cgi?id=956682).

- Services on SUSE Linux Enterprise Server 12 SP1 are started via the `systemctl` command (http://bugzilla.suse.com/show_bug.cgi?id=956683).

- New attributes for the *Appendix D, The Network Barclamp Template File* (http://bugzilla.suse.com/show_bug.cgi?id=956684).

- Added documentation for the new Web interface-based installation of the Administration Server to *Section 7.6.1, "Starting the SUSE OpenStack Cloud Crowbar Installation from the Web Interface".* (http://bugzilla.suse.com/show_bug.cgi?id=956869).

- Document the possibility to set the node file system at *Section 9.2, "Node Installation"* (http://bugzilla.suse.com/show_bug.cgi?id=956874).

- Horizon SSL options do not match (http://bugzilla.suse.com/show_bug.cgi?id=959335).

- The new backup procedure has been documented at *Section 11.5, "Backing Up and Restoring the Administration Server".* (http://bugzilla.suse.com/show_bug.cgi?id=962576).

- Added documentation about deploying HA for Compute Nodes (http://bugzilla.suse.com/show_bug.cgi?id=964205).

- Apache needs to be restarted before starting the installation from the Web interface (http://bugzilla.suse.com/show_bug.cgi?id=966158).

- Added *Appendix J, Recovering Clusters to a Healthy State* (http://bugzilla.suse.com/show_bug.cgi?id=966158).

- Provided additional information on bonding modes at *Section 7.3, "Network Mode"* (Doc Comment 29562).

- An HA setup of Ceilometer needs to be installed on a cluster with an odd number of nodes (Doc Comment 26861).

K.2 February, 2015 (Initial Release SUSE Cloud 5)

Chapter 2, Considerations and Requirements

- **Completely rewrote** *Section 2.5, "Software Requirements".* **Added information about subscriptions, optional features, media layout and repositories.**

Chapter 3, Installing the Administration Server

- Split the chapter into two separate parts.

- Transferred the optional SMT installation to the appendix (*Chapter 4, Installing and Setting Up an SMT Server on the Administration Server (Optional)*) to improve the readability.

Chapter 4, Admin Node Configuration

- Added information about SLES 12 and SUSE Enterprise Storage repositories and adjusted the repository paths to the new structure.

- Removed information about linking to local SMT repositories— this is now done automatically by the installation script.

- **Completely rewrote** *Chapter 5, Software Repository Setup* to make it easier to read.

Chapter 10, Deploying the OpenStack Services

- Updated screenshots where necessary.

- **Added** *Section 10.5.1.2, "Using Hybrid Authentication".*

- **Updated** *Section 10.6, "Deploying Ceph (optional)"* because of new configuration options, roles and the fact that Ceph needs SLES 12 nodes.

- **Updated** *Section 10.9, "Deploying Cinder"* by adding instructions on how to deploy multiple back-ends. Also added descriptions for additional back-ends Fujitsu EXTERNUS DX and VMware.

- **Updated** *Section 10.11, "Deploying Neutron"* because of changes in the barclamp.

- **Added** *Section 10.16, "Deploying Trove (Optional)".*

Chapter 12, Troubleshooting and Support

- **Added** *Q & A 12.1.3, "Miscellaneous".*

- **Added** *How to change the default keymap for instances?.*

Appendices

- Added VMware Compute Node system requirements to *Section G.1, "Requirements".*

- Added *Section G.4, "Making the Nova Compute VMware Node Highly Available".*

- Added *Appendix I, Crowbar Batch.*

Bugfixes

- Added a warning about old database files on shared storage to *Section 10.3.1, "HA Setup for the Database"* (https://bugzilla.suse.com/show_bug.cgi?id=875696).

- Added information about log files written during the upgrade procedure to *Section 11.3, "Upgrading from SUSE OpenStack Cloud 5 to SUSE OpenStack Cloud 6"* and *Appendix A, Log Files* (https://bugzilla.suse.com/show_bug.cgi?id=892497).

- Added *Section 10.16, "Deploying Trove (Optional)"* (https://bugzilla.suse.com/show_bug.cgi?id=893876).

- Fixed deployment order of barclamps (https://bugzilla.suse.com/show_bug.cgi?id=894063).

- Fixed wrong group names and file names in *Section 9.4.4, "Using an Externally Managed Ceph Cluster"* (http://bugzilla.suse.com/show_bug.cgi?id=894231).

- Added *Section 10.5.1.2, "Using Hybrid Authentication"* (https://bugzilla.suse.com/show_bug.cgi?id=894572).

- Fixed various minor issues in chapters *Chapter 2, Considerations and Requirements* and *Chapter 3, Installing the Administration Server* (https://bugzilla.suse.com/show_bug.cgi?id=895593).

- Updated *Section 10.9, "Deploying Cinder"* by adding instructions on how to deploy multiple back-ends. Also added descriptions for additional back-ends Fujitsu EXTERNUS DX and VMware (https://bugzilla.suse.com/show_bug.cgi?id=889729).

- Added a pointer to `man mount(8)` to *Section 10.3.1, "HA Setup for the Database"* (https://bugzilla.suse.com/show_bug.cgi?id=898538/).

- Documented the *Region Name* at *Section 10.5, "Deploying Keystone"* (https://bugzilla.suse.com/show_bug.cgi?id=900090).

- Added VMware Compute Node system requirements to *Section G.1, "Requirements"* (https://bugzilla.suse.com/show_bug.cgi?id=903676).

- **crowbar-backup** (*Section 11.5, "Backing Up and Restoring the Administration Server"*) is now officially supported by SUSE (http://bugzilla.suse.com/show_bug.cgi?id=904374).

- The YaST Crowbar module now supports adding custom repositories, which no longer makes it necessary to manually edit `/etc/crowbar/provisioner.js` (https://bugzilla.suse.com/show_bug.cgi?id=906267>).

- Added *How to change the default keymap for instances?* (https://bugzilla.suse.com/show_bug.cgi?id=906846).

- Corrected the number of nodes required for deploying `Ceph-mon` (https://bugzilla.suse.com/show_bug.cgi?id=907329).

- Added installation details for an HA database setup using a shared NFS directory to *Section 10.3.1, "HA Setup for the Database"* (http://bugzilla.suse.com/show_bug.cgi?id=910061).

- Added a link to the *CinderSupportMatrix* in *Section 2.2.1, "Cloud Storage Services"* (http://bugzilla.suse.com/show_bug.cgi?id=910843).

- Added *Q & A 12.1.3, "Miscellaneous"* (http://bugzilla.suse.com/show_bug.cgi?id=911336).

- Updated *Section 10.6, "Deploying Ceph (optional)"* (https://bugzilla.suse.com/show_bug.cgi?id=912609).

- Updated *Appendix A, Log Files* (https://bugzilla.suse.com/show_bug.cgi?id=912699).

- Documented changes in *Section 10.9, "Deploying Cinder"* regarding the NetApp backend (https://bugzilla.suse.com/show_bug.cgi?id=914711).

- Added *Section G.4, "Making the Nova Compute VMware Node Highly Available"* (https://bugzilla.suse.com/show_bug.cgi?id=914730).

- Added *Appendix I, Crowbar Batch* (https://bugzilla.suse.com/show_bug.cgi?id=915697).

- Updated *Section 10.11, "Deploying Neutron"* because of changes in the barclamp (https://bugzilla.suse.com/show_bug.cgi?id=916036).

- Corrected the SBD setup description in *Section 10.2, "Deploying Pacemaker (Optional, HA Setup Only)"* (https://bugzilla.suse.com/show_bug.cgi?id=916351).

- Added information on Ceph Calamari to *Section 10.6, "Deploying Ceph (optional)"* (https://bugzilla.suse.com/show_bug.cgi?id=916616).

- Added information about Ceph requiring SLES 12 nodes (https://bugzilla.suse.com/show_bug.cgi?id=916585, https://bugzilla.suse.com/show_bug.cgi?id=916907 **and** https://bugzilla.suse.com/show_bug.cgi?id=916918).

- Added a warning about not to set up shared storage in a productive SUSE OpenStack Cloud (https://bugzilla.suse.com/show_bug.cgi?id=917334).

K.3 August, 2014 (Initial Release SUSE Cloud 4)

Admin Node Installation

- Added the section *Section 7.5.1, "Providing Access to External Networks"* (http://bugzilla.suse.com/show_bug.cgi?id=882795).

Node OpenStack Service Deployment

- Updated the barclamp descriptions where necessary.

- Updated screenshots where necessary.

- Added the section *Section 10.1.2, "Queuing/Dequeuing Proposals"* (http://bugzilla.suse.com/show_bug.cgi?id=882825).

Bugfixes

- Added an explanation for the new option *Policy when cluster does not have quorum* to *Section 10.2, "Deploying Pacemaker (Optional, HA Setup Only)"* (http://bugzilla.suse.com/show_bug.cgi?id=875776).

- Added a list of Neutron plugins which can be used with VMware (http://bugzilla.suse.com/show_bug.cgi?id=880128).

- Added the section *Section 7.5.1, "Providing Access to External Networks"* (http://bugzilla.suse.com/show_bug.cgi?id=882795).

- Added an annotation to *Section 5.1, "Copying the Product Media Repositories"* explaining why not to use symbolic links for the SUSE Linux Enterprise Server product repository (http://bugzilla.suse.com/show_bug.cgi?id=886196).

- Added an explanation explaining the need to use a sub-domain in *Section 2.1.4, "DNS and Host Names"* (http://bugzilla.suse.com/show_bug.cgi?id=886563).

- Added the section *Section 10.1.2, "Queuing/Dequeuing Proposals"* (http://bugzilla.suse.com/show_bug.cgi?id=882825).

- Cleaned up network ranges in *Section 2.1.1, "Network Address Allocation"* (http://bugzilla.suse.com/show_bug.cgi?id=885807).

- Corrected annotation on VLAN settings (http://bugzilla.suse.com/show_bug.cgi?id=885814).

- Fixed an error about using openvswitch with Windows server integration in *Section 10.11, "Deploying Neutron"* (http://bugzilla.suse.com/show_bug.cgi?id=889602).

- Updated the upgrade procedure in *Section 11.3, "Upgrading from SUSE OpenStack Cloud 5 to SUSE OpenStack Cloud 6"* (http://bugzilla.suse.com/show_bug.cgi?id=889663).

K.4 April 21, 2014 (Maintenance Release SUSE Cloud 3)

Included information on how to make SUSE Cloud highly available.

The following new sections have been added:

- *Section 1.5, "HA Setup".*

- *Section 2.6, "High Availability".*

- *Section 10.2, "Deploying Pacemaker (Optional, HA Setup Only)"*

- *Section 11.4, "Upgrading to an HA Setup"*

- *Section 11.5, "Backing Up and Restoring the Administration Server"*

- *Appendix C, Roles and Services in SUSE OpenStack Cloud*

Various smaller additions and changes throughout the document. New terms have been added to *Terminology*.

K.5 February 17, 2014 (Initial Release SUSE Cloud 3)

Admin Node Installation

- Re-wrote *Chapter 7, Crowbar Setup* because YaST now supports Crowbar user management, setting up a bastion network and configuring external repository URLs.

Node Installation

- Added the section *Section 9.4.4, "Using an Externally Managed Ceph Cluster"*.

- Added the section *Section 9.3, "Converting Existing SUSE Linux Enterprise Server 12 SP1 Machines Into SUSE OpenStack Cloud Nodes"*.

- Added the FAQ *How to change the default disk used for operating system installation?* to *Section 12.1, "FAQ"*.

OpenStack Service Deployment

- Updated *Appendix G, VMware vSphere Installation Instructions*.

- Lots of minor changes in *Chapter 10, Deploying the OpenStack Services* because of changes in the Web interface.

- Added *Section 10.14, "Deploying Heat (Optional)"*.

- Added *Section 10.15, "Deploying Ceilometer (Optional)"*.

- Added instructions on how to use the Cisco Nexus plugin with Neutron (*Appendix H, Using Cisco Nexus Switches with Neutron*.

- Added instructions on how to configure NetApp for Cinder to *Section 10.9, "Deploying Cinder"*.

- Updated all screenshots because of an updated Web interface theme.

Maintenance

- Added the section *Section 11.3, "Upgrading from SUSE OpenStack Cloud 5 to SUSE OpenStack Cloud 6".*

General

- Added *Chapter 11, SUSE OpenStack Cloud Maintenance.*

- Added definition of user roles to *About This Guide.*

Bugfixes

- Added instruction on adjusting the CD-ROM drive letter for deploying Windows Compute Nodes when the Administration Server has got multiple hard disks to *Section F.2, "Providing a Hyper-V Netboot Environment"* (http://bugzilla.suse.com/show_bug.cgi?id=863978).

- Added a notes on the VLAN configuration at various places (http://bugzilla.suse.com/show_bug.cgi?id=863829 and http://bugzilla.suse.com/show_bug.cgi?id=861523).

- Adjusted the memory recommendations for the Control Node(s) at *Section 2.4.2, "Control Node"* (http://bugzilla.suse.com/show_bug.cgi?id=862312).

- Add bind mount instructions for the Hyper-V Server deployment to *Section F.2, "Providing a Hyper-V Netboot Environment"* (http://bugzilla.suse.com/show_bug.cgi?id=861462).

- Updated *Appendix G, VMware vSphere Installation Instructions* (http://bugzilla.suse.com/show_bug.cgi?id=859173).

- Added *Section 12.2.1, " Applying PTFs (Program Temporary Fixes) Provided by the SUSE L3 Support "* (http://bugzilla.suse.com/show_bug.cgi?id=855387).

- Corrections in *Section 10.6, "Deploying Ceph (optional)"* (http://bugzilla.suse.com/show_bug.cgi?id=850477).

- Corrected network name in the *SUSE Cloud Network Overview* image in *Section 2.1, "Network"* (http://bugzilla.suse.com/show_bug.cgi?id=846877).

- Added instructions on how to disable route verification to *Section 12.1, "FAQ"* (http://bugzilla.suse.com/show_bug.cgi?id=841214).

K.6 September 25, 2013 (Maintenance Release SUSE Cloud 2.0)

OpenStack Service Deployment

- Added instructions on how to set up support for Microsoft Hyper-V (*Appendix F, Setting up a Netboot Environment for Microsoft* Windows*).

- Screenshots for node allocation and for all barclamps have been added to *Chapter 9, Installing the OpenStack Nodes* **and** *Chapter 10, Deploying the OpenStack Services*.

Bugfixes

- Added the FAQ *What to do when install-suse-cloud fails on deploying the IPMI/BMC network?* to *Section 12.1, "FAQ"* (http://bugzilla.suse.com/show_bug.cgi?id=782337).

- Completely restructured the FAQ section in *Chapter 12, Troubleshooting and Support* (http://bugzilla.suse.com/show_bug.cgi?id=794534).

- Added a note about VLANs on the admin network to *Section 2.1, "Network"* (http://bugzilla.suse.com/show_bug.cgi?id=835065).

K.7 September 11, 2013 (Initial Release SUSE Cloud 2.0)

Admin Node Installation

- Re-wrote *Setting Up a Bastion Network*.

- Completely re-wrote the repositories chapter. It now also contains information on how to use an external SMT or SUSE Manager server.

- Renamed the commands `smt repos` and `smt mirror` to `smt-repos` and `smt-mmirror` because of a conflict with the `smt` command from the `star` package (*Chapter 4, Installing and Setting Up an SMT Server on the Administration Server (Optional)*).

Networking

- Added a chapter on how to adjust the SUSE OpenStack Cloud network settings (*Appendix D, The Network Barclamp Template File*).

- Added a snippet on the os_sdn network, that was introduced in SUSE Cloud 2.0 (*Section 2.1, "Network"*).

Node Installation

- Added *Section 9.4.3, "Mounting NFS Shares on a Node"*.

- Added *Section 9.4.2, "Configuring Node Updates with the SUSE Manager Client Barclamp"*.

- Added *Section 9.4.1, "Deploying Node Updates with the Updater Barclamp"*.

- Re-wrote *Section 9.4.6, "Enabling SSL"*.

- Added information on the new *Public Name* and *Target Platform* attributes on the *Node Dashboard* to *Section 9.2, "Node Installation"*.

OpenStack Service Deployment

- Added *Section 10.5.1, "LDAP Authentication with Keystone"*.

- Added instructions on how to deploy Neutron (*Section 10.11, "Deploying Neutron"*).

- Added instructions on how to set up support for VMware ESX (*Appendix G, VMware vSphere Installation Instructions*).

- Added instructions on how to deploy Cinder in *Section 10.9, "Deploying Cinder"*.

- barclamp descriptions have been updated—almost all configurable attributes are now described in *Chapter 10, Deploying the OpenStack Services*.

Bugfixes

- Added a note on debugging and adding additional repositories the update repositories chapter (http://bugzilla.suse.com/show_bug.cgi?id=838096).

- Fixed an error in *Section 2.1.2.2, "Dual Network Mode"* that claimed two NICs are required on the Administration Server (http://bugzilla.suse.com/show_bug.cgi?id=838412).

- Clarified in *Section 10.9, "Deploying Cinder"* that *cinder-volume* can be deployed on several block storage nodes (http://bugzilla.suse.com/show_bug.cgi?id=835921).

- Added the role name for the Administration Server to *Example D.3, "Network Modes for Certain Roles"* (http://bugzilla.suse.com/show_bug.cgi?id=838354

- Added information on how to access nodes from the outside by using the Administration Server as a jump host via the bastion network in *Section 2.1.3, "Accessing the Administration Server via a Bastion Network"* (http://bugzilla.suse.com/show_bug.cgi?id=838341).

- Added a short description on how to change the host name during the installation in the section *Chapter 6, Service Configuration: Administration Server Network Configuration* (http://bugzilla.suse.com/show_bug.cgi?id=826163).

- Dropped snippets about how to activate the bastion network (http://bugzilla.suse.com/show_bug.cgi?id=832952).

- Fixed a syntax error in a program listing at *Chapter 4, Installing and Setting Up an SMT Server on the Administration Server (Optional)* (http://bugzilla.suse.com/show_bug.cgi?id=826833).

- Added the FAQ *I have installed a new hard disk on a node that was already deployed. Why is it ignored by Crowbar?* to *Section 12.1, "FAQ"* (http://bugzilla.suse.com/show_bug.cgi?id=779733).

- Added the FAQ *What to do if a node hangs during hardware discovery after the very first boot using PXE into the SLEShammer image?* to *Section 12.1, "FAQ"* (http://bugzilla.suse.com/show_bug.cgi?id=788156).

- Corrected the IP address in *Chapter 6, Service Configuration: Administration Server Network Configuration* (http://bugzilla.suse.com/show_bug.cgi?id=817957).

- Made various improvements throughout the document (http://bugzilla.suse.com/show_bug.cgi?id=806698)

Terminology

Active/Active

A concept of how services are running on nodes in a High Availability cluster. In an active/active setup, both the main and redundant systems are managed concurrently. If a failure of services occurs, the redundant system is already online, and can take over until the main system is fixed and brought back online.

Active/Passive

A concept of how services are running on nodes in a High Availability cluster. In an active/passive setup, one or more services are running on an active cluster node, whereas the passive node stands by. Only in case of the active node failing, the services are transferred to the passive node.

Administration Server

Also called Crowbar Administration Node. Manages all other nodes. It assigns IP addresses to them, boots them using PXE, configures them, and provides them the necessary software for their roles. To provide these services, the Administration Server runs Crowbar, Chef, DHCP, TFTP, NTP, and other services.

AMI (Amazon Machine Image)

A virtual machine that can be created and customized by a user. AMIs can be identified by an ID prefixed with `ami-`.

Availability Zone

An OpenStack method of partitioning clouds. It enables you to arrange OpenStack Compute hosts into logical groups, which typically have physical isolation and redundancy from other availability zones, for example, by using separate power supply or network equipment for each zone. When users provision resources, they can specify from which availability zone their instance should be created. This allows cloud consumers to ensure that their application resources are spread across disparate machines to achieve high availability if the hardware fails. Since the Grizzly release, availability zones are implemented via host aggregates.

AWS (Amazon Web Services)

A collection of remote computing services (including Amazon EC2, Amazon S3, and others) that together make up Amazon's cloud computing platform.

Barclamp

A set of Chef cookbooks, templates, and other logic. Used to apply a particular Chef role to individual nodes or a set of nodes.

Ceilometer

Code name for *Telemetry*.

Cell

Cells provide a new way to scale Compute deployments, including the ability to have compute clusters (cells) in different geographic locations all under the same Compute API. This allows for a single API server being used to control access to multiple cloud installations. Cells provide logical partitioning of Compute resources in a child/parent relationship.

Ceph

A massively scalable, open source, distributed storage system. It consists of an object store, a block store, and a POSIX-compliant distributed file system.

Chef

An automated configuration management platform for deployment of your entire cloud infrastructure. The Chef server manages many of the software packages and allows the easy changing of nodes.

Cinder

Code name for *OpenStack Block Storage*.

cloud-init

A package commonly installed in virtual machine images. It uses the SSH public key to initialize an instance after boot.

Cluster

A set of connected computers that work together. In many respects (and from the outside) they can be viewed as a single system. Clusters can be further categorized depending on their purpose, for example: High Availability clusters, high-performance clusters, or load-balancing clusters.

Cluster Partition

Whenever communication fails between one or more nodes and the rest of the cluster, a cluster partition occurs: The nodes of a cluster are split into partitions but still active. They can only communicate with nodes in the same partition and are unaware of the separated nodes. As the loss of the nodes on the other partition cannot be confirmed, a *Split Brain* scenario develops.

Cluster Resource Manager

The main management entity in a High Availability cluster responsible for coordinating all non-local interactions. The *SUSE Linux Enterprise High Availability Extension* uses Pacemaker as CRM. Each node of the cluster has its own CRM instance, but the one running on the *Designated Coordinator (DC)* is the one elected to relay decisions to the other non-local CRMs and process their input.

Compute Node

Node within a SUSE OpenStack Cloud. A physical server running a Hypervisor. A Compute Node is a host for guest virtual machines that are deployed in the cloud. It starts virtual machines on demand using `nova-compute`. To split virtual machine load across more than one server, a cloud should contain multiple Compute Nodes.

Container

A container is a storage compartment for data. It can be thought of as a directory, only that it cannot be nested.

Control Node

Node within a SUSE OpenStack Cloud. The Control Node is configured through the Administration Server and registers with the Administration Server for all required software. Hosts the OpenStack API endpoints and the OpenStack scheduler and runs the `nova` services—except for `nova-compute`, which is run on the Compute Nodes. The Control Node coordinates everything about cloud virtual machines: like a central communication center it receives all requests (for example, if a user wants to start or stop a virtual machine) and communicates with the Compute Nodes to coordinate fulfillment of the request. A cloud can contain multiple Control Nodes.

Cookbook

A collection of Chef recipes which deploy a software stack or functionality. The unit of distribution for Chef.

Corosync

The messaging/infrastructure layer used in a High Availability cluster that is set up with SUSE Linux Enterprise High Availability Extension. For example, the cluster communication channels are defined in `/etc/corosync/corosync.conf`.

Crowbar

Bare-metal installer and an extension of Chef server. The primary function of Crowbar is to get new hardware into a state where it can be managed by Chef. That means: Setting up BIOS and RAID, network, installing a basic operating system, and setting up services like DNS, NTP, and DHCP. The Crowbar server manages all nodes, supplying configuration of hardware and software.

Designated Coordinator (DC)

One *Cluster Resource Manager* in a High Availability cluster is elected as the Designated Coordinator (DC). The DC is the only entity in the cluster that can decide that a cluster-wide change needs to be performed, such as fencing a node or moving resources around. After a membership change, the DC is elected from all nodes in the cluster.

DRBD (Distributed Replicated Block Device)

DRBD* is a block device designed for building high availability clusters. The whole block device is mirrored via a dedicated network and is seen as a network RAID-1.

EBS (Amazon Elastic Block Store)

Block-level storage volumes for use with Amazon EC2 instances. Similar to OpenStack Cinder.

EC2 (Amazon Elastic Compute Cloud)

A public cloud run by Amazon. It provides similar functionality to OpenStack Compute.

Ephemeral Disk

Ephemeral disks offer machine local disk storage linked to the life cycle of a virtual machine instance. When a virtual machine is terminated, all data on the ephemeral disk is lost. Ephemeral disks are not included in any snapshots.

Failover

Occurs when a resource fails on a cluster node (or the node itself fails) and the affected resources are started on another node.

Fencing

Describes the concept of preventing access to a shared resource by isolated or failing cluster members. Should a cluster node fail, it will be shut down or reset to prevent it from causing trouble. The resources running on the cluster node will be moved away to another node. This way, resources are locked out of a node whose status is uncertain.

Fixed IP Address

When an instance is launched, it is automatically assigned a fixed (private) IP address, which stays the same until the instance is explicitly terminated. Private IP addresses are used for communication between instances.

Flavor

The compute, memory, and storage capacity of `nova` computing instances (in terms of virtual CPUs, RAM, etc.). Flavors can be thought of as "templates" for the amount of cloud resources that are assigned to an instance.

Floating IP Address

An IP address that a Compute project can associate with a virtual machine. A pool of floating IPs is available in OpenStack Compute, as configured by the cloud operator. After a floating IP address has been assigned to an instance, the instance can be reached from outside the cloud by this public IP address. Floating IP addresses can be dynamically disassociated and associated with other instances.

Glance

Code name for *OpenStack Image*.

Guest Operating System

An instance of an operating system installed on a virtual machine.

Heat

Code name for *Orchestration*.

High Availability Cluster

High Availability clusters seek to minimize two things: system downtime and data loss. System downtime occurs when a user-facing service is unavailable beyond a specified maximum amount of time. System downtime and data loss (accidental deletion or destruction of data) can occur not only in the event of a single failure, but also in case of cascading failures, where a single failure deteriorates into a series of consequential failures.

Horizon

Code name for *OpenStack Dashboard*.

Host

A physical computer.

Host Aggregate

An OpenStack method of grouping hosts via a common set of metadata. It enables you to tag groups of hosts with certain capabilities or characteristics. A characteristic could be related to physical location, allowing creation or further partitioning of availability zones, but could also be related to performance (for example, indicating the availability of SSD storage) or anything else which the cloud administrators deem appropriate. A host can be in more than one host aggregate.

Hybrid Cloud

One of several deployment models for a cloud infrastructure. A composition of both public and private clouds that remain unique entities, but are bound together by standardized technology for enabling data and application portability. Integrating SUSE Studio and SUSE Manager with SUSE OpenStack Cloud delivers a platform and tools with which to enable enterprise hybrid clouds.

Hypervisor

A piece of computer software, firmware or hardware that creates and runs virtual machines. It arbitrates and controls access of the virtual machines to the underlying hardware.

IaaS (Infrastructure-as-a-Service)

A service model of cloud computing where processing, storage, networks, and other fundamental computing resources are rented over the Internet. It allows the customer to deploy and run arbitrary software, including operating systems and applications. The customer has control over operating systems, storage, and deployed applications but does not control the underlying cloud infrastructure. Housing and maintaining it is in the responsibility of the service provider.

Image

A file that contains a complete Linux virtual machine.

In the SUSE OpenStack Cloud context, images are virtual disk images that represent the contents and structure of a storage medium or device, such as a hard disk, in a single file. Images are used as a template from which a virtual machine can be started. For starting a virtual machine, SUSE OpenStack Cloud always uses a copy of the image.

Images have both content and metadata; the latter are also called image properties.

Instance

A virtual machine that runs inside the cloud.

Instance Snapshot

A point-in-time copy of an instance. It preserves the disk state of a running instance and can be used to launch a new instance or to create a new image based upon the snapshot.

Keypair

OpenStack Compute injects SSH keypair credentials that are injected into images when they are launched.

Keystone

Code name for *OpenStack Identity*.

libvirt

Virtualization API library. Used by OpenStack to interact with many of its supported hypervisors.

Linux Bridge

A software allowing multiple virtual machines to share a single physical NIC within OpenStack Compute. It behaves like a hub: You can connect multiple (physical or virtual) network interface devices to it. Any Ethernet frames that come in from one interface attached to the bridge is transmitted to all other devices.

Logical Volume (LV)

Acts as a virtual disk partition. After creating a *Volume Group (VG)*, logical volumes can be created in that volume group. Logical volumes can be used as raw block devices, swap devices, or for creating a (mountable) file system like disk partitions.

Migration

The process of moving a virtual machine instance from one Compute Node to another. This process can only be executed by cloud administrators.

Multicast

A technology used for a one-to-many communication within a network that can be used for cluster communication. Corosync supports both multicast and unicast.

Network

In the OpenStack Networking API: An isolated L2 network segment (similar to a VLAN). It forms the basis for describing the L2 network topology in a given OpenStack Networking deployment.

Neutron

Code name for *OpenStack Networking*.

Node

A (physical) server that is managed by Crowbar.

Nova

Code name for *OpenStack Compute*.

Object

Basic storage entity in OpenStack Object Storage, representing a file that your store there. When you upload data to OpenStack Object Storage, the data is neither compressed nor encrypted, it is stored as-is.

Open vBridge

A virtual networking device. It behaves like a virtual switch: network interface devices connect to its ports. The ports can be configured similar to a physical switch's port, including VLAN configurations.

OpenStack

A collection of open source software to build and manage public and private clouds. Its components are designed to work together to provide Infrastructure as a Service and massively scalable cloud computing software.

At the same time, OpenStack is also a community and a project.

OpenStack Block Storage

One of the core OpenStack components and services (code name: `Cinder`). It provides persistent block level storage devices for use OpenStack compute instances. The block storage system manages the creation, attaching and detaching of the block devices to servers. Prior to the OpenStack Grizzly release, the service was part of `nova-volume` (block service).

OpenStack Compute

One of the core OpenStack components and services (code name: `Nova`). It is a cloud computing fabric controller and as such, the main part of an IaaS system. It provides virtual machines on demand.

OpenStack Dashboard

One of the core OpenStack components or services (code name: `Horizon`). It provides a modular Web interface for OpenStack services and allows end users and administrators to interact with each OpenStack service through the service's API.

OpenStack Identity

One of the core OpenStack components or services (code name: `Keystone`). It provides authentication and authorization for all OpenStack services.

OpenStack Image

One of the core OpenStack components or services (code name: `Glance`). It provides discovery, registration, and delivery services for virtual disk images.

OpenStack Networking

One of the core OpenStack components or services (code name: `Neutron`). It provides "network connectivity as a service" between interface devices (for example, vNICs) managed by other OpenStack services (for example, Compute). Allows users to create their own networks and attach interfaces to them.

OpenStack Object Storage

One of the core OpenStack components or services (code name: `Swift`). Allows to store and retrieve files while providing built-in redundancy and fail-over. Can be used for backing up and archiving data, streaming data to a user's Web browser, or developing new applications with data storage integration.

OpenStack Service

A collection of Linux services (or daemons) that work together to provide core functionality within the OpenStack project, like storing objects, providing virtual servers, or authentication and authorization. All services have code names, which are also used in configuration files and command line programs that belong to the service.

Orchestration

A module (code name: `Heat`) to orchestrate multiple composite cloud applications using file-based or Web-based templates. It contains both a user interface and an API and describes your cloud deployment in a declarative language. The module is an integrated project of OpenStack as of the Havana release.

PaaS (Platform-as-a-Service)

A service model of cloud computing where a computing platform and cloud-based application development tools are rented over the Internet. The customer controls software deployment and configuration settings, but not the underlying cloud infrastructure including network, servers, operating systems, or storage.

Pacemaker

An open source cluster resource manager used in SUSE Linux Enterprise High Availability Extension.

Port

In the OpenStack Networking API: An attachment port to an L2 OpenStack Networking network.

Private Cloud

One of several deployment models for a cloud infrastructure. The infrastructure is operated exclusively for a single organization and may exist on or off premises. The cloud is owned and managed by the organization itself, by a third party or a combination of both.

Private IP Address

See *Fixed IP Address*.

Project

A concept in OpenStack Identity. Used to identify a group, an organization, or a project (or more generically, an individual customer environment in the cloud). Also called `tenant`. The term `tenant` is primarily used in the OpenStack command line tools.

Proposal

Special configuration for a barclamp. It includes barclamp-specific settings, and a list of nodes to which the proposal should be applied.

Public Cloud

One of several deployment models for a cloud infrastructure. The cloud infrastructure is designed for use by the general public and exists on the premises of the cloud provider. Services like applications, storage, and other resources are made available to the general public for free or are offered on a pay-per-use model. The infrastructure is owned and managed by a business, academic or government organization, or some combination of these.

Public IP Address

See *Floating IP Address*.

qcow (QEMU Copy on Write)

A disk image format supported by the QEMU virtual machine manager. A `qcow2` image helps to optimize disk space as it consumes disk space only when contents are written on it and grows as data is added.

`qcow2` is a more recent version of the `qcow` format where a read-only base image is used, and all writes are stored to the `qcow2` image.

Quorum

In a cluster, a *Cluster Partition* is defined to have quorum (is "quorate") if it has the majority of nodes (or votes). Quorum distinguishes exactly one partition. It is part of the algorithm to prevent several disconnected partitions or nodes from proceeding and causing data and service corruption (*Split Brain*). Quorum is a prerequisite for *Fencing*, which then ensures that quorum is indeed unique.

Quota

Restriction of resources to prevent overconsumption within a cloud. In OpenStack, quotas are defined per project and contain multiple parameters, such as amount of RAM, number of instances, or number of floating IP addresses.

RC File (openrc.sh)

Environment file needed for the OpenStack command line tools. The RC file is project-specific and contains the credentials used by OpenStack Compute, Image, and Identity services.

Recipe

A group of Chef scripts and templates. Recipes are used by Chef to deploy a unit of functionality.

Region

An OpenStack method of aggregating clouds. Regions are a robust way to share some infrastructure between OpenStack compute installations, while allowing for a high degree of failure tolerance. Regions have a separate API endpoint per installation.

Resource

In a High Availability context: Any type of service or application that is known to the cluster resource manager. Examples include an IP address, a file system, or a database.

Resource Agent (RA)

A script acting as a proxy to manage a resource in a High Availability cluster. For example, it can start, stop or monitor a resource.

Role

In the Crowbar/Chef context: an instance of a *Proposal* that is active on a node.

In the *OpenStack Identity* context: concept of controlling the actions or set of operations that a user is allowed to perform. A role includes a set of rights and privileges. A user assuming that role inherits those rights and privileges.

S3 (Amazon Simple Storage Service)

An object storage by Amazon that can be used to store and retrieve data on the Web. Similar in function to OpenStack Object Storage. It can act as a back-end store for Glance images.

SaaS (Software-as-a-Service)

A service model of cloud computing where applications are hosted by a service provider and made available to customers remotely as a Web-based service.

SBD (STONITH Block Device)

In an environment where all nodes of a High Availability cluster have access to shared storage, a small partition is used for disk-based fencing.

Security Group

Concept in OpenStack Networking. A security group is a container for security group rules. Security group rules allow to specify the type of traffic and direction (ingress/egress) that is allowed to pass through a port.

Single Point of Failure (SPOF)

An individual piece of equipment or software which will cause system downtime or data loss if it fails. To eliminate single points of failure, High Availability systems seek to provide redundancy for crucial pieces of equipment or software.

Snapshot

See *Volume Snapshot* or *Instance Snapshot*.

Split Brain

Also known as a "partitioned cluster" scenario. Either through a software or hardware failure, the cluster nodes are divided into two or more groups that do not know of each other. *STONITH* prevents a split brain situation from badly affecting the entire cluster.

Stateful Service

A service where subsequent requests to the service depend on the results of the first request.

Stateless Service

A service that provides a response after your request, and then requires no further attention.

STONITH

The acronym for "Shoot the other node in the head". It refers to the fencing mechanism that shuts down a misbehaving node to prevent it from causing trouble in a cluster.

Storage Node

Node within a SUSE OpenStack Cloud. Acts as the controller for cloud-based storage. A cloud can contain multiple Storage Nodes.

Subnet

In the OpenStack Networking API: A block of IP addresses and other network configuration (for example, a default gateway, DNS servers) that can be associated with an OpenStack Networking network. Each subnet represents an IPv4 or IPv6 address block. Multiple subnets can be associated with a network, if necessary.

SUSE Linux Enterprise High Availability Extension

An integrated suite of open source clustering technologies that enables you to implement highly available physical and virtual Linux clusters.

SUSE OpenStack Cloud Administrator

User role in SUSE OpenStack Cloud. Manages projects, users, images, flavors, and quotas within SUSE OpenStack Cloud.

SUSE OpenStack Cloud Dashboard

The SUSE® OpenStack Cloud Dashboard is a Web interface that enables cloud administrators and users to manage various OpenStack services. It is based on OpenStack Dashboard (also known under its codename `Horizon`).

SUSE OpenStack Cloud Operator

User role in SUSE OpenStack Cloud. Installs and deploys SUSE OpenStack Cloud.

SUSE OpenStack Cloud User

User role in SUSE OpenStack Cloud. End user who launches and manages instances, can create snapshots, and use volumes for persistent storage within SUSE OpenStack Cloud.

Swift

Code name for *OpenStack Object Storage*.

TAP Device

A virtual networking device. A TAP device, such as `vnet0` is how hypervisors such as KVM and Xen implement a virtual network interface card (vNIC). An Ethernet frame sent to a

TAP device is received by the guest operating system. The tap option connects the network stack of the guest operating system to a TAP network device on the host.

Telemetry

A module (code name: `Ceilometer`) for metering OpenStack-based clouds. The project aims to provide a unique point of contact across all OpenStack core components for acquiring metrics which can then be consumed by other components such as customer billing. The module is an integrated project of OpenStack as of the Havana release.

Tenant

See *Project*.

Unicast

A technology for sending messages to a single network destination. Corosync supports both multicast and unicast. In Corosync, unicast is implemented as UDP-unicast (UDPU).

User

In the OpenStack context, a digital representation of a person, system, or service who uses OpenStack cloud services. Users can be directly assigned to a particular project and behave as if they are contained in that project.

Veth Pair

A virtual networking device. The acronym veth stands for virtual Ethernet interface. A veth is a pair of virtual network interfaces correctly directly together. An Ethernet frame sent to one end of a veth pair is received by the other end of a veth pair. OpenStack Networking uses veth pairs as virtual patch cables to make connections between virtual bridges.

VLAN

A physical method for network virtualization. VLANs allow to create virtual networks across a distributed network so that disparate hosts (on independent networks) appear as if they were part of the same broadcast domain.

VM (Virtual Machine)

An operating system instance that runs on top of a hypervisor. Multiple virtual machines can run on the same physical host at the same time.

vNIC

Virtual network interface card.

Volume

Detachable block storage device. Unlike a SAN, it can only be attached to one instance at a time.

Volume Group (VG)

A virtual disk consisting of aggregated physical volumes. Volume groups can be logically partitioned into logical volumes.

Volume Snapshot

A point-in-time copy of an OpenStack storage volume. Used to back up volumes.

vSwitch (Virtual Switch)

A software that runs on a host or node and provides the features and functions of a hardware-based network switch.

Zone

A logical grouping of Compute services and virtual machine hosts.